THEMES IN
ECONOMIC ANTHROPOLOGY

Edited by Raymond Firth

TAVISTOCK PUBLICATIONS

London · New York · Sydney · Toronto · Wellington

First published in 1967
by Tavistock Publications Limited
11 New Fetter Lane, London EC4

Third impression 1970
SBN 422 72770 9
1.3

First published as a Social Science Paperback in 1970
Second impression 1970
SBN 422 72540 4
1.2

Printed by T. & A. Constable Limited, Edinburgh

This volume derives mainly from material presented at a Conference
on Economic Anthropology sponsored by the Association of Social
Anthropologists of the Commonwealth and held at St Antony's
College, University of Oxford, 28-30 June 1965

Distributed in the U.S.A.
by Barnes & Noble Inc.

Contents

Contents

Contents

Contents

Editor's Preface

This book originated in a conference on economic anthropology held by the Association of Social Anthropologists at Oxford in June 1965. To Raymond Firth was given the task of organizing the conference, and he was able to enlist as contributors the authors of the papers here published. It was agreed that discussion of each of the papers should be opened by a member of the Association who had been able to prepare a critical evaluation of the paper concerned, and that the results of this and of the general discussion should be used by the authors in the revision of their contributions for publication. In a very real sense, then, this book takes account of the thinking of two score or so social anthropologists on some aspects of economic anthropology.

Major acknowledgement must be given to the primary contributors: Lorraine Barić, Fredrik Barth, Percy Cohen, Mary Douglas, Scarlett Epstein, Ronald Frankenberg, Leonard Joy, and Sutti Ortiz. Cheerfully they contributed ideas to the planning of the conference, and undertook the preparation and revision of their papers amid the many other calls upon their time. To the 'discussants' of the papers: Edwin Ardener, Burton Benedict, Ronald Berndt, Abner Cohen, Ioan Lewis, and Barbara Ward, substantial thanks are also due for the care they devoted to their evaluations and the generous way in which they have allowed their ideas to be merged with others for this publication. A special word of appreciation should go to two contributors. Fredrik Barth, a member of the Association, took the trouble to travel over from Norway to deliver his paper, and played a very active part in the conference. Leonard Joy, an economist and not a member of the Association, spared time from a very busy teaching and research programme to prepare a paper of his own and to comment constructively upon the other contributions and upon the general discussion. Apart from giving this 'economic backing' to the arguments, his advocacy of linear programming developed into a cooperative effort with Barth, which appears in this volume as an experimental inquiry into some of the possibilities of this method for economic anthropology.

To Edward Evans-Pritchard and other Oxford hosts of the conference grateful thanks are due for many facilities and much hospitality.

The gratitude of the conference goes also to the Wenner-Gren Foundation for Anthropological Research. In pursuance of its policy of supporting 'growing points' in anthropology, the Foundation sponsored a conference on economic anthropology at Burg Wartenstein, in August 1960. (Some results of this appear in the volume on *Capital, Saving and Credit in Peasant Societies*, edited by Raymond Firth and B. S. Yamey, London, 1964.) In 1965 this Oxford conference used part of a grant-in-aid from the Wenner-Gren Foundation to the Association of Social Anthropologists; the Foundation has thus facilitated further exploration of empirical and theoretical issues in this important but still underdeveloped area of anthropology.

R. F.

London, May 1966

Raymond Firth

Themes in Economic Anthropology

A General Comment[1]

In the Introduction to earlier volumes of this series, presenting results of the Anglo-American Conference of 1963, Eggan and Gluckman point out that technical economics has had less influence on social anthropological research than other social sciences have had. They offer the opinion that this is possibly because of the highly abstract nature of the economic discipline (A.S.A. Monographs, 1, 1965, p. xv; 2, 1965, p. xvii; 3 and 4, 1966, p. xvii). I am no economist but, granting this, I think that other factors have also been involved in the relative lack of development of economic anthropology.

The radical difference in the nature of the empirical phenomena has clearly been one impediment. The characteristic Western institutional framework of business enterprise, with its machine technology, impersonal labour market, profit orientation, limited liability companies, international trading, banking and credit, shows marked contrast to the small-scale, highly personal, 'subsistence' economic systems, with little in the nature of a market economy and perhaps even no money medium, with which anthropologists have traditionally been concerned. Small wonder that economists have tended to ignore these 'simpler' societies and most anthropologists have seen little in common between 'primitive' and 'civilized' versions of an economy. Even Karl Marx, with his structural interest in 'pre-capitalist formations' could find relatively little 'primitive' material for his early studies and focused attention primarily on Western and Oriental peasant and feudal or quasi-feudal systems.[2] Again, anthropologists have often been so concerned to demonstrate the contribution which economic behaviour makes to the maintenance of social systems that they have tended to take the

1

economic phenomena for granted and to concentrate mainly on the social side of the equation.

The beginnings of the study of economic anthropology can be traced far back in the nineteenth and even into the eighteenth century. But it is only about fifty years since Wilhelm Koppers (1915-1916) and Max Schmidt (1920-1921) gathered the materials then existing from the work of Bücher, Cunow, Herment, Kohler, Lasch, Moszkowski, Sartorius von Waltershausen, and other long-forgotten writers, into synoptic and quasi-theoretical form. Following closely upon this came the more critical evaluation of Olivier Leroy (1925) and the various combinations of empirical inquiry and theoretical formulation by Richard Thurnwald, Bronislaw Malinowski, W. E. Armstrong, and the present writer. Most prominent among later general works was that of Melville J. Herskovits (1940) distinguished by its massive assembly of fact and its robust commonsense approach rather than by its command of economic theory. Over the last twenty years treatment of issues in economic anthropology has been more sophisticated, but threads of the discourse of those early years can still be discerned in the presentation and the controversies of today.

ECONOMIC VIEWPOINTS

Recognition of an analytical sphere which could be called economic was slow in anthropological studies. Symptomatic of the delay in appreciation of the character of the subject has been the relatively recent adoption of the term 'economic anthropology' instead of the older 'primitive economics'.[3]

The change in the title of the study has reflected a sharpening of interest in theoretical issues. One of these issues is the subject-matter of the study itself. In the earlier years the more theoretically minded students of the subject took over its definition from economics, regarding it simply as an extension of the field of economics into the material from technologically less well-developed communities. Since, as anthropologists, their perspective was comparative, they were very conscious of the way in which the form of the society was related to the form of the economy. But one of their preoccupations was to protect the notion of economy itself from confusion with technology and environmental influence so that it could be focused upon types of relationships between persons rather than between persons and things.

The role of 'things' – what Malinowski termed the material substratum – is basic in an economy. But rather different interpretations of their role have tended to emerge in the last decade or so, particularly in defining the subject-matter of economic anthropology. One aspect of this issue has been epitomized by Marshall Sahlins in a paper to an earlier conference (1965, p. 139): 'A material transaction is usually a momentary episode in a continuous social relation. The social relation exerts governance: the flow of goods is constrained by, is part of, a status etiquette.' Sahlins points out that the connection between material effort and social relation is reciprocal because a specific social relation may constrain a given movement of goods, but a specific transaction suggests a particular social relation. So much would be generally agreed by all economic anthropologists. Economists too might well concur. Indeed, in their insistence upon the significance not only of goods but also of services as elements of economic magnitude, economists have indicated their awareness of the importance of *relationship*, though they have been relatively uninterested in its social aspects.

Conventional treatment by an economist would lead to the consideration of the ways in which the wishes or demands of individuals to create or maintain social relations by means of transference of material goods and/or services are conditioned by the fact that such goods and services are not unlimited in quantity and quality. Therefore the individuals concerned must make choices regarding the persons with whom they wish to maintain social relations, the kinds of social relations they wish to maintain, and the kinds and amounts of goods and services which they can afford to involve in this transference. Clearly, the existing structure of their social relations and the ideas and expectations which they have of this must affect very deeply the nature of the transactions in which they engage. But the physical limitations on the number and type of objects available and on the time and energy of the persons concerned necessitate some channelling of goods and effort, as some selection of social relationships. There is in social anthropology an understandable view that it is the social relation which is primary, which dictates the content and form of the transaction. When this view is pushed to its extreme, notions of choice and decision among alternatives are played down and conformity to social pattern is regarded as paramount. So significant are deemed to be the socially received ideas about the nature and use of goods and services that it is asserted that the notion of scarcity can be dispensed with as an analytical concept.

It is not my purpose to evaluate the arguments on this issue here.[4] But a note on the position expounded or implied in the contributions to this book is in order. When the plan for our conference on economic anthropology was originally drawn up, it was decided that in order to get most effective discussion it was necessary to limit the field. Consequently, from among the various sectors open to examination it was agreed to focus our discussion primarily upon themes in the field of resource allocation and product distribution. As will be seen from the various essays, without expressing any very decided specific opinion, the contributions in general imply an acceptance of the view that the logic of scarcity *is* operative over the whole range of economic phenomena, and that, however deep and complex may be the influence of social factors, the notions of economy and of economizing are *not* basically separate. As Percy Cohen indicates in his contribution, however, the general viewpoint is that the issue in this abstract form is not highly relevant.

One element in the analysis is common ground throughout – while the material dimension of the economy is regarded as a basic feature, the significance of the economy is seen to lie in the *transactions* of which it is composed and therefore in the quality of *relationships* which these transactions create, express, sustain, and modify. Whether or not there is agreement with Sahlins (1965, p. 140) that in primitive conditions the place of 'transaction' in the total economy is more detached from production than it is in modern industrial communities, the emphasis of interest is still upon the transaction rather than upon the production. Again, interest tends to be concentrated as much upon the set of ideas and emotional attitudes associated with the transaction as upon its formal qualities. To an anthropologist the recognition that any specific economic system has a corresponding set of moral values is taken for granted. Where there is difference of view is on the quality of the commitment that can be inferred for participants in an alien economic system. Even if anthropologists discount the moral preconceptions of their own societies, their personal standpoints, embodying multiple and diverse cultural influences, can lead them to very different concepts of, say, the meaning of transactions or the basis of values in any particular economy they study.

Here one of the more critical issues for students of economic anthropology in recent years has been the concept of 'market'. The term market has had three rather different connotations in the literature of economics and associated studies. It has referred to the institutionalized locus of exchange, the market-place, with its booths and its traders, its competition and its conventions. Markets of this kind are very familiar to the economic historian, and have been studied to some extent by anthropologists.[5] Another concept of market is of a more abstract kind, non-locational, indicating the total field of interest of any good or service. In this sense one might talk of the 'standing' of a firm in the market, of a large firm driving a smaller out of the market, of the market for a particular type of labour or skill. The concept is used a great deal in this sense by economists and need imply neither any particular institutional structure nor any particular social or moral evaluation. Springing from this, however, is the use of the concept in still another sense, implying the allocation of resources by reference to impersonal criteria which disregard personal ties and social ends in favour of an immediate maximization principle of profit-making. It is this concept which has been selected particularly for distinction as the criterion separating the types of economic system studied by economists from those studied by anthropologists.

'Primitive' and even 'peasant' economic systems (though it is not clear how far in the latter case) are regarded as not operating in accordance with any 'market' principles of this order. They are asserted not to have a 'market mentality' or not to have the kinds of institution which allow individuals to operate in this way even if they wished. I think some confusion can easily arise here. Evidence of gross difference between primitive, peasant, and industrial economic systems is obvious. But absence of general markets for goods and services of all kinds and the lack of impersonal market relationships does not mean the lack of any concept of economic advantage. As the essays in this book demonstrate, the differences lie primarily in the structural and institutional fields. On the basic principles of choice in the use of resources and perception of relative worth in an exchange, there is a continuum of behaviour over the whole range of human economic systems. From this point of view it may be argued that the relation sometimes postulated as a disjunction between economics and anthropology is of the same order as the relation between economics and economic history. When the anthropologist or historian applies an empirical institutional test to theoretical economic propositions the propositions themselves may be found to need amplification or modification by specifying more precisely the conditions in which they operate. But anthropologist no more than historian needs to reject the whole apparatus of economic analysis.

One fairly obvious sphere in which the empirical observations of the anthropologist tend to qualify an economic assumption when it is translated into analysis of cases is in the concept of marginality, and the principle of diminishing returns. As impersonal general principles these may be taken as valid. But the personal perception and use of them by people engaged in economic transactions may vary greatly. People do not necessarily try to equate at the margin *all* sets of costs. Scarlett Epstein suggests from her examination of Indian rural communities that the behaviour of the agriculturalist is more easily explicable by assuming that he is working in terms of concepts such as those of average productivity than of a sensitive adjustment to the use of marginal factors. More generally, it would appear that in primitive economic systems the mobilizer of cooperative effort for enterprises such as house-building or team agriculture is more concerned to ensure a large labour supply for social reasons than to eliminate marginal workers. But even here, assuming some degree of continuity and certainty in the operations, the mobilizer may be concerned with the marginality of social factors. Moreover, granted the heavy institutional pressure on those who invite labour contributions to welcome all-comers and reward them equally, concepts of the marginality of technical factors still do not seem to be absent from the host's economic calculations. If the job is a relatively small one invitations are sent out to a relatively limited circle of people. The host *does* calculate, if only in rough terms, how much food or beer he has on hand or can mobilize in relation to the amount of labour force he requires and can entertain. As an hypothesis one may advance the notion that the perception and the operational use of marginality are to some extent a function of scale. If a labour force is very small, then there is more possibility of simple calculation about the effect of adding on one more person, and the differences in output and in reward are more significant. But if the labour force is large the addition of an extra hand is less economically significant, though refusal to employ may be socially of just as great importance. But even here the inclusion of one more worker may be of marginal social value; if he is omitted his resentment may not matter much.

Scarlett Epstein argues that in her Indian rural scene concern for marginal productivity arises with the change from a non-market to a market economy. In so far as this is so, it would seem to depend partly upon the relative amounts of land cultivated each season. If all land is under cultivation by a given labour supply for a single crop locally consumed each season, then one can understand the concern for fluctuations in productivity caused by seasonal factors rather than by variation in amounts of labour. As contact with a broader market economy develops, however, and the field for employment of factors both of land and of labour widens, so one would imagine that interest in alternatives sharpens and concepts of marginality come to the fore. But social as well as economic factors may be responsible for the change. As external market relations of a more impersonal character develop, local social bonds may weaken and make it less important if kinship and neighbourhood ties are ignored in the interest of margins in productivity. But even in a modern industrial society the flexible employment of the concept of marginality of units of labour is very much restricted by the influence of trade union organization. In its solidarity aspects this presents a broad analogy to the restrictive effects of

B   7

kinship organization in a primitive society. And in a family firm even nowadays, management may deliberately give a job to a kinsman whom strict marginality considerations would not lead them to employ.

In reaction against what they have imagined to be the traditional economists' view of 'economic man', with his rational, calculating, maximizing behaviour, anthropologists have often tended to stress the extent to which economic behaviour in 'primitive' societies has been governed by social criteria, moral rule, ritual proscription. They have sometimes overlooked the fact that, as Sutti Ortiz shows later in this volume, the economists' analytical assumption is not intended to deny the operation of emotional, irrational elements in economic thinking. It is concerned with drawing logical inferences from *consistent* behaviour in the treatment of resources, granted that these are limited in quantity and are capable of being put to various uses. It is really only in recent years that the economic anthropologist has focused upon the significance of choice-making and decision-taking from among the alternatives available in the economic systems he studies.

ECONOMICS OF THE GIFT

To illustrate the operation of these processes in an institutional milieu, I take as example the custom of gift, which has been illumined by the classic work of Malinowski and Mauss,[6] but which can still bear further study.

Mauss's general analysis has had a profound and most stimulating influence upon anthropologists. Stirred by Malinowski's presentation of the *kula* theme Mauss intended his theory to apply comparatively to the whole range of 'primitive or archaic' types of society. It is relevant, then, to see how far his conclusions are borne out when one considers societies other than those from which he has taken material. My own Tikopia evidence (Firth, 1965, p. 331) fully bears out Mauss's emphasis upon the triple significance of the obligation to give, the obligation to receive, and the obligation to repay. His insistence that every gift demands a counter-gift is illustrated by the fact that even when the Tikopia state that an object is given *sorimori*

8

fuere –'simply as a present'– this does not mean that they necessarily have ruled out the wish or the obligation for a return (cf. Firth, 1959b, p. 138). The distinction between this and *tauvi* – a 'payment' – is that the latter expresses a direct, overt exchange, with equivalents agreed in advance, not exchanges which may be indirect and covert. While reciprocity for a present may be long delayed, and is primarily at the discretion of the initial recipient, payment in overt exchange is usually expected to be immediate, and on the agreed terms.

Ethnographically, however, Mauss's account of the process of gift-making and return needs qualification. He cites 'Polynesian' material in support of his views that gift exchange takes place between groups in the form of 'total prestations' (1954, pp. 3, 6-12), and refers his triple scheme of obligation primarily to such group relations – though this is often overlooked by those who use his analysis. Now, in Tikopia, a Polynesian society, gift exchange takes place between individuals as well as between groups. It would be contrary to the facts to state that in Tikopia it is groups not individuals which carry on exchange, make contracts, and are bound by obligations. Often gifts, with all the accompanying transactions, are made by chiefs or other elders as heads of social groups, but on many other occasions individuals act upon their own responsibility and are not representative of a social unit. Again, the term 'total prestation' is often inapplicable to Tikopia transactions (cf. Sahlins, 1965, p. 177). Single items of objects or services are contributed, and involve single items in return. These may be caught up in an elaborate system of gift and counter-gift, but this does not necessarily involve in each case an exchange of the whole range of other social items included in the notion of 'total prestation'. Finally, I found in Tikopia no trace of the idea such as Mauss describes of the obligation to repay being based upon a belief that the thing initially given is not inert but embodies some part of the original owner's personality which afflicts the recipient if he does not repay the gift.[7] In so far as the Tikopia believe in the possibility of a ritual sanction for repayment, it lies in the concept of a personal mobilization of spirit forces, an energized reaction on the part of the original owner invoking 'sorcery' upon a recalcitrant debtor. But such ritual sanction would seem to be rare; I have no record of a case. With the Tikopia, the sanctions for reciprocity lie primarily in the field of economic, social, and moral attitudes.

Qualifications of a more analytical order may also be made to Mauss's views. Mauss has stressed the significance of the obligation to give, the obligation to receive, and the obligation to make a return as if they were each universally mandatory on the persons concerned and of the same weight. I am prepared to argue that, contrary to his implication, in all three fields there are significant areas of choice and uncertainty, and that in the existence of this uncertainty lie some of the most delicate problems of procedure for those engaged in the transactions. I would argue further that these problems are of particular concern in the interpretation of the moral aspects of the gift. Moreover, I would hold that the quality of the interpretation tends to vary according to the type of society under consideration.

Basically, the sanctions noted by Malinowski, Mauss, and other writers concerned to explain the widespread custom of the gift fall into three major categories: sanctions of economic and political advantage; sanctions of social status; and sanctions of ritual and religious belief. The obligation to give is based primarily upon sanctions of economic and political advantage and sanctions of social status, though in charitable giving the sanctions of religion may be very important. Economic and political sanctions appear with varying clarity in different types of transaction. Malinowski stressed the importance of the principle of reciprocity and conceded that even his category of free gift could be reinterpreted in terms of return for services. But he also made plain how in many Trobriand presentations the element of status involvement – or as he generally termed it, prestige – was highly significant, leading to some asymmetry between the value of gifts made ·and returned. Mauss, too, emphasizes the importance of the social sanction in the obligation to give, though he discusses this primarily in reference to the potlatch[8], and implies that the sanction of prestige – of losing 'face' – is as much institutionalized as personal in its effect. But what Mauss notes in essence, though he does not expand the idea, is that giving is an extension of the self, and hence the obligation to give is bound up with the notion of the self, its social bounds and social roles. When he points out that a refusal to give is a refusal of friendship and intercourse, the equivalent of a declaration of war, he is in effect pointing out that the refusal to give is a refusal to link one's personality in alliance with the would-be recipient. Mauss casts his thought in terms of religious ideas – to lose one's 'face' is to lose one's spirit. He was also led by the imagery of the Kwakiutl and Haida totemic mask to argue 'It is the veritable *persona* which is at stake' (p. 38). In focusing his analysis of giving and receiving on the exchange of 'things which are to some extent parts of persons', Mauss brings to mind Malinowski's expression about gifts in the Trobriands being acts with a social meaning rather than transmission of objects.

Mauss's theory of the gift applies most clearly to primitive and peasant states of society. But he himself points out that it also has some applicability to modern conditions in our own type of society. He ascribes to the operations of making and receiving gifts a kind of elemental morality of which he clearly approves. He would even like to see his analysis 'suggest a way to better administrative procedures for our societies' (1954, pp. 63-69). It is difficult to follow him in these somewhat optimistic conclusions. But there is point in considering a further example, one from present-day conditions, in which anthropologists have had good opportunity to make observations because they have been personally concerned.

A phenomenon that seems to be fairly general among field anthropologists is that many of them have been asked for gifts or money by informants and friends after their return from the field. Most of those asked seem to have assumed some responsibility in this way. To receive such requests is not simply an index to good rapport with the people among whom they work; various other conditions, especially the relative ease of communication, enter in here. Nowadays, with the growth of literacy and improvement in transport, every social anthropologist is apt to find himself maintaining social relations with some members of the society he has studied when his immediate period of residence among them is over. Like other anthropologists, my wife and I, when back in London, were not surprised to receive several requests for money from Malay people who had been our informants and friends in Kelantan. In polite phrases the letters (usually written in Malay, and by a kinsman or friend) asked for financial assistance because of the expense of a daughter's wedding, a house blown down, a village prayer house to be repaired, or a very poor fishing season. As a sample I give part of such a letter, in translation.

'Here is M- sending this letter. Because M- wishes to ask help from Tuan. Because M- at this time is in great difficulty. Because M-'s village has had a great monsoon and the rain has been exceedingly heavy. N- [her son] has not been able to get out to catch fish because the waves have been huge. Consequently M- requests aid in money; if Tuan and Mem have pity on M- send money as much as Tuan wishes. N- remembers well Tuan and Mem because Tuan and Mem were of kindly heart and very good to him. N- regards Tuan like a Father and Mem like a Mother. So too M- remembers the time when Tuan and Mem lived in her house and all the food she prepared Tuan liked. If Tuan wants some coconut sugar M- can send it. . . .'

Such letters, with their mixture of self-interest and sentiment, combining appeal to sympathy, to status relations, and to enjoyable memories of the past, are hard to resist, and personal factors here are very important in the decision.

Scientifically, it is interesting to examine some aspects of such a situation in the light of what Mauss has written. The first point to make in such a situation of gift-giving or considering requests for gifts or other assistance by the anthropologist is that commonly a considerable status differential is involved. Mauss for the most part considered cases of gift and return where the general social status of the parties concerned was broadly equivalent. In so far as their comparative status was involved in gift and reciprocity, it was in terms of competing for margins rather than starting from non-competitive statuses of very different kinds. (Mauss does refer to gifts between chief and a member of his community, but does not examine this to any degree.) As far as the anthropologist and the member of an exotic field community are concerned, their statuses, without being necessarily higher or lower than one another, are of different order. Commonly, one aspect of this difference is that the anthropologist is in a very superior economic position to that of all or most of the people he has studied. If he is to make a gift to one of them, then, the implications of this are different from those of gifts between members of the same community of approximately equal standing. (Different again are gifts from an inferior to a superior, made, as Tönnies states, as an expression of humility, with gratitude that they are accepted (1961, p. 92).)

To begin with, because of an anthropologist's superior economic position a gift may be solicited from him without loss of status by the asker. Most of the Malay peasants among whom we worked were very poor. Our resources appeared almost unlimited to them. To ask for assistance, then, was not necessarily demeaning, indeed could seem quite reasonable in their circumstances. This conditioned the attitude towards reciprocity. In very many cases there was clearly no intention of repayment in any material form whatsoever. The transaction took on the character of what may be described as a free gift, meaning by this not one that is spontaneous, as Malinowski describes it, but one that is made without the expectation of material return.

Let us take Mauss's major fields of obligation in turn. As regards the obligation to give, the situation is clearly complex. Leaving aside any personal sentiments between giver and recipient, three elements can be clearly distinguished. One is the view that a gift in these circumstances, when the anthropologist has left the field, is a continuation of the reciprocity which he gave in the field for past benefits. This is an imprecise item because the benefits received included many kinds of services, material and immaterial, the total effect of which is not really calculable. A second element in the obligation to give is certainly the anthropologist's interest in his own prestige – his feeling that failure to respond to an appeal will lower his status in the eyes of his appellant and possibly of the community. In a way, too, the issue is more subtle than this. Since he may never see the community or the appellant again, it is really the anthropologist's status in his own eyes that concerns him. Thirdly, there is the element of moral obligation. If people are poor

13

should one then not try to help, if they ask? But this characterization of the situation is inadequate. There is an obligation to give, but there are also elements which bear against making the gift. One of these is economic calculation. Illimitable as may be the anthropologist's resources from the point of view of his field informants, these resources could not long sustain a drain of gifts if many of the people he knew in the field were to request aid. Any series of gifts made, then, must have some relation to the total resources of the giver. But there is also the other side of the question. Any gift received should also bear some relation to the total requirements of the recipient. Here what may be regarded as a rationalization of the donor's unwillingness to give enters, mainly the view that since anything within the means of the donor is unlikely to relieve substantially the poverty of the recipient – and certainly could be only a minute contribution to alleviate the poverty of the community – therefore it is better not to give at all and so not encourage false hopes. I think that such a view is not wholly a rationalization and that many refusals of gifts sought have such a moral as well as an economic component. This is perhaps particularly true in cases where the anthropologist follows the 'Protestant ethic' and regards a person as primarily responsible himself for his own economic and social condition.

Again, dislike of pauperization – of contributing to a situation in which people are made to appear as begging, of soliciting goods which have not been offered, may also be an element. Again, there may be another moral aspect from the point of view of equity – why should A be given something which is not also given to B, who deserves it at least as much. The upshot of such consideration is, I would argue, that the 'obligation to give' is not simply a matter of status involvement, but has a number of complex elements involving choices of a significant, possibly painful, character before a decision is arrived at.

Now for the 'obligation to repay', involving the concept of reciprocity. In using the term 'reciprocity', one should distinguish concretely three types of transaction: those where the net effect is to restore the former economic equilibrium of the parties; those where the return transfer abates but does not neutralize the loss in the first transaction, or conversely more than makes up for such loss; and those where emphasis is laid upon the act of return rather than upon the quantity or quality of the goods returned. (Cf. Sahlins, 1965, for an elaborate scheme of a more formal order.) Linked with this last is the type of transaction where no material equivalent of any kind is rendered in return, but the giver is regarded as acquiring status or merit by his act. The recipient repays by serving as an 'instrument of enhancement' for the giver. In the present Malay instance mentioned, the obligation to repay any money given may be regarded as almost always of the last-cited order. Repayment is non-existent in material terms – or nearly so – but it is presumably conceived in terms of giving diffuse satisfactions – including verbal acknowledgement of the value of the gift. Long-term reciprocity, should the anthropologist ever return to the field, is conceivable but improbable. Certainly here no such ritual sanctions of the kind described by Mauss are applicable.

The 'obligation to receive' is also ambiguous. Presumably a gift once requested will be received, the obligation to receive it being the ordinary one of consistency in conduct. But two considerations may arise: one is that the amount of the gift may be either considerably more or considerably less than was expected. It may, therefore, be refused either as over-generous and unnecessary or as inadequate and humiliating. But although the gift may be regarded by the recipient as either too great or too small, he may still receive it because of the kind of sanctions that Mauss describes, a commingling of economic interest and respect for the relative social status of donor and recipient. On the other hand, a significant point appears here. If a gift is not solicited, then it may be refused on the grounds that receipt of it would not be consonant with the social status of the recipient, but would place him in an inferior position.

When, therefore, Mauss's argument is applied, as he himself has asked (p. 78), to concrete cases, then certain general conclusions can be drawn. First, it is clear that in any actual case motivation for donating, receiving, and repaying gifts may be much more complex than Mauss has allowed. In particular, presence or absence of status differentials and status competition is very significant. Again, while Mauss's view about the gift as an extension of the personality of the giver may be regarded as valid at the symbolical level, on the ethnographic evidence it is not so at the ritual level. In this field of symbolic expansion, Mauss's views would seem to be derived as much from first principles of psychological introspection as from sociological analysis. That this is probably so may be seen by reference to the brief treatment of the subject by C. G. Jung who, apparently without having read Mauss, put forward very much the same argument.

'To the extent that "Our" possessions are projection carriers, they are *more* than what they are in themselves, and function as such. They have acquired several layers of meaning and are therefore symbolical. When therefore I give away something that is "mine", what I am giving is essentially a symbol, a thing of many meanings; but owing to my unconsciousness of its symbolic character, it adheres to my ego because it is part of my personality. Hence there is, explicitly or implicitly, a personal claim bound up with every gift. There is always an unspoken "Give that thou mayest receive"' (Jung, 1958, p. 206).

Certainly, whether there has been derivation or not, the language of the psychologist and the sociologist is very similar.[9]

Moreover, Mauss has taken no account of the quantitative aspect of the gift situation. The proportion which the gift bears to the total resources of the giver, and to the resources and requirements of the recipient, may be very relevant in promoting or inhibiting the gift and its reciprocation. It is true that 'Give what you can afford' is a maxim that is simpler to enunciate than to work out in practice. But prudent calculation as much as status interest is often the determining factor of the time and size of a gift.

Then again, the moral aspect of gift-making may be much more complex than Mauss allows. Take what may be termed the *douceur*, the 'softening gift' of which officials, especially in Africa and the East, have learnt to be so wary. We know that what is sometimes called 'bribery' may be part gift-convention, not necessarily intended to secure undue personal advantage for the donor. At its best an expression of goodwill and esteem, or gratitude for past services rendered, at its worst a blatant attempt to secure favours at the expense of other people, such a 'softening gift' may be capable of various middle interpretations. But in the more rigorous administrations acceptance of any such gift is sternly discouraged. Incompatibility and conflict of obligation in regard to personal benefactor and impersonal State employer may easily arise. For an official to receive presents from a businessman to whom he afterwards let contracts would be in the eyes of his colleagues an act of decidedly negative morality. 'The obligation to receive' and the 'obligation to repay' are clearly out of place in such a situation. Public responsibility must take precedence over private transaction. There is an obligation quite definitely implied in the conditions of the official's service *not* to establish a social relationship by gifts.

Finally, Mauss has represented situations of gift exchange as those of conventional, almost automatic, behaviour and response. But what the social anthropologist sees in practice is often some degree of uncertainty as to whether to give and whether to reciprocate. Also, where group representation is involved, he may see differences of view among those concerned, not only as to the amounts of the gifts or recompense, but also as to their timing, their quality, and indeed whether they should be given at all.

In the light of the findings of economic anthropology over the last forty years since Mauss's monograph appeared, a new theoretical study of 'the gift' would now seem appropriate. Here anthropologists would probably agree with Mauss that there are elements of overlapping in gift behaviour from the primitive peasant field right through to industrial societies. The proportion of gift-making may be much less significant in an industrial type of society, but the basic types of behaviour would seem to have much in common. This seems to be one of the areas indeed, like that of kinship, where the studies of a social anthropologist should be pursued right through into his own society.

PROBLEMS OF VALUATION

It is obvious that highly significant factors in the interpretation of even relatively undeveloped economic systems are the processes

17

and the volume of the exchanges that take place. Some of these systems facilitate their exchange mechanisms by use of a general medium such as the shell strings and cowries described for some parts of Melanesia and Africa. It has long been recognized that, while some of these media may reasonably be classified as 'money', the restrictions and special attributions involved in the uses of others make it advisable to put them in another category. The analogy with coupons suggested by Mary Douglas in this volume offers an intriguing set of criteria for discussion. But the fact that in many primitive economic systems there is no mechanism whereby goods and services can be consistently and regularly exchanged for one another in relatively free style has definite restrictive effects (cf. Firth, 1959, pp. 23-24). It also raises a difficult problem for which no adequate solution has yet been found. In the absence of such pervasive exchange how can any system of evaluation of goods and services manifest itself? Can one identify prices? Certainly not in any very narrow sense. But using the term 'price' in the broadest sense, what kind of price can be assigned to, say, a wooden bowl or a day's work in helping to build a house? Economics can for many problems direct attention to opportunity costs at the margin, use of alternates, or substitutions – which is what some 'primitive' peoples themselves have in effect done. Where commodities are not in regular exchange for one another they still are commonly found to be arranged in a hierarchy or on a scale of estimations (see Firth, 1965, pp. 336-344). Concepts of equivalence, and of greater or less worth are formulated quite clearly and applied empirically. Goods and services are categorized as equivalent or not, and in the latter case as of more or less 'weight'. So for the Tikopia a wooden bowl is equivalent to a hank of sinnet cord and will be so exchanged on ceremonial occasions – the quality of cord and bowl being carefully scrutinized on both sides. But a bowl is not equivalent to a day's work on house-building, nor to a canoe. It would be regarded as a gross overpayment in the first case and a ludicrous underpayment in the second. These principles of valuation in terms of substitution are equally valid whether one is dealing with price in the strict sense or with non-price conditions. But in the latter situation determination of these values is a very complex matter. It may be argued indeed that only by the refined techniques of modern economic analysis can the problem be adequately handled.

The problem is further complicated in some of these primitive economic systems by the convention that spheres or circuits of exchange are highly differentiated. In such case objects in one sphere may not be directly exchangeable against those in another. (This is so at the ethnographic level. Analytically the spheres interpenetrate, if only because labour and food enter into both spheres at the stage of production.)

So in Tikopia wooden bowls and canoes are never directly matched. Since the economy lacks a common medium of exchange the value of one object cannot be then fully expressed in terms of another. The ranking system allows commodities to be put in some kind of hierarchical order of estimation, but no precise measurement of differences between them is feasible.

There is nothing very startling in this conclusion. Even in a highly complex modern industrial society there are certain kinds of goods, such as religious symbols, and certain kinds of services, such as many jobs within the family, which are never brought to the bar of exchange in any directly measurable way. It is indeed part of the peculiarity of every social system that it preserves certain of its sacra from direct incorporation into the economic system. What characterizes many primitive economic systems is that in accordance with their small scale and lack of impersonal relationships they can manage to run the system with so little confrontation of items in direct regular exchange. This theme has been demonstrated and elaborately analysed by Salisbury, who has argued that the presence in non-monetary societies of discrete scales of value, each dependent upon a different standard of evaluation, is not an unfortunate accident. It is a relatively simple mechanism which helps to maintain a basic standard of life at the same time as an allocation of status and power in the society (1962, p. 212).

Attempts have been made to find a more generally applicable measure of value in primitive economic systems lacking monetary media. One of the most sophisticated has been the use of the concept of time as a measure. Belshaw in 1949, and again in 1954, put forward the opinion that perhaps the nearest measure

19

of real cost in Melanesian conditions would be the use of the elasticity of demand for time. He pointed out that

'in a modern Western society it is reasonably safe to use money as a measure representing the resultant of the subjective balancing of ends achieved against ends sacrificed. The range of uses to which money may be put is extremely wide, and the values which are not satisfied by the use of money may conveniently be disregarded for many purposes. In addition, it may safely be presumed that the major institution examined, the firm, has money-making as its primary, if not its sole, end. In Melanesia today this is not the case. . . . We must therefore find some other more universal element which may be subjected to measurement. Such a universal element is time.'

Belshaw points out that time has the great advantage that it is measurable and that it must be used in the satisfaction of any ends whatsoever. On the other hand, it is not itself a direct measure of preference as between ends, since the amount of time spent on an activity depends upon the intensity of labour, skill, and technique employed and other resources available, as well as on the possible alternative use of time. Moreover, when we have ranked the goods in an elasticity of demand according to the time required to obtain them, we still are not ranging them in order of preference or value in any ultimate sense (C. S. Belshaw, 1949, Appendix IX; 1954, pp. 149-150). A similar position has been adopted by Salisbury, who has argued for the Siane that time is the only resource that can be used for competing ends, and the cost of any activity is what has to be forgone by using the time for that particular activity. 'Time then is *the* Siane measure of cost' (op. cit., p. 144). Difficulties that arise because of differences in intensity of labour, for example, are regarded by Salisbury as being dealt with in average terms by aggregates. The difficulty that arises through the lack of small units recognized by the people concerned was met by Salisbury's making his calculations in terms of man-days.[10]

All this touches on a well-worn theme in economics. It does seem that time is the most adequately measureable item available to the economic anthropologist who is studying non-monetary economic systems. But what does it measure? While in a general way time spent can be regarded as a measure of real cost, this still touches only part of the attribution of value. The concept can be linked, of course, as Frankenberg has indicated, with Karl Marx's view of the labour-cost theory of value. Marx was concerned to demonstrate the difference between three concepts: the amount of labour power (measured in time) put into the production of a commodity (what he regarded as its intrinsic value), the amount of support (primary subsistence) necessary to provide for the labourer in order that the commodity may be produced, and the difference of both of these in given historical conditions from the market price of the commodity (its relative value). Marx was particularly concerned to argue that in a capitalist system the labourer can produce more than the equivalent of what it costs to support him, and that by the structure of the system this 'surplus value' is acquired by the capitalist – hence class antagonism (cf. Dobb, 1931, pp. 605 *et seq.*). There is no need to traverse the arguments in regard to this theory.[11] But it must be made clear that labour – or labour-time – as a measure of *cost* is very different from labour or labour-time as a measure of *value*. The calculation of units of labour or of labour-time expresses just what it states. The notion of 'intrinsic' value attributed to these units is derived from elsewhere. And for them to have any significance in evaluation of the product, some assumption of the *relevance* of what the labour produces must be introduced.[12] The notion of time measurement as an index to relative values in a primitive economic system then, takes the analyst only a very short way.

ECONOMIC ANTHROPOLOGY IN THE MODERN WORLD

One of the major interests in economic anthropology has been descriptive – to find out how people in relatively simple technical conditions and with social fabrics very different from our own actually manage their economic affairs. Allied to this has been an interest of a more theoretical order – to try to elucidate the principles that underlie such economic systems and their relation to a more general body of economic thought and thought about the nature of society. In recent years, however, other trends of interest have also come to the fore. With rapid development in technology and communications, large numbers of primitive and peasant communities have been brought into increasing contact with industrial economy and with new and powerful political and social forces. Social anthropologists have of necessity turned their attention to the analysis of the changes taking place. Titles of studies such as *From Stone to Steel* or *Machine Age Maya* epitomize a host of studies in this field; in this volume Lorraine Barič has analysed a very interesting example.

Alongside this development has grown an increasing interest in the study of concepts hitherto regarded as a primary concern of economists and economic historians. Among these is the notion of the entrepreneur. Earlier anthropological studies could see little use to be made of this concept. (In my first study of the Tikopia economy I used the concept to only a very limited degree (Firth, 1965, pp. 134n, 308).) But as C. S. Belshaw has pointed out (1955, p. 146), there are several ways in which anthropologists may legitimately interest themselves in the study of entrepreneurs. They may assess the function of enterprise in the economies of primitive or peasant peoples, and examine the ways in which leadership embodies enterprise and is reflected in organization. With the growing modern preoccupation with processes of social change and problems of economic growth, anthropologists may study entrepreneurs as persons involved in these processes. Further, though it is as yet a relatively unchartered area for our study, anthropologists may deal with the complex problems of modern business administration as an aspect of the working of small groups, more or less integrated with cultural elements external to the firm. Reviewing the various meanings of the term 'entrepreneur', as indicated by L. M. Fraser (1937), Belshaw points out that from the point of view of an anthropologist interested in social change, extensive management is more important than innovation in the function of an entrepreneur. An important feature of the anthropological analysis is the study of entrepreneurs as they fulfil social roles in relation with other elements of the society. Studies by Scarlett Epstein, Salisbury, and Pospisil have added to our knowledge of entrepreneurship in societies of relatively

Themes in Economic Anthropology

simple technology, while Fredrik Barth and his collaborators (1964) have analysed entrepreneurship in complex European conditions.[13]

In line with this general anthropological interest in the characteristics of entrepreneurs has been an increased concern with processes of choice and decision-making – a trend visible in other aspects of social anthropology as well. Here the economic anthropologist does two things: reveals empirically just what factors, in what combination, enter into situations of choice; and indicates along what lines resolution of the choice is most commonly effected. Such analysis of actual processes of decision-making by Sutti Ortiz (pp. 191-226 below) yields results of interest to economists as well as to anthropologists.

It is from the point of view of the significance of what Lorraine Barić has termed the social variables, perhaps more than any other, that studies in economic anthropology can be significant in the applied field.[14] Economic planners, for instance, not infrequently lack a knowledge of the structure and norms of the community for which they plan. Here the provision of knowledge by anthropologists may be a very important component of the developmental process – though so far as a rule such provision has been conspicuously absent.[15]

Justification for the study of economic anthropology does not have to be found only in its possible contribution to the solution of problems of economic growth. One can defend the pursuit of 'pure' knowledge here as elsewhere, even if not as an end in itself, at least as essential for the proper development of an intellectual discipline – and ultimately for the proper development of human personality. But even if one rejects utilitarian criteria as the index of worth, one must recognize, as economists have already done, that to direct intellectual exploration towards the analysis of some concrete practical problem can give a powerful stimulus to abstract theoretical inquiry.

In my view two major sets of problems above all confront anthropologist and economist alike in this developing situation. One set of problems relates to economic viability. As modernization advances and the full range of consumption goods and services of industrial society tends to be presented before the people of even the most remote 'underdeveloped' areas of the world, these people will need to make a radical redeployment of their resources, especially their labour resources, if they are going to attempt to achieve the consumption levels which almost certainly they are going to demand. Traditional economic systems are changing with almost explosive force, but it is not at all clear that such changes will be effective in securing the new wants. Hence another set of problems relates to the possibility of radical realignment of existing systems of control of resources and economic choices. Enough examples are available of such redeployment and realignment in recent history of African and Asian societies to indicate a range of possible alternatives. But the analysis of the processes involved offers a challenge of great interest and importance to economic anthropology.[16]

NOTES

1. I am indebted to Leonard Joy and Percy Cohen for very useful suggestions at several points in this essay. I have given elsewhere (Firth, 1959a, pp. 25-48; 1965, pp. 1-31) other comments on the study of economic anthropology.
2. See Hobsbawn (1964, p. 25). Similarly, Max Weber's observations on primitive economic life, as reported in Chapter 2 of his *General Economic History* (1961) are fragmentary and old-fashioned. The more formal analysis of non-exchange economies by Schumpeter, though it deals primarily with an isolated manorial estate and an isolated communist society, is more suggestive (e.g. 1961, pp. 138-150).
3. See exemplification of this in the change of title of Herskovits's book, originally published in 1940 as *The Economic Life of Primitive Peoples*, in 1952 retitled as *Economic Anthropology: A Study in Comparative Economics*. Cf. Firth, who in 1939 referred to the possible future of 'economic anthropology' (p. 29), but for the most part discussed 'primitive economics'.
4. In addition to the stimulating but controversial work of Karl Polanyi and his collaborators (1957), interesting argument has been presented by Sahlins (1960), Meillassoux (1960), and Godelier (1965). There is not space to examine their more critical statements here.
5. E.g. R. Thurnwald (1927); Bronislaw Malinowsky y Julio de la Fuente (1957); S. W. Mintz (1960); Alice G. Dewey (1962); P. Bohannan & G. Dalton (1962); Clifford Geertz (1963). An elaborate study of the impact of a modern economy on a system of traditional markets in Oaxaca, Mexico, is being made by Ralph L. Beals and associates at present (1967).

It may be noted that in some relatively underdeveloped economies the local physical market may also be virtually equivalent to the total, i.e. the conceptual market for some kinds of goods and services.
6. A valuable commentary upon Mauss's work has been given by Lévi-Strauss (1950, pp. xxxii-xl). I would, however, credit Malinowski with having supplied Mauss with more theoretical stimulus in this field than Lévi-Strauss allows.

For interesting observations on gift and exchange, especially on prestation,

Themes in Economic Anthropology

see C. S. Belshaw (1965, pp. 11-51; cf. also Firth, 1963). The interpretation of social behaviour in terms of exchange has been pursued to great lengths by Homans (1961) and by Blau (1964). The latter in particular has attempted to apply marginal analysis to processes of social exchange in groups.

7. Lévi-Strauss has pointed out, cogently in my view, that the concept of essence of personality (*hau*) being involved in a return gift is unnecessary to Mauss's theory of exchange (1950, pp. xxxviii-xl). But whereas he chides Mauss gently for having adopted and generalized a specific 'native' theory, that of the Maori, the fact is that Mauss not only reinterpreted the Maori notion but also misread the text he cited. I have given a critical examination of Mauss's handling of this material, with some further consideration of gift exchange, in my study of the Maori economy (Firth, 1959, pp. 418-421, 425-426 – originally given in 1929). Mauss also made some errors in his use of Malinowski's material on the *kula*; see Firth (1957, p. 222).

8. Reinterpretation of the Northwest Coast potlatch in more specifically economic terms than Mauss used has recently been given by Suttles, Vayda, and Piddocke (see, e.g., Piddocke, 1965).

9. The language of literature has also many analogies, e.g. 'The only gift is a portion of thyself. The gift to be true must be the flowing of the giver into me'. Cf. 'He is a good man who can receive a gift well . . . the expectation of gratitude is mean and is continually punished by the total insensibility of the obliged person'. (From the essay on 'Gifts' in Emerson, 1876, Vol. I, pp. 220-223.) Note also 'It is rare indeed that people give. Most people guard and keep; they suppose that it is they themselves and what they identify with themselves that they are guarding and keeping, whereas what they are actually guarding and keeping is their system of reality and what they assume themselves to be. One can give nothing whatever without giving oneself – that is to say, risking oneself. If one cannot risk oneself, then one is simply incapable of giving' (James Baldwin, 1963, p. 100).

10. I myself have used time measure in terms of 'net days' to indicate variation between fishing-net teams in Kelantan, and the existence of alternative social and economic preferences (Raymond Firth, 1946, pp. 93-97).

11. Elsewhere I have indicated briefly the general relevance of Marx's views for 'dynamic theory' in social anthropology (Firth, 1964, pp. 19-25).

12. That the labour-cost theory of value is found unsatisfactory by an eminent modern economist not prejudiced against a Marxist view may be epitomized by the comments of Joan Robinson. She points out that for manufacturing industry differences in price are more or less, though not exactly, proportional to labour costs, but that this is not true of natural commodities. Moreover, this is not the same thing as a scheme of values. We cannot estimate the total value of the goods produced in a year by simply totting up the hours of labour that have gone into them. Some labour is highly productive, other is much less so. The value of the product is not only the labour expended upon it, but it also includes the contribution made by capital goods in which labour-time has been embodied in the past. Moreover, units of value conceived as labour-time do not measure the really significant quantities. 'In terms of *value*, an hour is an hour. A constant quantity of labour-time, year after year, produces the same *value*. But who cares? What we want to know is how much *stuff* it is producing.' Marx's notion of 'abstract labour', like Ricardo's 'absolute value' or Edgeworth's measurement of utility, is a 'mirage' (1962, pp. 40-46, 68).

13. For further observations on entrepreneurship in 'underdeveloped' economies see Hirschman (1961, pp. 3-4, 16-19).

14. Reference to the work of anthropologists in this field is given, e.g., by Schultz (1964, pp. 6, 40, etc.) and Hirschman (1961, pp. 2, 138). Various contributions to conferences on economic growth and allied topics have also been made by anthropologists – see, e.g., *Report of an Expert Working Group on Social Prerequisites to Economic Growth* (UNESCO, SS/38, 1964).
15. A striking instance of clarification by an anthropologist after the event shows how lack of communication between technical experts and Africans in such apparently simple matters as the measurement of fields, and of time-periods, inhibited agricultural development in Basutoland (Sandra Wallman, 1965).
16. For examination of these issues in the small-scale economy of Tikopia see Firth (1959b, pp. 339-349). For a recent broad treatment in a setting of discussion of the scope and findings of economic anthropology see Manning Nash (1966).

REFERENCES

BALDWIN, JAMES. 1963. *The Fire Next Time*. New York: The Dial Press.

BARTH, FREDRIK (ed.). 1963. *The Role of the Entrepreneur in Social Change in Northern Norway*. Bergen; Oslo: Norwegian Universities Press.

BELSHAW, CYRIL S. 1949. Economic Aspects of Culture Contact in Eastern Melanesia (Unpublished Ph.D. Thesis. London.)

—— 1954. The Cultural Milieu of the Entrepreneur: A Critical Essay. *Explorations in Entrepreneurial History* 7: 144-146.

—— 1965. *Traditional Exchange and Modern Markets*. Englewood Cliffs, N. J.: Prentice-Hall.

BLAU, PETER. 1964. *Exchange and Power in Social Life*. New York: Wiley.

BOHANNAN, PAUL & DALTON, GEORGE (eds.). 1962. *Markets in Africa*. Evanston: Northwestern University Press.

DEWEY, ALICE G. 1962. *Peasant Marketing in Java*. New York: Free Press of Glencoe.

DOBB, MAURICE. 1931. An Introduction to Economics. In William Rose (ed.), *An Outline of Modern Knowledge*. pp. 593-623. London: Victor Gollancz.

EMERSON, RALPH W. 1876. Gifts. In *The Complete Works of Ralph Waldo Emerson*. Vol. I. London.

FIRTH, RAYMOND. 1946. *Malay Fishermen: Their Peasant Economy* (2nd edn. 1956). London: Kegan Paul.

—— 1957. The Place of Malinowski in the History of Economic Anthropology. In Raymond Firth (ed.), *Man and Culture: An Evaluation of the Work of Bronislaw Malinowski*. pp. 209-227. London: Routledge & Kegan Paul.

—— 1959a. *Economics of the New Zealand Maori* (2nd edn. of *Primitive Economics of the New Zealand Maori*, 1929). Wellington, New Zealand: R. E. Owen, Government Printer.

—— 1959b. *Social Change in Tikopia*. London: Allen & Unwin.

—— 1963. Offering and Sacrifice: Problems of Organisation. *Journal of the Royal Anthropological Institute* **93**: 12-24.

—— 1964. *Essays on Social Organization and Values*. London School of Economics Monographs on Social Anthropology. London: Athlone Press.

—— 1965. *Primitive Polynesian Economy* (2nd edn. London: Routledge & Kegan Paul.

FRASER, L. M. 1937. *Economic Thought and Knowledge*. London: Black.

GEERTZ, CLIFFORD. 1963. *Pedlars and Princes: Social Change and Economic Modernization in Two Indonesian Towns*. Chicago & London: University of Chicago Press.

GODELIER, MAURICE. 1965. Objet et Méthodes de l'Anthropologie Économique. *L'Homme*, Avril-Juin: 32-91.

HERSKOVITS, MELVILLE J. 1940. *The Economic Life of Primitive Peoples*. New York: Alfred A. Knopf.

HIRSCHMAN, ALBERT O. 1961. *The Strategy of Economic Development*. New Haven, Conn.: Yale University Press.

HOBSBAWM, E. J. 1964. Introduction to *Karl Marx: Pre-Capitalist Economic Formations* (trans. Jack Cohen). London: Lawrence & Wishart.

HOMANS, GEORGE CASPAR. 1961. *Social Behaviour: The Elementary Forms*. London: Routledge & Kegan Paul.

JUNG, C. G. 1958. Transformation Symbolism in the Mass. Violet S. de Laszlo (ed.). In *Psyche & Symbol: A Selection from the Writings of C. G. Jung*. New York: Doubleday.

KOPPERS, WILHELM. 1915-1916. Die Ethnologische Wirtschaftsforschung. *Anthropos* **10-11**: 611-51, 971-1079.

LEROY, OLIVIER. 1925. *Essai d'introduction critique à l'étude de l'économie primitive*. Paris: Guenther.

LÉVI-STRAUSS, CLAUDE. 1950. Introduction à l'oeuvre de Marcel Mauss. In *Sociologie et anthropologie par Marcel Mauss*. Paris: Presses Universitaires de France.

MALINOWSKY, BRONISLAW, & DE LA FUENTE, JULIO. 1957. *La Economía de un Sistema de Mercados en México. Acta Anthropologica*, ep. 2, Vol. 1.

MAUSS, MARCEL. 1923-1924. Essai sur le don. *L'Année sociologique* 1 (i): 30-186. (Trans. Ian Cunnison, 1954, as *The Gift*. London: Cohen & West.)

MEILLASSOUX, CLAUDE. 1960. Essai d'interprétation du phénomène économique dans les sociétés traditionnelles d'autosubsistance. *Cahiers d'Etudes Africaines* 4: 38-67.

MINTZ, SIDNEY W. 1960. A Tentative Typology of Eight Haitian Market Places. *Revista de Ciencias Sociales* 4: 15-17.

NASH, MANNING, 1966. *Primitive and Peasant Economic Systems.* San Francisco: Chandler Publishing Company.

PIDDOCKE, STUART. 1965. The Potlatch System of the Southern Kwakiutl: A New Perspective. *Southwestern Journal of Anthropology* 21: 244-264.

POLANYI, KARL, ARENSBERG, CONRAD M. & PEARSON, HARRY w. 1957. *Trade and Market in the Early Empires.* Glencoe, Ill: Free Press.

ROBINSON, JOAN. 1962. *Economic Philosophy.* London: C. A. Watts.

SAHLINS, MARSHALL D. 1960. Political Power and the Economy in Primitive Society. In Gertrude E. Dole & Robert L. Carneiro, *Essays in the Science of Culture,* pp. 390-416. New York: Thomas Y. Crowell Company.

—— 1965. On the Sociology of Primitive Exchange. In M. Banton (ed.), *The Relevance of Models for Social Anthropology,* pp. 139-236. A.S.A. Monographs, 1. London: Tavistock Publications.

SALISBURY, R. F. 1962. *From Stone to Steel: Economic Consequences of a Technological Change in New Guinea.* Melbourne University Press on behalf of the Australian National University.

SCHMIDT, MAX. 1920-1921. *Grundriss der Ethnologischen Volkswirtschaftslehre.* 2 vols, Stuttgart.

SCHUMPETER, JOSEPH A. 1961. *The Theory of Economic Development* (trans. Redvers Opie). New York: Oxford University Press.

SCHULTZ, THEODORE W. 1964. *Transforming Traditional Agriculture.* New Haven & London: Yale University Press.

THURNWALD, RICHARD. 1927. Markt. In Max Ebert (ed.): *Reallexikon der Vorgeschichte,* vol. 8, pp. 34-42. Berlin: Verlag Walther Greuter & Co.

TÖNNIES, FERDINAND. 1961. *Custom: An Essay on Social Codes* (trans. A. Farrell Borenstein). New York: Free Press of Glencoe.

WALLMAN, SANDRA. 1965. The Communication of Measurement in Basutoland. *Human Organization* 24: 236-243.

WEBER, MAX. 1961. *General Economic History* (trans. Frank H. Knight). New York: Collier Books.

Leonard Joy

One Economist's View of the Relationship between Economics and Anthropology

'. . . the different social and human sciences may be different realms, in whose borderlands trespass is dangerous save for the genius.

'But we do not advise that a writer in prose should not read poetry, or a poet prose: and a social or human scientist may profit by studying disciplines other than his own. It is dangerous to practise them without training and appropriate skills.' ELY DEVONS AND MAX GLUCKMAN (1964, p. 261)

'. . . we again state emphatically that there is a *duty of abstention*, which requires that if we are to solve certain problems we have to abstain from studying other, though apparently related, problems, and leave these to our colleagues, whether in the same or in some other discipline.' (Ibid, p. 168)

These two quotations from Devons and Gluckman – one an economist, the other a social anthropologist – seem to raise central issues about the relationship of economics to anthropology to which I must address myself. However, before asking to what extent an anthropologist may profit by studying economics and how far he should leave its study to economists, it is worth discussing the nature of economics and its bearing on anthropology.

Let us accept from the outset that there are broad topics of common interest to the two disciplines. Economists and anthropologists have both been interested in analysing the determinants of resource allocation and product distribution. Typically, however, economists pursue their studies in relation to different communities from those in which anthropologists pursue theirs. It has been argued that it is the very difference between these communities that puts the study of the same topics within the purview of economics in one set of communities but within the purview of anthropology in the other.

The differences that distinguish two sets of communities and are supposed to justify this division of labour should be noted.

It is to be found in the impersonality or otherwise of exchange (Polanyi, 1957), or, more generally, the 'low level of differentiation of the economic subsystem from other subsystems' in primitive as compared to advanced economies (Parsons, 1953). This is not by any means the same as saying that the role of production and exchange possibilities, as compared to that of social values and institutions, in determining behaviour is *insignificant* in primitive economies. So far as I know, this has not been argued. On the contrary, the importance of the material environment has often been emphasized.[1] While the ready differentiation of economic from other sub-systems in advanced economies may be taken to justify the neglect of social variables in the study of production and distribution in advanced economies, it cannot be used to justify the neglect of economic variables in the study of primitive communities.

SOCIAL AND ECONOMIC DETERMINANTS OF BEHAVIOUR

It has been argued that in primitive societies the prime determinants of behaviour are social rather than economic. This argument has been most explicitly related to primitive exchange (Dalton, 1961), where it is observed that participants in primitive markets do not appear to seek immediate material advantage in exchange, but concern themselves more with considerations of role and status. The primacy of social factors has not to my knowledge been explicitly argued in relation to the determination of production and resource allocation in primitive societies. Nevertheless, it appears to be widely assumed to govern all economic activity and to be regarded as sufficient reason for treating economic and other variables as exogenous to social theories of the determination of production and exchange. This does not mean that economic variables are neglected by anthropologists. Indeed, economic, ecological, and technological data are among those which anthropologists almost invariably record. They are the context in which society is seen to operate. Yet analytical criteria of significance for the selection of data to be recorded seem absent or weak. Goods and services are discussed because they are what are being produced and exchanged. The bearing that the conditions of their production and properties for exchange have upon behaviour, while generally recognized in principle, seems to me to be given too little significance in analysis. Even if one takes the view that economic variables should be regarded as exogenous to theories of social determination of behaviour, one must recognize a prior need to determine the role of the variables exogenous to the system. I would question whether this role has been adequately defined and whether it could be so defined without recourse by anthropologists to economics.

While it might be satisfactory to treat economic variables as exogenous for the analysis of equilibrium situations, I am sceptical of the possibilities of progress by this means in the analysis of some aspects of social dynamics. For that matter, I am no less sceptical of the possibilities of progress in the study of economic dynamics while social variables are treated as exogenous to the economic system. Take, for example, questions of land reform (or is a society no longer primitive when land reform is imposed upon it?). An economist might analyse the effects of a proposed reform in terms of changes in the opportunities open to various people involved. (In this context, 'opportunities' is a neutral word indicating simply 'possibilities'.) Predicting the economic consequences of a land reform involves predicting what people will do in the face of new opportunities. Given an understanding of their values and customs, the direction – if not the speed – of response might be predicted. But values themselves – and social institutions, too – may change in the face of new opportunities. A model of change in this situation would need to incorporate, endogenously, both economic and social variables. Economists are gradually becoming aware of the significance of this interdependence. A study of development economics reveals values and social institutions to be of unavoidable significance and models of economic development must allow for changes in social values and institutions resulting from, and affecting the process of, economic development. What is true for the economist is equally true for the anthropologist. One cannot take economic opportunities as given. They are changing and will continue to change, not only exogenously, but in response to changes in values and social institutions. A study of the mutual interrelationships of economic and social factors seems ultimately to demand a joint approach by the two disciplines.

IMPLICATIONS OF ECONOMIC MODELS FOR ANTHROPOLOGY

It seems wise to pause at this point to consider the nature of economics in relation to anthropology. There can be no doubt that the conventional textbook economics models commonly relate to the explanation of phenomena which do not occur in primitive economies – at least in the sense in which they are seen to occur in advanced economies. Money, interest, employment, boom, and slump are convenient examples. In so far as comparable phenomena can be found in primitive economies the contrasts are usually more striking than the similarities. Some would argue (Dalton, 1961) that there are no economics models that relate to the phenomena of primitive economies. I would dispute this, but, even if it were true that no such models at present exist, it would not deny the possibility that they could be developed.

It seems that some anthropologists would have difficulty in agreeing with this view on the grounds that the behavioural implications of economics models are unacceptable. Much of the discussion on the relevance of economics to anthropology has centred on the issue of whether it is reasonable to assume the existence of economic man in primitive societies. Most of this discussion has assumed that economics depends on an assumption of rational, maximizing behaviour directed to 'economic ends' (see especially Cohen's discussion of Malinowski, Polanyi, Dalton, and Sahlins and, of course, their own works to which he refers (*infra*, pp. 92-99)). It is necessary to make the point here that, whatever economists implicitly assume, they would almost universally deny the existence of 'economic ends'. The choice of ends is not a subject of study to the economist: it is data to him in the same category as data concerning technological possibilities. That it is something he can advise on has been explicitly denied by Robbins (1932, pp. 135-136), and this view appears to be generally accepted. Profit maximizing is certainly not a necessary postulate for the analysis of producers' behaviour. Indeed, economics can proceed a fair way without making any assumptions at all about behaviour, for it can be used to study simply the nature of alternatives available in any situation. Such alternatives can, of course, be described only in material terms by the economist, but he can at least calculate the direct material opportunity cost of any activity. With assistance from the anthropologist, he might also measure the indirect costs where these involve, for example, the sacrifice of reciprocal rights.

In so far as economists have been interested in the behaviour of producers and consumers (always separated in economics textbooks but only for convenience), it has largely been because they were interested in examining the implications of falling demand and rising supply curves. Diminishing utility, diminishing returns, and economic rationality are what these turn out to be. Economists have been generally happy to accept these assumptions underlying their aggregative models. In general, they have given reasonable predictions of the direction in which changes of supply, demand, and price might be expected. Even so, there is a substantial literature questioning the adequacy of the behavioural assumptions of micro-economics (especially in relation to production theory). Some have argued that it is not sufficient to regard non-optimizing behaviour as abnormal. Instead, it has been suggested that behaviour is generally different from what is supposed. It has been urged that there is a need to look more closely at the way decisions are made – especially in relation to production, prices, sales, and inventories – and it has been suggested that a new look at the behaviour of microcosms would indicate needed modifications to aggregative models. By and large, however, the chief success of this line of argument has been to convince many economists of the importance of an emphasis on the measurement of aggregative relationships in the belief that these can be understood independently of an understanding of the behaviour of microcosms they involve.

In spite of this there has been a good deal of work in recent years on studying decision-making behaviour – especially in relation to farmers and manufacturing businesses (Renborg,

1962; Johnson *et al.*, 1961; Cyert & March, 1963). This work has been concerned with analysing both the nature of decisions that are faced and the nature of managerial decision-making processes. Indeed, decision-making is a major topic for study in economics these days, although it scarcely gets a mention in most textbooks.

It cannot be too strongly emphasized that economics is not an immutable body of knowledge contained in universal laws and general theories. Indisputably, economics theorizing is concerned to explain things which do not occur in many societies. Indisputably, too, the assumptions of many of its models are inappropriate to many societies. Equally, the assumptions of its models may be found to be, or may become, inappropriate to the societies where the models are now claimed to have relevance. In this event, we shall not scrap economics; still less shall we all turn anthropologists. (Though this has been the response of some economists who have studied societies new to them.) We shall, I hope, modify the models by looking for new hypotheses to identify relevant variables and their inter-relationships. In part, we shall find our hypotheses by observing the way people and institutions actually do behave. No doubt we shall continue to test our hypotheses with techniques – albeit improved – similar to those we now use. In short, we shall continue to use the tools of economics – simulation, measurement, and testing – to investigate economics problems as our society changes, and we shall extend our applications not only in time but also to the study of different forms of societies – especially to poor countries and to socialist economies.

I have agreed that Polanyi's concern that economics is 'trying to explain things that do not occur' in primitive societies is likely to be valid in relation to existing conventional economics models. However, the mere elucidation of similarities and differences between conventional models and observed reality might in itself be simulating. The papers in this volume by Mary Douglas, Sutti Ortiz, and Scarlett Epstein demonstrate this handsomely. Ortiz and Epstein demonstrate furthermore that there is a need to modify the conventional economics model from which they start. Even if the necessary modification amounts to a rejection of the initial model, the resulting model may still be an economics model. If it is, then the conclusions of Polanyi and Dalton are especially unfortunate. They would be unfortunate enough if they discouraged the development of anthropological models from economics models. They would clearly be wrong if they discouraged anthropologists – or economists – from developing the required economics models.

RELEVANCE OF ECONOMIC ANALYSIS

But I am perhaps making too clear a distinction between economics and anthropological models; in relation to behavioural decision-making models it has already been recognized that it is difficult, if not impossible, to distinguish 'material' from 'social' determinants of behaviour. If we attempted to set up a utility function which was postulated to govern behaviour, some of its dimensions might be distinguished as referring to 'material' satisfactions and some to 'social' satisfactions. In so far as 'material' and 'social' satisfactions were interdependent (i.e. satisfaction in one dimension affecting the degree of satisfaction in the other) it would be impossible to distinguish these for separate analysis. Yet this seems to be the position *most especially* with the societies (economies) studied by anthropologists. Thus there can be no separation of 'economics' from 'social' models. I am arguing that, so far as economics is concerned, decision-making need not be by an individual nor be continuous or consciously maximizing; behaviour may be constrained by custom, the breach of which involves a cost; and it may be guided by any beliefs or values whatsoever.

In short, I am arguing that economics is readily adaptable to the recognition of the interdependence of 'material' and 'social' dimensions of behaviour.

In a market economy, selling rice may involve no more than the exchange of one simple asset for another. In a primitive economy, an exchange involving rice may involve other complex assets and liabilities – or rights and obligations. But the fact that the exchange is more complex does not make it beyond the scope of economics. Neither does the fact that it has social significance. In advanced economies, choice has psychological significance if not social significance, but this does not mean that only psychologists study choice or that economics is irrelevant to its study. Economists have always insisted that it is not their concern to explain preferences. They have been content to explore the nature of alternatives in choice situations in relation to the material aspects of production and exchange possibilities. If anthropologists have an interest in these questions, economics would seem to be relevant to them.

I have argued that economics might be useful in the understanding of choice situations. Let us consider, for example, the problem of understanding the farming systems of technologically underdeveloped communities and the significance of the social institutions which they embody. I would go so far as to say that such farming systems might even be 'predicted' with the aid of economic analysis which could also be used to explore the significance of, for example, customary sexual division of labour, or reciprocal working parties. This would be done by examining the implications of their abandonment. As I myself observed when I worked among the Acholi and peasant Punjabis, the range of choices of farming system, even in the most constraining environment, can be large and complex, involving as it does a nearly infinite permutation of cropping patterns and sequences, fallowing and cultivation practices, and so on. Yet given such data as yields – and their variability in relation to planting date, cultivation practices, position in sequence – and the labour requirements of alternative practices, etc., the economist will be able to define fairly clearly the nature of the choices confronting farming communities. In all probability he will be able to narrow down effective choices of farming systems to give a fairly clear prediction of holding size, crops grown, and so on in relation to size of family, land availability, and customs affecting production and distribution. In order to perform such an exercise the economist must seek data from outside his own discipline – agronomic data, anthropological data, climatological data, and so on. But he has a clear idea of the significance of these data for his model. Moreover, he is able to say something about the consequences of variations in these data. While it may not throw much light on climatology to know how farming systems might be varied if rainfall were less unreliable, it might throw considerable light on anthropology to know what the consequences would be of neglecting social custom. This is one of the major senses in which, I believe, economics can contribute to anthropology.

The significance of a community's values might be explored in comparable fashion. For an understanding of values implies an understanding of alternatives forgone.[2] Sometimes this may be a fairly simple matter, but often it is not, even in relation to direct material alternatives. Where questions of allocation of time or choice of techniques in farming are involved, the issues may be most complex. In analysing the significance of customs in terms of the consequences of their abandonment, customs regarding product distribution might also be investigated using economics models. Situations in Africa and India come readily to mind which would defy 'common-sense' interpretation and demand systematic analysis. Since we do not offer any generalized model appropriate for all situations, a knowledge of the wide range of economics models and their implicit assumptions may be required. So, also, will a knowledge of the reality that the assumptions are required to match.

It bears repeating that economics is not as lacking in adaptability as the textbooks make it seem. Anyone who thinks that all economics has to offer for the analysis of production is a two-dimensional profit-maximizing production function, is bound to conclude that it is useless and irrelevant to the problems of primitive economies. Unfortunately, a corollary of this observation is that the level of analysis which is relevant may be very sophisticated indeed.[3] This will be particularly so in relation to institutions which have significance in terms of insurance in the face of uncertainty. This seems to be the case with many social institutions (including those reported by Epstein in the present volume). Some examples of African reciprocal labour customs may also be included in this category, especially where they have the effect of regulating the staggering of planting dates – a practice which seems to ensure for the community the straddling of the optimum planting date and the staggering of the harvest peak. A relevant tool of analysis for such situations might well be quadratic programming – a technique first applied in economics for optimizing investment portfolio selections (Markovitz, 1959; Das Gupta, 1964).

In considering the sorts of economics models that might have relevance to anthropology, we might profitably refer to the analysis used in the other contributions to this volume. In her paper on the Páez, Sutti Ortiz concludes that decision-making is neither continuously maximizing (as implied by neo-classical economic analysis) nor rigidly exercised at periodic intervals – as implied by, for instance, linear programming. What she seems to need is a flow decision model in which behaviour is normally automatic by habitual reference to constant principles and where it becomes the result of conscious choice only under the impact of external stimuli. The simulation of such decision models is an economist's field of interest. At present, I know of no work published on individual decision-making models of this sort – excluding publications in the closely related field of dynamic programming (Throsby, 1964). But I do know of work in progress. It might be argued that such work is outside the mainstream of economic analysis and that development in this field will not depend on a grounding in conventional economic analysis. This is possible, but I believe that a solid grounding in micro-economics and its recent applications would be an enormous advantage to anyone working on such models.

EQUILIBRIUM ANALYSIS

A field of particular interest to economists is general equilibrium analysis, i.e. a study of the properties of systems of interdependent microcosms.[4] The study of general equilibrium need not be confined to aggregates where the number of microcosms approaches infinity. Anthropology seems to me to be bristling with general equilibrium problems including those relating to the supplies and demands of goods and services and the conditions under which these are distributed. Included within such problem fields might be the study of the equilibrium conditions of polygamous systems and the effects of changes of population, for example, or the opportunities for earning bride-price. Neoclassical economics studies prices and quantities using assumptions of diminishing marginal utilities, diminishing returns to factors, and continuous adjustment towards utility maximization. There are no uncertainties; all goods and services are infinitely divisible and marketable and there are no social constraints on behaviour (except that, implicitly, theft is not permitted). These are, to repeat a point, convenient assumptions. Economics does not disappear when they are relaxed but it may become more complicated. There is no reason that I can see why general equilibrium models derived from economics cannot be modified to analyse problems in primitive societies.

Anthropologists might well be interested in the dynamics of general equilibrium systems as well as their stationary states. Firth (1959b, pp. 341 *et seq.*) discusses social change in terms of 'the structure of ideals', 'the structure of expectations', and 'the structure of action'. He thereby distinguishes what people think they ought to do from what they have been expecting themselves to do and from what they have been observed to do in fact. He says:

> 'Social change is made possible by alteration in the external circumstances. With this may be associated a modification in patterns of expectations and closely followed by modification in the patterns of social action. The ideals of a community may not be seriously affected for a long time' (p. 342).

Acceptance of this view – if only as an hypothesis for testing – will demand an analysis of the 'alteration in external circumstances'. Any study of the changing significance of custom in the face of changing circumstances (e.g. of customary sexual division of labour or of polygamy or of customary labour services or extended family obligation, in the face of new market opportunities or crops or technologies or relative resource scarcities) is likely to find economic analysis relevant if not indispensable.

In this connection anthropology might be able to develop the concept of 'degree of disequilibrium'[5] to analyse patterns of change. It may also find it useful to incorporate into its tool-kit as economics has done, such items as Markov Process analysis – which might be used, for example, to study the pattern of adoption of new techniques (Lee *et al.*, 1965).

COMPLEXITY OF CHOICE SITUATIONS

I have already made the point that primitive choice situations are not necessarily – nor even typically – simple. Typically, they are exceptionally complex. Almost all choice situations in cultivating communities that I have considered have been highly complex. By this I mean two things: first, that there is a high degree of interdependence between activities such that quite small changes in cropping patterns, or the timing of operations, may have major ramifications through the whole farming system and affect related activities such as house-building, visits to market, hunting operations, ceremonials, and so on; secondly, that complexities arise because of the existence of uncertainties caused by variations in weather, incidence of pests, etc.[6] It is the existence and extent of such complexities that requires the application of economic analysis.

From the point of view of economic anthropology the simulation of behaviour is of central interest. In this context, some sort of behaviour must be postulated. But, as we have already indicated, it need not be defined in terms of any *single* objective. Objective functions (i.e. preference systems or utility functions) may be *n*-dimensional and the dimensions may include 'power', 'status', and other experiences besides consumption interpreted in the more conventional economic sense. They may be bounded by constraints which confine some activities, e.g. minimum provision against famine or for hospitality for unexpected guests; or by prohibitions or upper limits on other activities. Where objective functions have more than one dimension or are constrained, they are taking account of 'conflicts of principle' (see Cohen in this volume, p. 107). It is perfectly conceivable that the 'objective function' may be highly constrained in this sense and that the constraints leave little room for choice. It seems that this may have been the sort of situation that Sahlins had in mind when he proposed that a concept of 'provisioning society' should replace the concept of maximization (1965, p. 225).

Even though it may be reasonable to represent behaviour as determinate and not the product of conscious choice when we

40

are studying equilibrium situations with unchanging opportunities, such a representation may become questionable in the face of change. New opportunities may stimulate choice; constraints may be modified or abandoned. The objective function itself may change. Those who would argue against the existence of maximizing man would seem to assume that choice has long been resolved and continues with inertial momentum – unchanging behaviour in a context of unchanging opportunity. Even where this is true, the significance of forgotten choice is something to be explained. Where it is not true, and opportunities are changing, it is the inflexibility or adaptability of behaviour that has to be explained.

The observation that there are no such things as 'economic' motives does not perhaps entirely satisfy the anthropologist who cannot see how patently 'non-economic' motives – and activities – can be incorporated into economic models. Conceptually, at least, there is no problem here. For example, ritual exchange, reciprocal exchange, redistributive exchange, and market exchange can each be included separately in the pattern of activities open to individuals or groups. To be sure, one could not calculate an individual's optimizing behaviour unless one knew both his utility function and the rates of return to different activities in respect of each of the dimensions of the utility function. But one could say something about *implicit* revealed preference from the observation of behaviour. This sort of model might, of course, be a poor behavioural analogue, implying as it does conscious decision-making by thought processes which may not take place. This is the point raised by Ortiz. But, whatever the behavioural analogue used, the economic model can readily incorporate supposedly 'non-economic' activities, and the attempts by some researchers (e.g. Bohannan and Dalton) to distinguish *separate* 'spheres' of activity are in part misguided. The fact that they need to be differentiated as activities does not mean that they should be separated. The concept of 'spheres' tends to imply independence and to deny the interdependence of these activities. The Joy-Barth note (*infra*, pp. 175-189) shows the economic homologue of the anthropological model and brings out both the distinctions and the interdependence.

Leonard Joy

COMMUNICATION OF ANTHROPOLOGISTS WITH ECONOMISTS

This essay began with quotations from Devons and Gluckman which posed some of the key questions for discussion in this context. I have as yet scarcely attempted to tackle the important questions of how far the anthropologist may profit from studying a discipline other than his own, and how far this should be regarded as dangerous and for geniuses only. Nor have I tried to ask at what point the anthropologist has a duty of abstention and an obligation to leave the field to economists instead. What I have argued is that there is a common borderland which does belong to one or both of these disciplines and that the economist is far more involved than some would accept. Having argued that the subjects have a bearing on each other in terms both of topics of common interest and techniques of common value, I have now to consider how far anthropologists should invest in economics.

The papers in this symposium by Epstein and Ortiz are in effect discussions of the relevance of economics models to particular situations. The models hypothesize behaviour, and the discussion asks how far observed behaviour matches up to the model – how far the models have explanatory relevance to the observed situations. In both cases the authors conclude that the models are not satisfactory. They both make suggestions for models which would more nearly represent reality. To my mind the development of the models they suggest demands a considerable competence in micro-economics. But even if I am right this still does not lead to the conclusion that anthropologists in this field should train to build their own models. Perhaps they need simply to be able to communicate with sympathetic economists. Alternatively, it might be that they should leave this field solely to economists, but this I do not believe. The development of relevant models will require not only skill in the construction and analysis of models but also the ability to match the properties of the models to reality. The economist's method of testing by results is likely to be especially unrewarding because here he is not testing the effect of marginal adjustments to a basically

42

sound model but is trying to create wholly new models based on behavioural representation. This requires training in objective observation such as is aimed at for anthropologists, as well as a feel for where to look for relevant social variables.

Thus I believe that partnership is required here between anthropologists and economists. This implies two-way communication. If this cannot be achieved on the ground it will be desirable at least to ensure a two-way communication of results. What is required is constructive comment from each side on the other's works. This could involve fundamental revision of ideas for both parties; if it did not there would indeed be little need for any getting-together.

Even those who accept the convergence of interest of economics and anthropology might argue that the appropriate procedure for each of the separate disciplines is one of those listed by Devons and Gluckman (seen from the point of view of the anthropologist), viz.:

(a) the *incorporation* of economic 'facts' e.g. opportunity costs expressed in physical or monetary terms.

(b) the *abridgement* of economic 'facts' (postulated or validated) e.g. that resource allocation is 'economically' inefficient (assuming that meaningful content is given to this phrase).

(c) postulating *naïve assumptions*, e.g. as the economist does, that behaviour is maximizing. (I have been unable to think of any naïve assumption that anthropologists might derive from economics that would not be covered by (a) or (b) above.)

The paper by Lorraine Barić starts from a 'postulated abridgement' (that resource allocation is 'economically' inefficient) to explore possible hypotheses of social variables important in the determination of resource allocation. This seems to be a perfectly reasonable procedure though it is not strictly necessary to make any assumptions about the efficiency of resource allocation in order to do so. However, a comprehensive model of decision-making with regard to resource allocation would doubtless include economic variables as well as social variables. Thus in so far as hypotheses about social variables are to be tested, cooperation between the disciplines seems inevitable.

Prior to such a synthesis and the relevant measurement and testing, care is necessary to emphasize the status of the untested hypotheses.

An issue of substance that emerges from this point is that purely anthropological or purely economic models built by the use of the *ceteris paribus* assumptions by one discipline in relation to variables deriving from the other may be:

(a) untestable, and therefore of doubtful validity, without reference to the other discipline;

(b) invalid because of the interdependence of social and economic variables.

Thus my own conclusion is that, for the analysis of some situations, more than one discipline *must* be actively invoked if progress is to be made. I consider too that anthropologists might well find themselves in a situation where an investment in some familiarity with a limited field of economics research might be profitable in so far as it suggests – directly or indirectly – appropriate methods of analysis or models which might be enlightening. But the venturesome should look for guidance from economists specialist in the relevant field. Textbooks – and economists in the wrong field – are likely to prove unhelpful and disappointing.

NOTES

1. For example, Firth (1951 p. 147) has stresed that the material side of the economic situation is very intimately bound up with its social correlate.
2. I think I am making the same point here as Firth:

'Thus it is useless to know how many hours a man has spent over a month in agriculture if one does not know also what alternatives were open to him, what he did with the rest of his time, and what relation this expenditure of time, both totally and marginally, bore to his agricultural labour and to the yield derived therefrom' (1959a, p. 45).

Firth's main purpose here is to argue against descriptive as opposed to analytical recording of technologies.
3. But complicating the conventional theory does not always help. See, e.g., Nakajima (1965).
4. Anyone who has taken a shower in a hotel room at the same time as the person in the next room will know what a general equilibrium problem is. The settings of the hot and cold taps of both showers necessary to produce the required pressures and temperatures, the existence of such settings, and the dynamic consequences of different adjustment patterns and different initial

states are some aspects of general equilibrium properties that might be studied in this case.

5. One aspect of this idea is implicit in Barth's paper in this volume: '. . . entrepreneurs will direct their activity pre-eminently towards those points in an economic system where the discrepancies of evaluation are greatest . . .' (p. 171). I am stressing the need to study changes in behaviour (and thence of values) through the measurement of 'discrepancies of evaluation' or at least of changing opportunities.

6. These remarks apply especially to areas where annual crops are cultivated. Rainfall variability is a particularly complicating factor affecting e.g. Acholi, Lango, Teso, and Kamba farming systems. Irrigation brings different complications. I have seen these only in Punjab and the Sindh but, by their nature, these complications would apply equally to purely subsistence systems also.

REFERENCES

CYERT, R. M. & MARCH, J. G. 1963. *A Behavioral Theory of the Firm.* Englewood Cliffs, N.J.: Prentice-Hall.

DALTON, G. 1961. Economic Theory and Primitive Society. *American Anthropologist* **63**: 1-25.

DAS GUPTA, S. 1964. Producers' Rationality and Technical Change in Agriculture with special reference to India. London (Unpublished Ph.D. Thesis).

DEVONS, ELY & GLUCKMAN, MAX. 1964. Conclusion: Modes and Consequences of Limiting a Field of Study. In M. Gluckman (ed.), 1964, pp. 158-261.

FIRTH, R. 1936. *We, the Tikopia.* London: Allen & Unwin.

—— 1951. *Elements of Social Organization.* London: Watts.

—— 1959 a. *Economics of the New Zealand Maori.* 2nd edn. Wellington, New Zealand: R. E. Owen, Government Printer.

—— 1959 b. *Social Change in Tikopia.* London: Allen & Unwin.

GLUCKMAN, MAX (ed.). 1964. *Closed Systems and Open Minds: The Limits of Naïvety in Social Anthropology.* Edinburgh & London: Oliver & Boyd.

JOHNSON, G. L. et al. (eds.). 1961. *Managerial Processes of Mid-Western Farmers.* Ames, Iowa: Iowa State University Press.

LEE, T. C., JUDGE, G. G. & TAKAYAMA, T. 1965. On Estimating the Transition Probabilities of a Markov Process. *Journal of Farm Economics* **47**(3).

MARKOWITZ, H. 1959. *Portfolio Selection.* New York: Wiley.

NAKAJIMA, C. 1965. The Subsistence Farmer in Commercial Economics. (Unpublished paper presented to Agricultural Development Corporation Seminar on Subsistence and Peasant Economics. February/March 1965. East-West Centre, Honolulu).

PARSONS, T. 1953. *The Integration of Social and Economic Theory*. The Marshall Lectures 1953. Cambridge: Cambridge University Press.

POLANYI, K., ARENSBERG, C. & PEARSON, H. W. (eds.). 1957. *Trade and Markets in the Early Empires*. Glencoe, Ill.: Free Press.

RENBORG, U. 1962. *Studies on the Planning Environment of the Agricultural Firm*. Upsala: Almqvist & Wiksell.

ROBBINS, LIONEL. 1932. *An Essay on the Nature and Significance of Economic Science*. London: Macmillan.

SAHLINS, MARSHALL D. 1965. On the Sociology of Primitive Exchange. In M. Banton (ed.), *The Relevance of Models for Social Anthropology*, pp. 139-236. A.S.A. Monographs, 1. London: Tavistock Publications.

THROSBY, C. D. 1964. Some Dynamic Programming Models for Farm Management Research. *Journal of Agricultural Economics* 16(1).

Ronald Frankenberg

Economic Anthropology

One Anthropologist's View

A PREFATORY THOUGHT

'Where speculation ends – in real life – there real, positive
science begins: the representation of the practical activity, of the
practical process of the development of men. Empty talk about
consciousness ceases, and real knowledge has to take its place.
When reality is depicted, philosophy as an independent branch
of knowledge loses its medium of existence. At the best its place
can only be taken by a summing-up of the most general results,
abstractions which arise from the observation of the historical
development of men. Viewed apart from real history, these
abstractions have in themselves no value whatsoever. They can
only serve to facilitate the arrangement of historical material, to
indicate the sequence of its separate strata. But they by no
means afford a recipe or scheme, as does philosophy, for neatly
trimming the epochs of history. On the contrary, our difficulties begin only when we set about the observation and the
arrangement – the real depiction – of our historical material,
whether of a past epoch or of the present.' MARX & ENGELS
(1845, p. 38)

WHAT IS ECONOMIC ANTHROPOLOGY?

Theological students versed in the differences between Methodism and Calvinism are dismayed to find that in Wales the Pres-
byterian Church describes itself as Calvinistic Methodist.
Similar feelings beset some social scientists faced with the idea
of economic anthropology.

This was implied by Arthur Lewis (1955, p. 6) when (before,
as shown in his Foreword, he was converted by Scarlett Epstein
(1962)) he wrote: 'Economists and sociologists deal in generalizations, where anthropologists and historians deal in particular
cases'.

Dalton makes the same point in more literary terms when he

accuses Armstrong (1928) of having brought Mycroft's tools to Sherlock's subject:

'All social scientists are either Sherlock or Mycroft Holmes. Anthropologists are Sherlock: they go to the scene, observe minutely, gather their threads of evidence from what they observe, and – like Sherlock – sometimes reach Paddington before reaching conclusions. Economic theorists are Mycroft; they do not go to the scene to observe minutely. They have no equivalent to fieldwork because economists are not concerned with social organization or human behavior, but rather with the behavior of prices, income determinants, capital-output ratios, and other impersonal matters relating to the performance of nationally-integrated, industrialized market economies (for which fieldwork is unnecessary). Institutional matters, personal roles, and the social implications of economic organization have long since been consigned to the limbo of sociology. Neither the problems of interest nor the methods of analysis are the same in economics and economic anthropology' (1965, p. 58).

Mycroft and Sherlock were, however, brothers, and Sherlock regarded an evening with Mycroft as by no means wasted. Indeed he assured Watson that some of his most interesting cases had come to him through Mycroft. Dalton's over-rigid view of their relationship is reflected in his views of anthropology and economics. To me these subjects seem to have opposing but converging lines of development. If I am correct, classical economics saw the economic process as embedded in the social. The writings of Marx are the culminating point in relating the two together. After Marx, Marshall and his successors moved away as Dalton suggests, consigning the social concomitants – Marx's question, *cui bono?* – to the limbo of sociologists and Marxism. The depression of the thirties, however, and the advent of Keynes to some extent brought sociology back. In Baran's words (1957, p. 8) the political came back into political economy:

'[Keynesianism] implicitly repudiated the zealously guarded "purity" of academic economics by revealing the paramount importance for the comprehension of the economic process of the structure of society, the relations of classes, the distribution of income, the role of the state, and other exogenous factors.'

What crisis and Keynes began, concern with economic growth and development has continued. Modern economists seem to turn not merely to the classics, but also to sociology and anthropology for help. Economy turns once more to ecology and ekistics. Sociology itself has pursued a less devious course. While economists took the sociology out of political economy, sociologists took out the economy. A line of theoretical argument can be traced from Marx through Weber to his translator Parsons, and then to Smelser. Nevertheless an absence of detailed empirical study makes it possible for MacRae (1965) to feel he can put the two disciplines together when he writes: 'Sociologists have too much neglected economic institutions. So too have economists save when concerned with their formal and/or financial aspects. To this Marx is a constant corrective.'

He might have added so too are Malinowski and Firth, for the anthropological tradition has neglected neither the social nor the economic. Theoretical interactions are noted by Parsons (1957) on Malinowski, and Firth (1951) on Weber. Just as in economics, however, Marx and Engels's writings on economic anthropology were shunted off the mainline and only allowed to return when no longer considered to travel at a dangerous speed.

Malinowski (1922, p. 85n.) himself acknowledged his admiration, with reservations, for Bücher; and Firth has briefly spelled out this influence (Firth, 1957b, p. 209). Malinowski demonstrated that the laws of supply and demand in exchange were modified by social relationships. He showed the interrelation between social relations and economic relations in the *Kula* and in Trobriand chieftainship. Sometimes it was the economic relationships that were primary and sometimes the social.

As fieldwork studies and detailed analysis of individual small-scale societies became the standard practice of ethnography, Bücher's reproach becomes less appropriate:

'Our travellers have hitherto devoted little special attention to the economy of primitive peoples. In the midst of their

49

attention to dress, forms of worship, morals, religious beliefs, marriage customs, art and technical skill, they have often overlooked what lay closest at hand, and in the gossipy records of ethnographic compilations the word 'economy' has no more found a place than has the word 'household' in the chronicles of the numerous investigators into the constitution of the family' (1901, p. 39).

If, in Arthur Lewis's phrase (T. S. Epstein 1962, p. vii), 'Economics is concerned with the phenomena of production and of distribution', nearly all anthropological monographs began with economics. Few, however, centred their analysis on economic ideas and concepts, and many missed the point (Firth 1951, p. 130).

Technology, ecology, and economics were three possible frameworks for arranging such material and some chose one and some the other. Raymond Firth in Britain and Herskovits in the United States presented all three and formed the nucleus of thought upon which modern economic anthropology is based. Evans-Pritchard, Forde, Gluckman, Stanner, and Richards are also among senior British anthropologists who have made major contributions in this field. It is no mean achievement of anthropology and of their consistent emphasis that the literature on, for example, the social relations in primitive and peasant markets (Bohannan and Dalton, 1962; Dewey, 1962; Epstein, T. S., 1961; Cohen, 1965) is so much fuller than that for analogous phenomena in advanced industrial society.

Just as the hard facts of economic life forced economists in the thirties to the realization that their theories were insufficiently empirical and hence into intellectual crisis, so the multiplication of empirical data in economic anthropology in recent years points to a need for classification and theory.

Among American anthropologists critique and classification have gone hand in hand. In the rest of this paper I propose, first, to outline the neo-classical view of economic anthropology as exemplified by Firth. Secondly, I shall consider the various critiques that have been levelled at this approach especially by Burling, Dalton, and Sahlins. Finally, I shall suggest possible lines of synthesis.

NEO-CLASSICAL VIEWS: E.G. THE CONTRIBUTION
OF RAYMOND FIRTH[1]

As I see it, Firth has applied economic theory most explicitly to the study of anthropology. To him (1951, p. 125):

'The basic concept of economics is the allocation of scarce, available resources between realizable human wants, with the recognition that alternatives are possible in each sphere. However defined, economics thus deals with the implications of human choice, with the results of decisions.'

He goes on to emphasize that such choices involve personal and social relations. As he has written earlier (1951, p. 83):

'A theoretical framework for the analysis of social change must be concerned largely with what happens to social structures. But to be truly dynamic it must allow for individual action.'

Although his economics begin from scarcity he still argues and recognizes (cf. Robbins Burling, 1962, and below) that the main concern of economics 'by a convention', is with those fields of choice 'which involve goods and services, and primarily those which have a price put upon them. In this sense relations between persons in virtue of their association in the production or exchange of these goods and services are "economic" relations' (1951, p. 130).

From these beginnings Firth has, over the years, established a number of points which must here be summarized briefly:

1. Economic relations and the choices involved in them are patterned in any one society – they form a system (1951, p. 123).

2. Exchange relations are fundamental in all human society (1965, pp. 18-21). In this (as he says) he follows Malinowski. Separate papers have, of course, been written on the classification of types of exchanges (e.g. Sahlins, 1965; Steiner, 1954).

3. While all societies (and their economies) are unique, it is necessary and useful to adopt a simple classification to enable

51

discussion to proceed. Societies are primitive, peasant, and industrial.

(a) *Primitive societies*

Thus Firth says of Tikopia:

'The economy of Tikopia in the form in which I observed it in 1928/29 can reasonably be categorised as of "primitive" type. The term primitive is a relative one. More closely applicable to an economic than to a social system, it has no very precise defining character and is variously used. My own view is that it implies a system of simple non-mechanical technology, with little or no innovation, directed to maintenance rather than increase of capital assets, and with relatively low differentiation of economic roles of people in production, entrepreneurial and management functions. Usually it is without overt market institutions or generally acceptable media of exchange for rapid conversion of one type of resource into another' (1965, p. 17).

He convincingly rejects the term 'subsistence economy' to describe it as being misleading. Tikopia produces more than food, clothing, and shelter. Exchange does occur, and – even without money – Tikopia can be (and indeed has been) studied as an economic system.

(b) *Peasant economies*

Much more common in the modern world and of increasing interest to the practical economist are what Firth calls peasant economies (1951, pp. 87, 88).

'. . . a system of small-scale producers, with a simple technology and equipment, often relying primarily for their subsistence on what they themselves produce. . . . Such a small-scale productive organization, built upon a use of or a close relation to primary resources, has its own concomitant systems of capital accumulation and indebtedness, of marketing and distribution. *The necessary relation of this peasant economy to particular types of social structure gives a characteristic shape to life in peasant communities'* (Frankenberg's italics).

Firth considers that a peasant economy is characterized by its type of social relationships rather than type of technological production. Therefore he does not confine the term to agricultural peasants (Firth & Yamcy, 1964, pp. 17-18): we can 'speak not only of peasant agriculturalists but also of peasant fishermen, peasant craftsmen and peasant marketers, if they are part of the same social system. In any case, such people are often in fact part-time cultivators as well.' He might have added, citing Arensberg (1937), peasant shopkeepers and peasant publicans.

The peasant social system thus described can (as Firth's reference to the Middle Ages (1951, p. 137) implies) be embedded in various kinds of external social relations – feudal, capitalistic, or other.

From the point of view of the local society

'. . . economic ties are personalized – that is relationships as economic agents depend on the social status and relationships of the persons concerned. Put another way, labour is given as a social service, and not simply an economic service. Its reward is therefore apt to be calculated in terms of the total social situation, and not merely the immediate economic situation. Economic means tend to be translated into social ends' (1951, p. 137).

This, I believe is precisely the point about the "embeddedness" (Polanyi's term) of pre-capitalist economy that Marx is making in the famous passage in *Capital* (cited by Firth, 1965, p. 20) which refers to the development of commodity exchange at the boundaries of such communities. The full paragraph from the Everyman Edition of *Capital* throws a different light on Marx's views from that here suggested by Firth and accepted by many other writers (Marx, 1930, p. 63). (The sentences quoted by Firth are italicized.)

'The first step by which a useful object is enabled to become an exchange-value is that it should have an existence as something which has not a use-value for its owner; and this happens when it forms a superfluous portion of some article that satisfies his immediate wants. Objects in and by themselves exist apart from man, and are therefore alienable by him. If this alienation of objects is to be reciprocal, all that is requisite is that human beings shall tacitly confront one another as the individual owners of such alienable objects, and shall thus confront one another as mutually independent persons. But *no such relation of mutual independence exists for the members of a primitive community*, whether this take the form of a patriarchal family, or that of an ancient Indian commune, or that of the Inca state in Peru etc. *Commodity exchange begins where community life ends*; begins at the point of contact between a community and an alien community, or between the members of two different communities. But as soon as products have become commodities in the external relations of a community, they also become, by repercussion, commodities in the internal life of the community.'

It is now more widely recognized that Marx was less dogmatic than had been supposed. The recent publication of hitherto unpublished works of Marx has thrown further new light on his views on the development of pre-capitalist societies (see Hobsbawm, 1964, p. 60; Godelier, 1965, pp. 90, 91; and compare Firth, 1965, p. 362).

(c) *Industrial society*

Consideration of peasant society leads Firth to the contrasting characteristics of modern industrial society.

'In the latter the individual has normally a high degree of anonymity, of impersonality in the economic situation. Even if he is not merely a number on a payroll, it is his function as an energy factor, a provider of capital, or of organizing capacity that is of prime importance. As such it is his specific industrial characteristics, not his total social characteristics that matter. He is deemed to be replaceable. It is the magnitude and quality of his contribution to the economic process, irrespective of his personal status or position in the society, that defines him. In primitive (*sic*) communities the individual as an economic factor is personalized, not anonymous. He tends to hold his economic position in virtue of his social position. Hence to displace him economically means a social disturbance' (1951, p. 137).

4. Firth uses his classification to illuminate his own empirical researches and those of others. It leads him, *inter alia*, to stress, in his own practice, programmatically and in criticism of Malinowski, the importance of quantitative data. He is concerned with discussing incentives, scarcity, capital, choice and decision-making, saving, investment, interest, and credit, as they operate not only within various individual societies but also within various types of society. He sees the role of the economic anthropologist as applying the concepts used by economists in industrial society to primitive and peasant society. The economic anthropologist, however, has the additional task, which extends even into industrial society, of examining 'the economic role of a person in a particular situation against his social role, and against that of the system of groups of which he is a member' (1951, p. 138).

5. Finally, Firth is concerned with the problems of how in specific cases and in general, one type of society changes to another (Firth, 1959; 1957b, p. 106 *et seq.*; 1951, p. 96).

This view of economics, anthropology, economic anthropology, and anthropological economics is not universally accepted nor indeed always understood. I now consider some critiques and their implications.

BERLINER'S CRITIQUE

While Firth (1951, p. 130) questioned the economic relevance of the fact that 'cracked feet are treated with cow dung', Berliner (1962) seems a little shocked that Firth (1936, p. 14) should mention feet at all. He writes as a professional economist criticizing economic anthropology in the course of criticizing anthropology as a whole. He is a gentle critic.[2]

Berliner's main concern is to elucidate by a simple application of matrix analysis and the logic of sets what cultural and social anthropologists do with their data. In the process of doing so, however, he throws light on the 'Calvinistic Methodist' aspect of our subject-matter. His omissions and oversimplifications regarding social anthropology do not concern us here and emerged in the *Current Anthropology* discussion.

The columns of his matrix represent the characteristics of what he calls a particular culture; one may represent, for example, the Navaho, one the Chinese, one the Trobriands. His rows consist of particular aspects of culture – language, kinship, art, religion, economy. Each box therefore contains data on a particular cultural aspect of a particular culture. (He distinguishes between culture and society in a way that proved unacceptable to many of his readers, including myself, but this is not relevant here.) Thus Navaho economy is in one box, Trobriand religion in another. He suggests that there are four anthropological ways of analysing data. Column analysis – all about the Navaho – is the method of cultural anthropology – the contents of all the boxes in one column are compared, the question asked is: what is there about Navaho stories that makes them like Navaho pottery and Navaho songs? Row analysis compares the boxes in one row – how is the Navaho kinship system like the Trobriand kinship system and how is it different? He suggests that this is the method of social anthropology.

Those who lean most heavily on the column analysis method say, in effect: to understand the Navaho kinship system, one must understand Navaho culture. There is another point of view that argues in effect: to understand the Navaho kinship system, one must understand kinship systems.

Gluckman and Devons's statement partly confirms this view of social anthropology, when they write: 'We would indeed contend that knowledge of South American and European villages might be more useful for the analysis of Indian villages, than is knowledge of Sanskrit' (1964, p. 195).

The third possibility is classification and comparison of whole columns – the typing and grouping of cultures. He calls this comparative cultural anthropology and cites Ruth Benedict as an example. He might have taken Herskovits's work (1926) on

56

the cattle complex of East Africa. Finally, he considers comparison of rows – comparative social anthropology, citing Leslie White and Chapple and Coon. Again, he might have chosen Gluckman (in Radcliffe-Brown & Forde, 1950) or Firth (1964). There is, Berliner suggests, a fifth possibility, frowned on by anthropologists and used by economists, to wit, the detailed analysis of the contents of a single box. He summarizes:

'If all economists were anthropologists by training, we should know a great deal more about the relations between changes in economic variables and changes in other cultural variables (column analysis). And we should know a great deal more about those properties of an economic system that are universal in character and those that are peculiar to our culture (row analysis). But we should know very much less about the systematic regularities among economic variables themselves (box analysis)' (1962, p. 53).

In the study of economic growth and development he suggests that anthropology could be used to shrink the prediction triangle. I will return to his dynamic models later.

ATTACK I: ROBBINS BURLING AND THE INDIVIDUAL

After citing this mild analytical critique, I turn to the first attack – by Robbins Burling (1962). His argument is that anthropologists do not know what they are doing in economics. Most of them, he claims, do not understand what economics is about because they have not read Lionel Robbins's *Nature and Significance of Economic Science*. Those who have read him either have not understood him, as he claims Dalton did not, or have not applied him consistently, as he claims Firth and Herskovits did not.

Burling suggests that there are five possible ways of regarding economics that could be and have been used by anthropologists:

(a) the study of material means to man's existence;

(b) the production, distribution, and consumption of goods and services;

(c) the study of things that economists study;

57

(d) the study of systems of exchange however they are organized; and

(e) the study of the allocation of scarce means to alternative ends.

He goes on to argue that the first is better called technology, subsistence, or ecology; the second is so general as to be meaningless; the third is ethnocentric; and the fourth is limited. Only the fifth is acceptable and useful and can be developed. It is not my intention here to argue that the fifth is useless in anthropology. With the additional illumination of focusing on the 'material', Firth has patently put it to good use. I shall also refer to a genuinely sociological maximization model used by Barth and his collaborators. I do intend to argue, however, that much of Burling's criticism is either wrong-headed or misplaced and certainly does not justify the generally contemptuous tone of his article.

First, it is questionable whether Lionel Robbins has really 'devastated these materialist definitions'. The familiar arguments about opera singers' wages and theatre tickets not being material, and about economic choices being between the material and the non-material, are valid warnings to the first-year student about the complexity of economic life (see Godelier, 1965, pp. 37-39). But they spring from an *individualistic* approach to social science which is too one-sided to be accepted by social anthropologists, and I suspect (and hope) by most modern economists (especially since Keynes and the revived interest in macro-economics). Whether the individual chooses a trip to Europe or a car, is a choice between non-material and material to the individual. But to the society in which he lives it is a choice that affects the disposal of material resources. The economic anthropologist, like any social scientist, has constantly to face the problem of seeing the individual in the social framework. Focusing on the entrepreneur as an individual outside a social context will only lead him, as it has led economics, into blind alleys. It is true that some anthropologists have interpreted both the study of material means to man's existence, and the production, distribution, and consumption of goods and services, as descriptive technology. Others, however, have correctly recognized that social organization related to the organization of material life is not only a proper field of study but also something about which one can talk to economists. Burling's criticism of anthropologists for looking at what economists do in advanced industrial society and then going and doing likewise, has at first sight a more convincing ring. He writes:

'What anthropologists have done, however, is to look upon the type of goods and services that we price and consider these to be economic even in other societies, instead of realising that it is the phenomenon of pricing itself which gives these particular goods and services their unity' (p. 807).

He suggests that this is mere illogical ethnocentrism. He continues:

'Some people, to be sure, price goods or services which we do not. Brides frequently are paid for, but because of our ethnocentric view that brides are not an economic commodity (because we do not happen to price them) anthropologists have resisted the idea that women can be bought and sold and have even suggested that it is somehow nicer to speak of "bride-wealth" than "bride-price". This magic with words does not obscure the fact that in some parts of the world wealth is transferred in exchange for brides. In many places monetary compensation is paid to redress injuries such as theft, adultery, or even murder, though since we do not happen to feel that it is appropriate to price such transactions, we usually feel that they are not "economic" ' (p. 807).

So, once again, he fails to see a phenomenon in its social aspects and misses the reasons that lead social anthropologists to think and write as they do (see Gluckman, 1965b, p. 47).

Burling allows that the study of systems of exchange of whatever kind is worth while, but denies that in themselves they are necessarily economic. He reaches at last the true perspective in Robbins, and maximization of satisfactions through the choice and allocation of scarce means to multiple objectives:

'Many anthropologists who have concerned themselves with economic problems have recently used similar definitions, including Firth in his latest discussion of anthropological economics, and Herskovits. But these authors, after indicating choice, allocation, and "economizing" to be the core of economic behavior, slip back to a consideration of "economizing" among material objects and ends, or only among the objects which *we* include in our market system. It is this mistake that Robbins avoids and it is for this reason that I have found his essay so valuable and so much more satisfying logically than the formulations of most anthropologists who have dealt with these problems' (p. 810).

He continues to chide Firth and Herskovits for the narrowness of the topics which they cover, again, I think, revealing that he is concerned one-sidedly with the individual rather than society. The analogy which he draws between what he calls Freudian psychological man and economic man confirms this view. He alleges that Freudian man maximizes pleasure just as economic man maximizes profit (and, he suggests, Leachian man maximizes power. It is true that he apologizes in the next sentence for this simplification of Leach (p. 814, and Leach, 1954)).

The crucial economic question to Burling is the actual behaviour of the *individual* in situations of choice. Thus, this leads to a conception of social organization as a whole as a system of exchange '. . . and would identify economics with anthropology if it were not the case that economists are concerned with *how* people economize and anthropologists *whether* they economize'.

His final conclusion, which he considers is only marred by the difficulty of quantification, is that:

'It should be possible to speak of the supply of prestige, the demand for power, and the cost of authority. I see no reason why one should not even speak of the marginal utility of loving care. Each man can be regarded as an entrepreneur, manipulating those around him, trading his products of labor, attention, respect etc. for the most he can get in return' (p. 819).

To Burling, alone among the writers I here consider, no classification of societies is necessary, since fundamentally he does not work within a social context at all.

That is not to say that analysis in terms of the entrepreneur is not valuable, but it has to be put in a social context as Barth has done.[3]

COUNTER-ATTACK I: FREDRIK BARTH, ROBERT PAINE, AND THE ENTREPRENEURIAL PROCESS

Fredrik Barth has shown the possibility of using the concept of entrepreneur within a social context.

'It is essential to realize that "the entrepreneur" is not a *Person* in any strict sociological sense though inevitably the word will be used, also in the present essays, in a way that may foster this impression. Nor does it seem appropriate to treat entrepreneurship as a status or even a role, implying as it would a discreteness and routination in the materials we wish to analyse. Rather its strict use should be for an *aspect of a role*: it relates to actions and activities, and not rights and duties. Furthermore it characterizes a certain quality or orientation in this activity which may be present to greater or lesser extent in the different institutionalized roles found in the community. . . . It is with the factors encouraging and channelling, or inhibiting such activity, that we shall be concerned' (Barth, 1963, p. 6).

Barth and his colleagues reject a structural view of society and seek means to analyse social behaviour in terms of dynamic processes. As economists have before them, they call the theory of games to their aid. Barth distinguishes entrepreneurial aspects of behaviour because

(*a*) The entrepreneur has a more single-minded concentration on the maximization of one type of value, namely profit (not necessarily economic profit).

(*b*) The entrepreneur acts on the basis of the *deductive prognosis* of results instead of expectations based on accumulated institutionalized experience.

Ronald Frankenberg

(c) The entrepreneur has a willingness to take risks by committing his assets, trusting in his deductive reasoning, and acting against the odds.

However, the entrepreneur does all this in a specific social environment – his niche. Barth's scheme may be represented diagrammatically.

Niche		*Assets*
position occupied in relation to resources, competitors, clients	*Instrumental restrictions*	sum total of capital, skills, and social claims
	limitations of freedom of choice	

The instrumental restrictions, however, must be seen as modified by social and moral restrictions.

'Activities have ramifying implications beyond what is considered under their relationship to initial assets and niche; to represent these, the entrepreneur's alternative tasks and techniques must somehow be permuted against the structure of the community' (p. 10).

This involves taking into account the social costs and 'a consideration of the place of the product of an enterprise in the whole system of circulation of value that characterizes the community'. This system of circulation may not be unitary but divided into discrete spheres leaving the entrepreneur with the task of finding or creating channels of conversion from one to the other.

Thus Paine (1963), in a subtle descriptive analysis of three economic developments in a northern Norwegian community, shows how two types of entrepreneurial activity emerge – free-enterpriser and free-holder. The distinction is very similar to Merton's functional analysis of local and cosmopolitan influentials in a small American town (Merton, 1957, pp. 387-420).[4]

The free-enterpriser may well be born outside the community in which he operates, but that is not his fundamental characteristic. His goals have in common with those of other free-enterprisers offence against neighbourly values. They make themselves by their actions.

'Entrepreneurs of the freeholder type are prepared to accept responsibility in associations in order to help raise the productivity of the community. Their industrious engagement on their own farms and in fishing demonstrate the legitimacy of their intentions. Those of the free-enterpriser type may not work in either of the principal livelihoods of the community. Their characteristic interests are of a speculative kind and they pursue them in disregard of local values' (p. 52).

Like Merton's cosmopolitans they do not identify with any particular community, and, as Paine expected and predicted, he learnt after he had left the field that those free-enterpriser entrepreneurs who could afford to had gone to exercise their entrepreneurial skills elsewhere. Since free-enterprisers have different goals and different standards of success from freeholders, they are not rivals, and in fact form natural allies, as Paine's account shows. Free-holders use free-enterprisers to gain support in the outside world, and free-enterprisers hope partially to legitimate their activities within the community by the respectability that association with free-holders may bring. Both types of entrepreneur are rivals to those with the same goals. Both pursue self-interest, but only free-enterprisers are interested in power over persons as a means to status and wealth; free-holders are content to seek to influence. The 'real' leader (*Breivik*) was not an entrepreneur at all but the embodiment of norms. For even free-holder entrepreneurs need a surplus of time, and to repudiate to some extent the duties of reciprocal obligation in an egalitarian community. One of Paine's examples (the Rasmussen brothers) owed their emergence as free-holding entrepreneurs to the same thing as their lack of success in the role – namely the unmarried state which made them economically successful and socially unpopular. Virtues for the rest of the community were vices when practised by them.

Again in more general terms, as Barth points out in his introduction (p. 9):

'The occasional need for repudiating relationships points to a possible connection between entrepreneurship and factionalism or social stratification. Both these forms of social division imply limitations or discontinuities of obligation and commitment. They are thus social barriers which may give strategic scope to certain kinds of enterprise, and may even be *generated* by the entrepreneur where the advantages he gains (*and* can offer to those who follow him) outweigh the costs of repudiating the relevant relationships.'

Paine's analysis is a particularly fruitful example of the usefulness of the concept of entrepreneur when put in a sociological setting. In terms of the discussion of economic innovation, it enables us to see that because the free-holder is an innovator rather than a revolutionary, his role in externally imposed change may be that of active opponent rather than ally. It may also help to analyse an even more dynamic situation. Thus the cooperative manager in Rudie's paper in the same volume can be seen using a free-holder entrepreneurial position to establish himself or his son as a free-enterpriser (Rudie, 1963, p. 69). Similarly Paine helps to throw light on Arensberg's two-stage process from peasant-peasant, through peasant-shopkeeper, to big-town capitalist entrepreneur (Arensberg, 1937, pp. 146-180).

Thus it will be remembered that the family shop of the small Irish town operates like the family farm within a context of kindred and reciprocity. 'Money buys the shop, credit may stock its shelves, but it is the social alliance, contracted in a country marriage, which supplies the trade upon which business rests' (p. 161).

The farmer who becomes a small shopkeeper or publican is a free-holder entrepreneur. This, however, is not a stable state. Individuals or their children either fall back into the countryside or advance another stage to the larger eastern towns and to the free-enterpriser entrepreneur status. 'The country people flock into the towns and the townspeople all die out of them' (p. 152). This two-stage process of escape from the 'embeddedness' of community economics is not uncommon.

The maximization approach as interpreted by Barth and his

colleagues is therefore a fruitful one. But I do not think it is as distinct from what 'structuralist' and 'functionalist' anthropologists do as they think it is (see, for example, T. S. Epstein in Firth and Yamey (1964)). It may, of course, be quite distinct from what functionalists and structuralists say they do.

ATTACK II: DALTON, POLANYI, AND THE
INAPPLICABILITY OF ECONOMIC THEORY[1]

Dalton summarizes his own view (1961, p. 20) thus:

'Primitive economy is different from market industrialism not in degree but in kind. The absence of machine technology, pervasive market organization, and all-purpose money, plus the fact that economic transactions cannot be understood apart from social obligation, create, as it were a non-Euclidean universe to which Western economic theory cannot be fruitfully applied. The attempt to translate primitive economic processes into functional equivalents of our own inevitably obscures just those features of primitive economy which distinguish it from our own.'

Burling's attack on economic anthropology started from the assertion that the twin prophets, Herskovits and Firth, failed to understand economic theory. He only succeeds in showing (in my view) that he doesn't understand anthropology. Dalton follows Polanyi in a more sophisticated approach. He argues that economic theory is purpose-built for a specific kind of economy – that is, the market economy – and is based on the analysis of price (Dalton, 1960, 1961; Bohannan and Dalton, 1962). He seems to me to show the limitations of formal economics (cf. Godelier, 1965, pp. 60, 61) rather than damage the anthropologists' use of it, for – as he says himself – the anthropologist has been eclectic and creative. And wisely so.

'The question arises, if it is thought that Western price theory is relevant to primitive economy, why not other branches of Western theory – say Keynesian income and employment theory – as well? The answer, perhaps, is that in the attempt to apply Keynesian theory to primitive economy it would become evident that the assumption of functional similarity of economic organization between the primitive and the West is empirically indefensible. In a word, it cannot be done' (1961, p. 16).

Precisely, but then no one said it could: the classical statement of Firth's, quoted by LeClair (1962), was both much more modest and much more demanding.

'What is required from primitive economics is the analysis of material from uncivilized communities in such a way that it will be directly comparable with the material of modern economics, matching assumption with assumption and so allowing generalizations to be ultimately framed which will subsume the phenomena of both civilized and uncivilized, price and non-price communities into a body of principles about human behavior which will be truly universal' (LeClair, 1962, p. 1187; Firth, 1939, p. 29).

The fundamental premise of Dalton's argument is that modern economics arose historically in, and continues to analyse, a society in which 'Everyone derives his livelihood from selling something to the market' (1961, p. 1). There are not only market-places for this purpose but there is also an all-embracing abstract market – the market for motor-cars or wheat futures – or the labour market. In a later publication with Bohannan he develops this further to suggest the fruitful paradox that in a given society the absence of market-places may well be indicative of the extreme importance of production for a market (Bohannan & Dalton, 1962). Dalton emphasizes that a system of production for the market compels a particular kind of interdependence ('market prices rearrange labour and resource uses'); and he points out what Burling misses, namely that:

'The "economic man" of 19th century economics was not a myth, but a succinct expression of this institutional fact; the necessity for each of the atomistic units in an impersonal, market exchange system to acquire his livelihood through market sale' (1961, p. 2).

He poses the question, why is it believed that economic theory applied in this way is universally relevant? He answers that it is because classical economists and their successors considered such economic ideas as scarcity to be quasi-biological universals. Whereas in fact, as he correctly states, economic attitudes are *socially determined*.

He considers (following Polanyi) that the illusion persists because there are some economic phenomena that all societies do have in common. There are material goods that are necessary to satisfy fundamental biological and social wants. The provision of them is the substantive meaning of the term 'economic'. All societies have economic systems in this sense.

'The existence of some type of *systematic* economic structure is implied for the following reasons: the exploitation of natural resources requires the use of technique for the acquisition or creation of material goods (horticulture, farming, hunting, manufacture). The use of technique and of natural resources, together with the need for distributing material goods among all the inhabitants, require definite institutional arrangements – structured rules of the game – to assure continuity of supply, that is, to assure repetition of performance. The participants are mutually dependent for other reasons as well: the use of technique, division of labor, natural environment, and the fact that economic processes take place within a social community, all make necessary the utilisation of some pattern of recognised rights and obligations. It is the rules which integrate the use of natural resources and technique and assure continuous co-operation in the provision of material goods that we call an economic "system" ' (1961, p. 6).

But, he goes on, there is another analytical use of the term economic – meaning economical or economizing: 'It denotes a special set of rules designed to maximize the achievement of some end or to minimize the expenditure of some means.' He claims that it is because this denotation of 'economic' is confused with the substantive meaning cited above that there arises the illusion that economic theory can be applied to all societies. The confusion arises because market-organized industrialism has precisely the characteristic that both meanings are relevant.

Once again the accusation of ethnocentricity is made. Empirically, he follows Polanyi in suggesting that there are other integrative mechanisms than market exchange found in pre-industrial society. They are:

1. reciprocity, that is material gift and counter gift-giving induced by social obligation derived typically from kinship, and

2. redistribution – the channelling upward of goods or services to socially determined allocative centres (usually king, chief, or priest) who then redistribute . . .'

Dalton goes on to list and contrast the major types of question asked of the same material by anthropologists and economists, a point which I need not deal with again here, since these questions are common ground, have already been touched upon, and are well enough observed (Dalton, 1961, pp. 10-12; and Percy S. Cohen in this volume).

He has, however, to concede that although the integrative mechanisms of substantive economics differ, the economic processes appear on the surface to be the same.

'It is true that many economic mechanisms and practices either are universal or very frequently found in primitive, historical, and modern economics. But their presence is not prima facie evidence of organizational, operational or functional similarity. Division of labor, money uses, external trade and market places are best regarded as adaptable devices (like language and mathematics) capable of varied use for different purposes in a variety of organizational contexts. Here, the poverty of our terminology is a source of built-in ambiguity' (p. 20).

This line of argument leads him to chide Herskovits for asking who owns the means of production and to suggest, echoing his own previous paper on 'surplus' (1960), that questions about a society can and should only be posed in terms of the society's own values.

Dalton was answered in formal terms by LeClair (1962), who produces a recipe for the analysis of economic systems which he claims evolves from Firth and Herskovits, and does not seek to supersede them. Although LeClair's paper may be useful as a fieldwork guide on what to look for, it makes no additional theoretical point relevant to us here.

It seems to me that Dalton argues himself into a dead stop – particularly in the last extreme relativistic view that all our terms are so biased that they cannot be used. He is clearly right when he says that the blind application of market terms to primitive economics is not fruitful, but then, as he himself points out, the theory of price is only one part of modern economics. A view of modern society based on it alone fails adequately to explain modern economy.

I would suggest that he has two ways out. The one, which he almost takes, is to see the problem historically. Do non-market economies ever change into market economies? Do reciprocal become redistributive, or redistributive become market, economies? If so, what happens in the process? His last paragraph suggests that he is moving this way and, while I think it is self-evident to the social anthropologist, it may prove a revelation to at least some economists.

The phrase 'economic growth' joins together two different kinds of change which go on simultaneously in underdeveloped areas: institutional transformation from indigenous socio-economic forms such as reciprocity and redistribution, to market-organized industrialism; and additions to real material output generated by the new economic and technical apparatus (and see Firth, 1951, p. 137; Hobsbawm, 1964, p. 17).

The second way out is not unrelated to the first. In his most recent paper (1965), Dalton first praises Firth for distinguishing between peasant and primitive, but then writes: 'If one puts the questions of market economy and economic theory to Nuer, Lele or Trobriands economy one comes up with parody, not analytic insights' (p. 122).

Now this sounds as if it ought to be true, and yet in practice is not. The explanation, I suggest, is that, because of the nature of the societies anthropologists study, they are forced to do in microcosm what Marx advocated in discussing the problem of

69

value in capitalist society – i.e. look beyond the market to production. Like Marx we

'take leave for a time of this noisy sphere, where everything takes place on the surface and in view of all men and follow (capital and labour) into the hidden abode of production, on whose threshold there stares us in the face "no admittance except on business" ' (Marx, 1889, p. 155).

This may lead us to yet another escape from Dalton's despair. He quotes with approval Boulding's view (1957, p. 318) that the basic abstraction of economics is that of the commodity, and I shall return to the importance of commodities below. Meanwhile I wish to recall Marx's definition of the value of commodities in terms of the *socially necessary labour-time* needed to *produce* them.

The association of time and production within a cultural framework, the discussion of the allocation of the ultimate in scarce resources – time – may well be the key to the further theoretical development of economic anthropology. This is a point to which I return below in the discussion of Salisbury's *From Stone to Steel* (1962).

COUNTER-ATTACK II: SALISBURY AND THE CRITERION OF LABOUR-TIME[6]

'One must start from ethno-economic analysis – with Malinowski, not Ricardo – in order to choose those transformation paths to industrialization which entail only the unavoidable social costs' (Dalton, 1961, p. 21).

It is perhaps unfortunate for Dalton's view of the relevance of Ricardo, that Salisbury, in the most sophisticated attempt yet to deal with the problem of value and capital in a primitive economy, should have arrived apparently independently at a labour theory of value based, like Ricardo's and Marx's, on the socially necessary labour-time needed to produce.

Salisbury also provides a corrective to Sahlins and White in that he includes a third term between technological and social – the economic. His theoretical chapters seek to give 'a fuller understanding of how a technological change has produced economic changes, which in turn have led to changes in the basic structure of the society'.

Salisbury describes how, in the indigenous economic system, three nexuses 'of activity' could be isolated – subsistence, luxury, and *gima* – ceremonial exchange (cf. Gluckman, 1965a, pp. 134-135; Goody, 1962, Uberoi, 1962). The first involved people working by themselves but with generalized obligations to help one another within the clan. All members of the clan have equal access 'to both the factors and the products of production'. As Gluckman has pointed out, individual production for communal consumption is a very frequently occurring form of economic organization in Africa (Gluckman, 1965b, Chapter II, *passim*). The choice of how to meet subsistence ends appears to be made on technological grounds, but is actually traditionally determined. The individual has little freedom of choice. Production is planned to produce fixed quantities of food over a period, a margin for entertainment, and occasionally a huge surplus for distribution (p. 83). (See Audrey Richards (1939) in a classic study.)

> 'Most competition between ends, however, occurs not between those subserved only by subsistence activities, but between those subserved by subsistence activities and those subserved by other activities.' (Salisbury, 1962, p. 84).

Luxury activities concerned production, distribution, and consumption by individuals not by groups. 'Luxury goods' are distributed by 'enlightened self-interest', since Siane are strongly egalitarian and maintain influence over each other by systems of obligation and counter-obligation in a way familiar to all anthropologists and well known through systematization by Mauss.

The exchange of *gima* valuables 'is concerned with the relations between corporate intermarrying groups' (p. 104). It involves formal exchange of non-utilitarian goods in a way that publicly expresses obligations and distinctions between groups. 'The three nexuses exist relatively independent of each other' (p. 106) (cf. Gluckman, 1965a, Chapter V, "The Vocabulary of Ownership", esp. p. 159). At least before the coming of Europeans, specific goods belonged specifically to a specific nexus. Specific situations required specific kinds of exchange. But there is a link between them.

'The one resource used in all activities is the time of the participants. At all moments an individual has to choose whether or not he will enter a situation where a specific activity would be appropriate. At all moments the cost of doing one activity is the activities of other kinds which must be forgone' (p. 106).

Salisbury shows the way in which men and women allocate their time among the Siane in terms of both the original stone technology and the introduced steel one (see Tables on p. 108).

Before steel, both men and women spent 80 per cent of their time on subsistence activity, now men spend only 50 per cent of their time on subsistence. For women there has been little change. As far as the men are concerned, the effect of a change in technology has been (as always) to reduce the socially necessary labour-time needed to produce their subsistence. In the absence of a market for subsistence goods, they do not therefore produce 8/5 times as much but allocate their time elsewhere. In the early period of indirect contact, warfare increased, and so did *gima* activities. The gap between the prestige and power of big men and others widened. Direct contact with the Europeans introduced one major change – money. But, Salisbury argues, the only new thing about money was its divisibility and hence the liquefying effect it had in promoting a flow of capital between the separate spheres and introducing uncertainty about what goods belonged in what spheres.

The overall situation in the future could either be the strengthening of corporate groups or the development of a more atomistic society. Which occurs depends on whether big men become more or less influential. This in turn is related to the question of whether a demand for cash crops becomes linked with a shortage of land. So far, however, 'native life is richer in colour, in variety and in material possessions', but the structure of society is unchanged.

I have presented a very contracted and concise summary of Salisbury's rich and careful analysis. In his last three chapters he shows in practice what Dalton and Sahlins have declared impossible in theory. He uses the concept of capital to show the relationship between technological and social change, and shows how a fourth nexus of economic activity in European hard goods is developing. He demonstrates how his impressions of the existence of nexuses can be analytically validated, since demand varies differentially for different categories of commodities (p. 171).

He suggests that this is because Siane have four different standards of evaluation according to whether the commodities concerned are subsistence, prestige, luxury, or novel capital investment. His table (p. 198) demonstrates their qualities.

Subsistence capital	Plentiful, durable, fixed, productive
Subsistence consumption	Plentiful, consumable, portable, utilitarian
Prestige	Scarce, durable, portable, nonuseful
Luxury	Scarce, consumable, portable, utilitarian
Novel capital investment	Scarce, durable, fixed, productive

He argues that this categorization applies to all societies, especially those 'where the distinction has not become blurred through the introduction of money'.

He finally claims that the existence of these four standards is 'not an unfortunate accident':

'It is a simple mechanism ensuring that subsidence goods are used to maintain a basic standard of life below which no person falls; that free floating power is allocated peacefully, with a minimum of exploitation (or disturbance of the individual's right to subsistence) and in accordance with the accepted standards; that the means of ensuring flexibility in the society do not disrupt the formal allocation of statuses in the society or the means of gaining power' (p. 212).

Thus he, surprisingly, reaches a functionalist viewpoint akin, as he himself says, to Parsons and Smelser. I think it is possible to accept his analysis without this conclusion, and without assuming that he reaches it because primitive society is different. His work could be re-analysed to reach a more dynamic conclusion in two ways. First, he does not push his own recognition of value in terms of time to its limits but instead backtracks to a modern orthodox view derived (*inter alia*) from Benham (quoted as the superscription to Salisbury's chapter on economic values (p. 184). Secondly, as he himself, of course, recognizes in a paragraph on monetary societies (p. 212), the Siane now live in a monetary world.

The conversion of goods in all four nexuses into commodities produced for exchange into money with a price linked by supply and demand but based on the socially necessary labour-time will set the Siane on the same kind of 'path from Rome' cited by Gluckman (1965a, p. 270).

'. . . a movement away from a situation where the law was mainly interested in commodities insofar as they conserved pre-established status relationships or established new status relationships. Commodities were no longer of primary value in discharging or creating debts in linked series between persons of linked status. Commodities began to develop an autonomous existence, entirely independent of their significance in multiple status relations.'

Like modern economists and Wildean cynics – Siane will soon know the price of everything and the value of nothing.

COUNTER-ATTACK III: SCARLETT EPSTEIN ON CHANGE
IN TWO PEASANT VILLAGES IN INDIA

'. . . Economic development may occur without any change in economic roles and relations, provided it does not result in a reallocation of resources or in an increased range of economic relations. Far from undermining the economic structure of any society such economic development may even strengthen the existing pattern of economic relations' (Epstein, T. S., 1962, p. 318; cf. Epstein, A. L., 1963, p. 211).
'Thus we have established a positive correlation between economic, political, ritual and organizational change, with

economic change being the determining variable' (*idem*, p. 334).

Like Salisbury, Scarlett Epstein is concerned with the effect of a seemingly accidental, externally imposed technological change on small-scale society. Her study makes an interesting contrast to his in that she is not only in a different tradition of anthropology – detailed description of dramatic social process – but also a different tradition of economics. Whereas Salisbury might be described as an empirically verifying theorist, Epstein is (like her economics teacher, W. Arthur Lewis) a theoretically informed empiricist.

She studied the economic effects of the introduction of a new modern irrigation system on two previously identical villages in Mysore. For topographical reasons, the one that she calls Dalena became a dry cultivation village on the fringe of the irrigation area. The other, Wangala, is right in the centre of the irrigation area and in terms of economic growth got a full and direct benefit. Paradoxically, she shows that Dalena underwent the most far-reaching economic change, defining economic change as a change in economic roles and relations.

Both villages have increased over a period of 25 years their output of goods and services. Both villages have moved from production for use to a money economy. Wangala, the wet village, has however remained a discrete agricultural economy. Dalena has become more closely integrated into a regional economy. Some Dalena men went to work in town or became small entrepreneurs either in agriculture or outside it.

'Thus as Dalena men increased the range of their economic relations, the interdependence between farmers and their agricultural labourers decreased and consequently the hereditary economic relations between Peasant masters and Untouchable clients disappeared' (p. 315).

In fact, in a whole series of ways, the existing economic structure of Dalena became incompatible with the new economic environment and was changed. It was, of course, not deliberately changed. Men simply ceased to make what they considered to be payments not in their interest.

Some aspects remained unchanged. Epstein recounts how the relationship between Peasants as a whole and Workmen as a whole was not changed, although a personal quarrel occurred and could have been used as a pretext. Similarly (as in the account of the Siane) the economic roles of Dalena women remained relatively unchanged. The division of labour by sex is compatible with men's participation in the wider economy (Frankenberg, 1966, *passim*).

In Wangala, economic development took what Epstein calls a 'unilinear form' – it could be summarized by saying, the same as before only more so. 'Peasant farmers now require more labour, so they employ their Untouchable clients and their Peasant debtors for more days per year. The greater requirement for cash cropping can be quite easily met under the traditional system of hereditary economic relations' (p. 317).

She goes on to show how the same services are required from Functionaries as before. There is not even in this case a redistribution of resources: '. . . irrigation in fact emphasised the existing economic differentiation and economic relations could continue unaltered.'

Interestingly enough, only wives of landowners benefited by a change of role in Wangala, since their labour in the fields was now considered undignified by their richer, higher-status, and prestigeful husbands. The difference in the economic changes in the two villages are reflected in political, ritual, and familial changes and in changes in cultural values. Thus, in dry Dalena, Panchayat members are no longer necessarily lineage elders. Dalena men take part in strikes and in regional political affairs.

'The increased economic mobility created by economic diversification led to a redistribution of wealth, which became incompatible with political leadership based on the hereditary principle' (p. 319). In Wangala, the only political changes concerned changes in the relative power of factions. Even this, however, was not fundamental, since here factions represent merely conflicting groups, whereas in Dalena they represent conflicting ideas and ideologies.

As far as ritual relations are concerned, ritual beliefs and practices are in this area intimately related to activity on the soil. '. . . no ritual is performed when a factory worker receives

his wages or a contractor his pay.' The division between innovators and conservatives put an end to joint village rituals in
Dalena. In Wangala, for a complex of reasons, there is an
increased number and intensity of rituals.

The value system of Wangala based on an attachment to the
land remained, like much else in the wet village, basically unchanged. In Dalena also, the change here was much slower than
in other spheres of life. Epstein considers this to be universal
and compares the action of industrialists in Britain in the
eighteenth and nineteenth centuries investing the proceeds of
industry in large estates. (I am by no means convinced that this
was not in fact a highly rational investment – it certainly turned
out to be a highly profitable one.) She considers this value
conservatism to be a brake on social change. Finally, she shows
how the struggle for prestige is intensified in both villages, but in
Wangala it remains a struggle for ritual prestige and in Dalena
it becomes concerned with economic prestige.

A logical continuation from Epstein's work would be to
consider the same problems in an industrial society. As W.
Arthur Lewis points out in his Introduction:

'Moreover in studying the market economy, economists have
tended to take institutions for granted, and have tended to
neglect inter-actions and conflicts between the market and
other social institutions. This has left a gap into which some
anthropologists are now sliding. They slip into factories, and
study how workers set or react to production norms; they
watch directors at work in the board-room; or they study the
effects of prestige on occupations. It is clear that the anthropologist's technique of observation, and his understanding of
the inter-relations of social institutions, have an important
contribution to make to the study of even the most advanced
market economies' (Lewis, in Epstein, 1962, p. vii).

Such a view has led British social anthropologists into
interesting and fruitful lines of research which, although outside
the traditional fields of social anthropology, are nevertheless
valuable extensions of its methods (e.g. Lupton, 1963; Allcorn,
1954). In a previous paper I attempted to construct a technologically based morphological continuum for Britain, as Sahlins

has done for Polynesia and Melanesia (Frankenberg, 1965; Sahlins, 1963).

Here, however, I want to pass to Sahlins's work on specifically primitive and peasant society.

ATTACK III: SAHLINS AND THE EVOLUTION OF CULTURE

Sahlins (1960, 1962a, 1962b, 1963, 1965) has produced, to my mind, a most interesting series of critiques of the classical economic anthropology. When he asserts for himself, however, he is often more cogent than when he attacks others. His first paper is the least moderate and the most outspoken – he leaves no doubt about what he means to say (1960, p. 391).

'It is incredible that anthropology – having at hand comparative materials from the whole range of human history and the entire gamut of cultural arrangements – should adopt, in dealing with primitive economics, a theoretical outlook relevant to historically recent, evolutionarily advanced systems of production and exchange. The fact remains that primitive economic behaviour is largely an aspect of kinship behaviour, and is therefore organized by means completely different from capitalist production and market transactions. The inference is clear: the whole of modern economic theory, resting on the assumption of the market and its concomitants, fails to apply to primitive economies.

To the initial failure to recognize the distinctiveness of primitive economies can be traced a whole compendium of economic fallacies in anthropological theories.'

Fighting words! He then lists as the two main fallacies those which we have already explored: (*a*) the Burling or Robbins-Burling approach with some injustice here attributed, *inter alia*, to Firth, and (*b*) the individualistic approach, attributed mainly to Herskovits.

He next turns his attention to capital and attacks its over-generalized use in economic anthropology as being metaphoric and misleading. I think that he is partly in error here and partly right. He praises Polanyi for showing the orthodox difference

78

between economic and economizing. What I think Sahlins is doing is confusing capital and capitalism. If his attack is on Herskovits and Bunzel for finding capitalism where none exists I am with him, but capital precedes capitalism and in itself does not imply either entrepreneurs or a propertyless wage-earning class. Sahlins, and I, and I suspect Firth, will agree with Marx (quoted Sahlins 1960, p. 394; Marx, 1889) when he says 'capital is not a thing but a social relation between persons, established by the instrumentality of things' (cf. Marx, 1930, p. 849). This is true of all capital, though what Marx was writing about specifically in *Capital* was capital with a capital C – or we might call it capitalist capital. Firth writes specifically of peasant capital (Firth & Yamey, 1964, p. 18) and implies that the role of capital in peasant producing and primitive society was different from that in industrial society. Indeed, even Marx was aware of this in 1845-1846. With certain obvious amendments what he then wrote about early towns could have been written by Firth of Tikopia.

'Capital in these towns was a naturally derived capital, consisting of a house, the tools of the craft, and the natural, hereditary customers; and not being realizable, on account of the backwardness of commerce and the lack of circulation, it descended from father to son. Unlike modern capital, which can be assessed in money and which may be indifferently invested in this thing or that, this capital was directly connected with the particular work of the owner, inseparable from it and to this extent estate capital' (Marx & Engels, 1845, 1965; p. 67).

Sahlins (at least in 1960) also out-Marxes Marx in his conviction and determination that, failing capitalist class relations, there can be no other kind of class relations. Lowie, Herskovits, and Bunzel all come under fire for suggesting 'capitalist' association between power and wealth in primitive society. Herskovits is attacked for applying Veblen's ideas of conspicuous consumption to the primitive field. Although by 1963, Sahlins himself is writing

'Palatial housing, ornamentation and luxury, finery and ceremony, in brief, conspicuous consumption, however much it seems mere self-interest always has a more decisive social significance. It creates those invidious distinctions between rulers and ruled so conducive to a passive – hence quite economical! – acceptance of authority. Throughout history, inherently more powerful political organizations than the Polynesian, with more assured logistics of rule, have turned to it – including in our time some ostensibly revolutionary and proletarian governments, despite every pre-revolutionary protestation of solidarity with the masses and equality for the classes' (1963, p. 300).

Sahlins shows himself a follower of Evans-Pritchard and Fortes (1940, p. 8).

'Most African societies belong to an economic order very different from ours. Theirs is mainly a subsistence economy with a rudimentary differentiation of productive labour and with no machinery for the accumulation of wealth in the form of commercial or industrial capital. If wealth is accumulated it takes the form of consumption goods and amenities or is used for the support of additional dependants. Hence it tends to be rapidly dissipated again and does not give rise to permanent class divisions. *Distinctions of rank, status, or occupation operate independently of differences of wealth*' (my italics).

Here, Sahlins falls into an error shared by Polanyi, Dalton, and others about the emergence of social classes. Godelier (1965, pp. 55-56) points out that the redistribution of goods by a minority can lead to classes emerging within tribal society.

Sahlins summarizes the essence of primitive economies as he saw them in 1960. First, they are systems which produce for use rather than exchange, with the corollary that control of the means of the production is decentralized, local, and familial. This, he says, implies (1) that relations of coercion, exploitation – dependence and mastery – 'are not created in the system of production', and (2) that in the absence of exchange there is a tendency to limit production to what can be used (see above).

It follows from this that a tribal-wide economy is only created by prestigeful chiefly administrators. Economy is embedded in kinship, and kinship minimizes the search for gain. Reciprocity and pooling are the principal forms of transaction. This is spelled out in more detail in his latest non-polemical and more convincing paper (1965). If the chief has prestige and power it is related to his status as redistributive agent. 'It is not, however, the possession nor consumption of goods that gives chiefly power, but their dispensation; hence generosity is the *sine qua non* of chieftainship' (1960, p. 411).

There is, however, a direct association between the growth of political power, a tribal (as opposed to a household) economy, and productivity.

'Considered, however, in general perspective, in the evolution of culture as a whole, productivity, the tribal economy, and political power proceed together. *The higher the productivity, the more differentiated and larger the tribal economy, and the more developed the chiefly powers*' (my italics) (Sahlins, 1960, p. 412).

Sahlins has consistently presented his material within an evolutionary framework – but like others of White's pupils he is concerned with the evolution of culture rather than the evolution of society. He sees (as in the passage above) a direct relation between technology and social change. If Burling threw out the bath-water of social relations and left the baby in shivering isolation, Sahlins, at least in his earlier work, may be said to have thrown out the baby and kept the bath-water. Individuals and even societies seem to be seen as passive recipients of exogenous pushes in the form of technological changes.

CONCLUSIONS – MAGNIFICENT DYNAMICS

I have dwelt perhaps unfairly on Sahlins's 1960 paper instead of his much more sophisticated later works. My justification for this may be, first, that Sahlins has not to my knowledge repudiated it and he refers to it in 1965.

Secondly, Sahlins relies heavily in 1960 on Marx. Berliner (1962, p. 60) specifically equates Marx and White. That I think that both sometimes misinterpret Marx is perhaps irrelevant; what is relevant is that they fail to take advantage of the method which another interpretation of Marx would give them. To argue this, I return to Berliner's paper and discuss the distinction he makes there between comparative static and dynamic types of analysis.

His argument is complex and mathematical and I do not propose to do more than quote his summary.

'. . . Static models in both anthropology and economics can deal only with the properties of equilibrium states, and can say nothing about the time path of change from one equilibrium state to another caused by the change in a parameter.' 'Dynamic models do all that static models do (describe the properties of end states) but in addition permit the analysis of the time-path of change from one state to another.'

Berliner's example of a dynamic theory which had the virtue of being disprovable and the vice of being disproved is 'Morgan-Tylor evolutionist theory'. He adds that while the disproof of unilinear evolutionism meant that 'magnificent dynamics' underwent eclipse in both anthropology and economics, White/Childe evolutionism and Harrod/Domar dynamics are bringing them back.

The new dynamics of White, however, he criticizes (correctly in my view) because the primacy of technology makes the system depend always on exogenous change.

'. . . Changes in technology are exogenous; they are external to the culture and cannot be explained by the culture, but they shape the changes in culture . . . . The system moves in spurts; each change in technology sets in motion a series of changes in the culture until the new culture is again consistent with the new technology. . . . Moreover in the absence of new pushes, the systems eventually settle down to stationary states; the systems are dampened in other words. In fact, all real societies are subject to a sufficient number of exogenous pushes, from diffusion for example, that they rarely reach stationary states.'

It is nevertheless useful, Berliner argues, to distinguish 'theories dependent on such pushes, from self-generating dynamic theories'. He argues that economists in their preoccupation with the business cycle have developed theories of endogenous change; anthropologists have not, he says, devoted so much attention to cyclical movements. (He is less than well informed on British social anthropology.)

With the already noted exception of Burling, all the general anthropological writers I have considered have been concerned with some kind of morphological continuum. We can represent them in tabular form.

Firth	Primitive		Peasant		Industrial[8]
Dalton	Markets		Peripheral markets		Market
Sahlins (1958)	Band	— Tribe —	Chiefdom	—	State
Polanyi	Reciprocal		Redistributive		Exchange
Sahlins (1965)	Generalized reciprocity		Balanced reciprocity		Negative reciprocity

In Berliner's terms, such 'scales' can be seen either as a series of end-states – comparative statics – or as arbitrary stopping-points on a continuous process through either real or notional time. We can incorporate the endogenous/exogenous variable within this scheme, thus:

1. Exogenous comparative statics
   The object was here, it was hit, now it's there.
2. Endogenous comparative statics
   The object was here, it moved itself, now it's there.
3. Exogenous dynamics
   The object was here, it was hit and moved first to there at velocity x, where it collided with y and moved on to there at velocity z.
4. Endogenous dynamics
   The object was here, it moved itself, touched that, changed, moved again.

It is a model of the fourth type that I am interested in. This is the kind of model that classification in terms of market behaviour alone cannot provide for Dalton, Bohannan, and Firth. It is also the model that Sahlins, and long before him Bücher, reject for themselves (and in the case of Sahlins, incorrectly, for Marx too).

'Herskovits repeatedly notes that the means of production are in the direct possession of producers, and obliges us by pointing out the most significant implication of this fact, viz., the primitive producer, "is the master of his own economic destiny" (1952, p. 31). To Marx, of course, this is the key difference between capitalistic and most pre-capitalistic economies. And Bücher tersely grasps its importance when he notes that from a household economy, relations of social dependence "manifestly cannot come" (1907, p. 318)' (Sahlins, 1960, p. 408).

It is, I think, the model to which Epstein and Salisbury would move if they carried their insight and analysis beyond the single society to attempt a 'magnificent dynamics' approach. Their separate empirical approaches have arrived at two of the basic concepts of Marx's theory – the labour (time) theory of value (Salisbury) and historical materialism (Epstein, 1962, p. 315; cf. Marx, 1859). It seems only reasonable to try the experiment of re-insertion in the total theoretical framework. I suspect some economists would welcome the opportunity of rediscovering Marxist views on development without the embarrassment of getting them from Marx (cf. Freedman, 1962).

Such a model, I believe, could be constructed if one took as the starting-point not the social concomitants of exchange but the social concomitants of production (including exchange as one of these).

The key questions are: what is produced, by what social groups? How are the groups organized and by whom? What is the purpose of production (e.g. use or exchange)? How are conflicts which arise in the process of production dealt with? What alternative uses could be given to time used in production? If we ask these specifically sociological questions about technological change, two things will follow. First, we shall rediscover that the interrelations of technology and society are very complicated, which is no surprise. Secondly, the exogenous comparative statics of cultural evolution can be transformed into a view of dynamic change, initially within individual societies and ultimately to a more sophisticated theory of social evolution.

It does not, of course, follow from my view that this is the way forward; that, with Dalton, Bohannan, and Sahlins, I believe Herskovits, Firth, and others have wasted their time. On the contrary, different problems require different approaches, and the many specific empirical studies, whatever their theoretical approach, provide valuable bricks for synthesis.

'The scholar of humanistic temperament attracted by the unique properties of the individual human being or human society, searches for culture patterns. To the scholar of scientific temperament, societies are specimens of which only the generalizable properties are of interest. For purposes of prediction or policy, or for the fullest understanding of mankind, the two types of scholarship are complementary rather than competitive. Indeed the anthropologist of grandest scope combines the "Two Cultures" in one person. To the outside reviewer, it is the fruitful union of humanist and scientific scholarship that provides the distinctive pleasure in the study of anthropology' (Berliner, 1962, p. 53).

NOTES

1. Raymond Firth does not necessarily accept any of my interpretations. He specifically rejects my view that he falls back on an evolutionary framework.
2. Compare the controversy on physical anthropology in the same issue of *Current Anthropology* where a writer is described as being 'in the position of a homeopath amateur writing a specialized treatise in the field of surgery' (p. 35).
3. See Gluckman (1965a, pp. 229-230), in which the allocation of scarce resources is seen as operating in Barotse kinship law.
4. This is different from my analysis of strangers, as Paine says, but not for his reasons – see Paine (1963, p. 52; Frankenberg, 1957, p. 43).
5. A detailed criticism of Dalton and Polanyi is to be found in Percy Cohen's paper in this volume. I have been highly selective in my comments. An evaluation of the 'surplus' controversy is in Godelier (1965, pp. 52-54).
6. The suggestion that the nearest approach to 'a standard element symbolizing real cost' might be 'the use of the elasticity of demand for time' is made by Belshaw (1954, pp. 149-150). He writes in a note that his Ph.D. thesis contains an Appendix devoted to this topic. In this, as in many other points, I find myself anticipated by Maurice Godelier in a paper published shortly after the present paper was read. He also emphasizes this point in relation to Salisbury (Godelier, 1965, p. 71-72), as did Worsley in his review of Salisbury (Worsley, 1963).
7. Godelier does not share my view on Firth here (1965, p. 62). He also sees Salisbury's difficulties as springing from his 'objectification' of the concept of capital.
8. See note 1 above.

REFERENCES

ALLCORN, D. H. 1954. Social Life of Young Men in a London Suburb. Manchester (Unpublished Ph.D. thesis).

Ronald Frankenberg

ARENSBERG, C. 1937. *The Irish Countryman*. New York: Macmillan.
ARMSTRONG, W. E. 1928. *Rossel Island, an Ethnological Study*. Cambridge: Cambridge University Press.
BARAN, P. 1957. *The Political Economy of Growth*. London: Calder.
BARTH, FREDRIK. 1963. *The Role of the Entrepreneur in Social Change in Northern Norway*. Bergen; Oslo: Norwegian Universities Press.
BELSHAW, C. S. 1954. *Changing Melanesia: Social Economics of Culture Contact*. Melbourne: Oxford University Press.
BENHAM, F. 1936. *Economics*. London: Pitman.
BERLINER, JOSEPH S. 1962. The Feet of the Natives are Large: An Essay on Anthropology by an Economist. *Current Anthropology* **3**: 47-61.
BOHANNAN, PAUL & DALTON, GEORGE (eds.). 1962. *Markets in Africa*. Evanston, Ill.: Northwestern University Press.
BOULDING, K. 1957. The Parsonian Approach to Economics. *Kyklos* **10**: 317-339.
BÜCHER, C. 1901. *Industrial Evolution*. New York.
BURLING, ROBBINS. 1962. Maximization Theories and the Study of Economic Anthropology. *American Anthropologist* **64**: 802-821.
COHEN, ABNER. 1965. The Social Organization of Credit in a West African Cattle Market. *Africa* **35**: 8-20.
DALTON, GEORGE. 1960. A Note of Clarification on Economic Surplus. *American Anthropologist* **62**: 483-490.
— 1961. Economic Theory and Primitive Society. *American Anthropologist* **63**: 1-25.
— 1965. Primitive Money. *American Anthropologist* **67**: 44-65.
DEWEY, A. 1962. *Peasant Marketing in Java*. Glencoe: Free Press.
DOBB, MAURICE. 1946. *Studies in the Development of Capitalism*. London: Routledge & Kegan Paul.
EPSTEIN, A. L. 1963. The Economy of Modern Matupit: Continuity and Change on the Gazelle Peninsula, New Britain. *Oceania* **33**: 182-215.
EPSTEIN, T. SCARLETT. 1961. A Study of Rabaul Market. *Australian Journal of Agricultural Economics* **5** (1).
— 1962. *Economic Development and Social Change in South India*. Manchester: Manchester University Press.
— 1964. Personal Capital Formation among the Tolai of New Britain. In Firth & Yamey, 1964, pp. 53-68.
EVANS-PRITCHARD, EDWARD E. & FORTES, MEYER. 1940. *African Political Systems*, London: Oxford University Press.
FIRTH, RAYMOND. 1936. *We The Tikopia: The Sociology of Kinship in Primitive Polynesia*. London: Allen & Unwin.

—— 1939. *Primitive Polynesian Economy* (1st edn.). London: George Routledge.

—— 1946. *Malay Fishermen: Their Peasant Economy* (1st edn.). London: Kegan Paul, Trench, Trubner.

—— 1951. *Elements of Social Organization.* London: Watts.

—— (ed.). 1957a. *Man and Culture: An Evaluation of the Work of Malinowski.* London: Routledge & Kegan Paul.

—— 1957b. The Place of Malinowski in the History of Economic Anthropology. In Firth (ed.), 1957a, pp. 209-227.

—— 1957c. Work and Community in a Primitive Society. *H.R.H. Duke of Edinburgh's Study Conference on the Human Problems of Industrial Communities within the Commonwealth and Empire, Oxford, 1956.* Oxford: Oxford University Press.

—— 1959. *Social Change in Tikopia.* London: Allen & Unwin.

—— 1964. Family and Kinship in Industrial Society. In Halmos, P. (ed.), 1964, pp. 65-87.

—— 1965. *Primitive Polynesian Economy* (2nd edn.). London: Routledge & Kegan Paul.

FIRTH, RAYMOND & YAMEY, B. S. (eds.). 1964. *Capital, Saving and Credit in Peasant Societies.* London: Allen & Unwin.

FRANKENBERG, RONALD. 1957. *Village on the Border.* London: Cohen & West.

—— 1965. British Communities: Problems of Synthesis. In M. Banton (ed.), *The Social Anthropology of Complex Societies.* A.S.A. Monographs, 4. London: Tavistock Publications, pp. 123-154.

—— 1966. *Communities in Britain.* Harmondsworth: Penguin Books.

FREEDMAN, R. (ed.). 1962. *Marx on Economics.* Harmondsworth: Penguin Books.

GLUCKMAN, M. 1950. Kinship and Marriage among the Lozi of Northern Rhodesia and the Zulu of Natal. In A. R. Radcliffe-Brown & D. Forde, 1950, pp. 166-206.

—— 1965a. *The Ideas in Barotse Jurisprudence.* Yale: Yale University Press.

—— 1965b. *Politics, Law and Ritual in Tribal Society.* Oxford: Basil Blackwell.

GLUCKMAN, M. & DEVONS, E. (eds.). 1964. *Closed Systems and Open Minds.* Edinburgh & London: Oliver & Boyd.

GODELIER, M. 1965. Objet et Méthodes de l'Anthropologie Économique. *L'Homme* Avril-Juin, 32-91.

GOODY, J. 1962. *Death, Property, and the Ancestors. A Study of the Mortuary Customs of the LoDagaa of West Africa.* Stanford, Calif.: Stanford University Press; London: Tavistock Publications.

Ronald Frankenberg

HALMOS, P. (ed.). 1964. *Development of Industrial Society*. Sociological Review Monographs No. 8. Keele.

HERSKOVITS, M. J. 1926. The Cattle Complex in East Africa. *American Anthropologist* **28**: 230-272, 361-388, 494-528, 633-664.

—— 1952. *Economic Anthropology*. New York: Knopf.

HOBSBAWM, E. J. 1964. Introduction to Karl Marx – *Pre-capitalist Economic Formations*. London: Lawrence & Wishart.

LEACH, E. R. 1954. *Political Systems of Highland Burma*. London: Bell.

LECLAIR, EDWARD E., Jr. 1962. Economic Theory and Economic Anthropology. *American Anthropologist* **64**: 1179-1203.

LEWIS, W. ARTHUR. 1955. *The Theory of Economic Growth*. London: Allen & Unwin.

LUPTON, T. 1963. *On the Shop Floor*. Oxford: Pergamon.

MACRAE, D. 1965. Karl Marx. *New Society*, 5, p. 122.

MALINOWSKI, B. 1922. *Argonauts of the Western Pacific*. London: Routledge & Kegan Paul.

MARX, KARL. 1859. *Critique of Political Economy*.

—— 1889. *Capital*. Allen & Unwin Edition.

—— 1930 (1890). *Capital*, 2 vols. Everyman Edition. London: Dent

MARX, K. & ENGELS, F. 1965. *The German Ideology* (1845) (New English Edition). London: Lawrence & Wishart.

MERTON, R. K. 1957. *Social Theory and Social Structure*. (Revised and enlarged edition) New York: Free Press.

PAINE, ROBERT. 1963. Entrepreneurial Activity without its Profits. In F. Barth, 1963, pp. 33-55.

PARSONS, TALCOTT. 1957. Malinowski and the Theory of Social Systems. In R. Firth, 1957a, pp. 53-70.

PARSONS, T. & SMELSER, NEIL, J. 1956. *Economy and Society*. London: Routledge & Kegan Paul.

POLANYI, K. 1946. *Origin of our Time: The Great Transformation*. London: Gollancz.

POLANYI, K., ARENSBERG, C. W. & PEARSON, H. W. 1957. *Trade and Market in the Early Empires*. Glencoe, Ill.: Free Press.

RADCLIFFE-BROWN, A. R. & FORDE, D. (eds.). 1950. *African Systems of Kinship and Marriage*. London: Oxford University Press.

ROBBINS, L. 1935. *An Essay on the Nature and Significance of Economic Science* (2nd rev. edn.) London: Macmillan.

RICHARDS, AUDREY I. 1939. *Land, Labour and Diet in Northern Rhodesia*. London, Oxford: Oxford University Press.

RUDIE, INGE. 1963. Two Entrepreneurial Careers in a Small Local Community. In F. Barth, 1963, pp. 56-69.

Economic Anthropology

SAHLINS, MARSHALL D. 1958. *Social Stratification in Polynesia.* American Ethnological Society. Seattle: University of Washington Press.

—— 1960. Political Power and the Economy in Primitive Society. In G. E. Dole and R. L. Carneiro, *Essays in the Science of Culture*, pp. 390-415. New York: Crowell.

—— 1962a. Review of B. F. Hoselitz, *Sociological Aspects of Economic Growth. American Anthropologist* **64**: 1063-1073.

—— 1962b. *Moala*, Ann Arbor: University of Michigan Press.

—— 1963. Poor Man, Rich Man, Big-Man, Chief: Political Types in Melanesia and Polynesia. *Comparative Studies in Society and History*, **5**: 285-303.

—— 1965. On the Sociology of Primitive Exchange. In M. Banton (ed.), *The Relevance of Models for Social Anthropology.* A.S.A. Monographs, 1, pp. 139-236. London: Tavistock Publications.

SALISBURY, R. F. 1962. *From Stone to Steel.* Melbourne: Melbourne University Press.

STEINER, FRANZ. 1954. Notes on Comparative Economics. *British Journal of Sociology* **5**: 118-129.

UBEROI, J. SINGH. 1962. *Politics of the Kula Ring.* Manchester: Manchester University Press.

WORSLEY, P. 1963. Review of Salisbury, 1962 in *Journal of Polynesian Society*, **72**(2) June.

ACKNOWLEDGEMENTS

Thanks are due to the authors and publishers concerned for permission to quote from the following works, of which full details are given in the References:

The American Anthropological Association in respect of papers by George Dalton and by Robbins Burling from the *American Anthropologist;* Professor Fredrik Barth and Universitetsforlaget in respect of *The Role of the Entrepreneur in Social Change in Northern Norway;* Thomas Y. Crowell in respect of the paper by M. D. Sahlins from *Essays in the Science of Culture* edited by G. E. Dole and R. L. Carneiro; the Editor of *Current Anthropology* and the author in respect of the paper by Joseph Berliner; Manchester University Press in respect of *Economic Development and Social Change in South India* by T. S. Epstein; Melbourne University Press in association with the Australian National University in respect of *From Stone to Steel* by R. F. Salisbury; the author and Routledge & Kegan Paul in respect of *Primitive Polynesian Economy* by Raymond Firth; the author and C. A. Watts & Company in respect of *Elements of Social Organization* by Raymond Firth.

Percy S. Cohen

Economic Analysis and Economic Man

Some Comments on a Controversy[1]

INTRODUCTION

For some time now, there has been disagreement among anthropologists concerning the applicability of economic analysis to primitive and peasant societies. One view is that economic principles are universally true and therefore serve to explain and analyse the conduct of men in primitive and peasant societies. The other view is that such principles apply only to complex market economies: that is, to commercialized and industrialized societies, and perhaps only to capitalist societies among these. But the controversy is also possibly about something else: for those who favour the wider applicability of economic theory tend to stress the common characteristics of human conduct in all societies, and possibly even the common characteristics of all societies; while those who deny the wider applicability of economic theory seem to suggest that human societies are fundamentally different in certain important respects.

I hope to show in this essay that the two questions are closely related; and that seeking an answer to one of them provides some hint of an answer to the other.

A BRIEF HISTORY OF THE DEBATE

Few arguments in anthropology have actually started with Malinowski. But it is often convenient to treat his views as though all major controversies stem from them, if only because he was so deliberately polemical. He used his genius, sometimes rather indiscriminately, to lay about him on all sides, armed with the massive weight of Trobriand ethnography. If the established views stressed the differences between primitive and civilized men – for example, in the sociology of law – then Malinowski stressed the similarities. If the proponents of another new discipline stressed the similarities – for example, Freud – Malinowski stressed the differences.

The economists – or so it seemed to Malinowski – were stressing the similarities. They thought that all men sought to maximize their gains, and that this was simply an expression of a universal human characteristic. Malinowski challenged this view by arguing that this was not a universal characteristic but simply a Western one, the product of a particular culture: primitive men – that is, Trobrianders – were often more concerned to fulfil their moral obligations than to maximize their gains. The Trobrianders engaged in three types of activity involving the exchange and distribution of material goods: *urigubu, kula,* and *gimwali.* The first was a form of payment in kind to women and children who had rights in the property of the matrilineage; the second was gift or ceremonial exchange, which might also accompany the third; only the third, simple trade, which was carried on largely with strangers and constituted a very small part of economic activity, could be said to be governed by the motive to maximize material gain. Culture, not human nature, conditioned men's economic conduct (Malinowski, 1922, pp. 63-65, 81-86, 189-191).

While Malinowski was right in denying the truth of a universal psychological assumption, he was mistaken in thinking that economic theory actually required this assumption. As Lionel Robbins has noted, the question of the truth or falsity of certain psychological hypotheses, which are believed to explain fundamental economic assumptions, is irrelevant to economics (Robbins, 1932, pp. 83-86). Malinowski's argument is therefore, at least in part, beside the point. But he seems to have stumbled across an important idea: that it is more difficult to abstract the economic aspect of social conduct in the study of primitive societies than it is in the study of industrial societies.

The defects in Malinowski's arguments were soon noted by Firth, who, like his teacher, has been profoundly concerned to rescue economic anthropology both from those who equated it with a study of material culture as well as from those who saw it simply as a means for documenting the hypothesis of primitive communism. Firth starts out from the assumption that all men in all societies are faced with the same economic problem: how to allocate scarce resources between alternate uses, given that some uses are more highly valued than others. He sees the main task of economic anthropology to be the study of how men organize their activities in solving the problem of allocation within the limits set by their physical environment, as transformed by culture, their technology and state of knowledge, their social structure and values. He denies that men in primitive and peasant societies are mere automata driven by the demands of their environment and social structure, and sees them as exercising choice in having to economize as men do in more complex societies. In analysing this aspect of conduct, anthropologists can use economic categories and economic analysis (see Firth, 1939, pp. 1-31, 352-365; also Firth, 1951, pp. 122-155; and Firth, 1957).

Firth agrees that most primitive and peasant economies lack specialized economic institutions, such as factories, banks, and commodity exchanges; but it is not these alone which provide the object of economic analysis. An economist may abstract certain economic processes from a number of concrete, institutional contexts; and, similarly, an anthropologist may abstract such processes from the 'concrete' contexts of family, kinship, and community.

Firth studies such economic processes as how men allocate their time and resources between the production of 'investment goods', such as canoes, 'durable consumer goods', such as pandanus mats, and other 'consumer goods', such as yams, and between different productive activities, such as horticulture, fishing, and the making and repairing of tools. He describes how they mobilize labour and reward it, how goods and services are distributed and exchanged, and what factors affect decisions on these matters.

He concedes that societies with a simple technology and a small scale and narrow range of social relationships do have certain characteristics which result from their simplicity: payments for services and rates of exchange are fixed by custom and scarcely fluctuate in the short run, though they may alter in the long run with changes in relative scarcities; and gift-giving is the most important form of distribution and exchange. He sees that these and other characteristics function as part of a system of moral involvement and familiarity, and notes that there is relatively little economic activity outside of the moral community (Firth, 1939, pp. 347-361). He illustrates these points not only in his earlier studies of Tikopia economy, but also in his later study of the far more complex economic system of Malay fishermen, among whom interest rates, for example, may be affected not only by the conditions of supply and demand, but also by the nature of the relationship between borrower and lender (Firth, 1946, p. 168). These forms of exchange reflect what Gluckman later called 'multiplex' structures of social relationships (Gluckman, 1955, p. 19). Despite all this, Firth concludes that these characteristics are to be found also in industrial societies and that the difference between types of economic system is one of degree, not one of kind (Firth, 1939, p. 355).

This view has been questioned by K. Polanyi and others in their discussion of the economies of classical and other ancient, civilized societies (Polanyi, 1957). They try to show that, while these societies had a number of characteristics associated with market economies, they lacked certain essential ones. For example, they had a complex division of labour in the urban sector, extensive trade, both internal and overseas, middlemen, money dealers, forms of banking, discounting, and arbitrage. But most of their trade was in luxury goods and was managed by the State. Manufacturers produced for known buyers in known quantities, and did not compete in an uncertain market; their decisions were not significantly affected by market fluctuations, and the market in factors of production did not significantly react to changes in the demand for final products. The factors of production were not themselves marketed or marketable. These authors conclude that the oft-stressed distinction between economies with markets and those without is less important than the division between economies which are governed fully by the market principle and those which are not. They maintain that the propositions of formal economics were devised to explain the processes of the genuine market economy and do not apply universally. They commend certain anthropologists for making an important start in the comparative study of economic systems, but think that they are partly misguided in their belief that they can use principles which have, in any case, only limited value for the analysis of market economies, since they say little about the working of the institutional structure of the economy (ibid., pp. 236-371).

These views were, in due course, taken up and amplified by Dalton, who argues as follows. In a society with a complex division of labour, the majority of individuals can satisfy their wants only by selling their labour. They cannot be paid in kind because their wants are manifold and diverse. The double need for a standardized system of payment, which will both ensure a supply of labour and enable labour to exchange its reward for commodities, creates a totally monetized economy. In such economies, changes in conditions in one market will lead to changes in the conditions in others; changes in the supply and demand for consumption goods produce changes in the market for factors of production. Such systems differ radically from those normally studied by anthropologists, in which groups satisfy their wants by cooperative production and joint consumption of the produce, exchanging only surpluses, if they do not give them away as gifts, but not producing much for exchange. The analysis of such systems is conducted in terms of the categories of reciprocity, not in terms of supply and demand (Dalton, 1961).

Dalton, in cooperation with Bohannan, applies these views to the study of African markets (Bohannan and Dalton, 1962, pp. 1-26). They distinguish three types of economic system: the marketless economy, the economy with peripheral markets, and the economy fully governed by the market principle. The first and second types are the only ones which are indigenous to Africa. Both these types are 'multi-centric, having several distinct transactional spheres . . . distinguished by different material items and services . . . by different principles of exchange and by different moral values' (ibid., p. 3). These different spheres may also be ordered in a moral hierarchy. In so far as money is used, there will be a different type for each sphere; a single, all-purpose money would destroy the divisions between moral spheres.

In economics with 'peripheral markets', the laws of supply and demand do sometimes operate, especially in the market for consumer goods or other final products, where there is barter or money payment. But prices may vary from one district to another – each one constituting a 'closed circuit' – and they may even vary within the same market at any one time: personal goodwill may be more important than material gain. Fluctuations in prices affect neither the value of productive factors nor the level of production. Most traders are themselves producers; there are few genuine middlemen who profit by buying cheap and selling dear (ibid., pp. 7-10).

Bohannan and Dalton have improved on the views of Polanyi: they recognize that the market principle operates in varying degrees and they abandon a simple, twofold classification; however, in the study of marketless economies they seem to find no place for the kind of economic analysis recommended by Firth.

There is support for Firth's view in a study of Javanese local markets by A. Dewey (1962, pp. 185-189). In addition to describing market activities and analysing the background to trading, the author tries to analyse the logic of market behaviour in economic terms.

In these markets, there are two sets of considerations: first, buyers are concerned to obtain good value and traders to make a profit; second, both buyers and sellers wish to maintain certain kinds of personal relations which embrace more than the commercial one. People have to reconcile these two principles, and in doing so they balance one set of advantages against another; in this, they are behaving quite rationally (ibid., p. 115). Dewey takes issue with those authors who find that economic conduct in peasant societies is noticeably different from that in industrial societies; and she argues for the wider use of economic analysis. What she seems to have in mind, apart from some limited use of supply and demand analysis, is the use of certain descriptive categories, such as 'capital', 'investment', 'opportunity cost'.

Two recent contributors to this debate, Robbins Burling and LeClair, have, like Dalton, sought to clarify the general issues rather than comment on particular cases (Burling, 1962;

LeClair, 1962). Burling, who is a critic both of Dalton and, in some ways, of Firth also, provides a useful survey of the different meanings of the term 'economic', and decides in favour of the study of the maximization of satisfactions. LeClair also disagrees with Dalton and, like Burling, sees the task of economic anthropology as the application of analytic principles and categories.

Most contributors to this debate concede that there are important differences between primitive and industrial economies; they disagree only as to whether these are to be called differences in kind or of degree. However, at least one writer, L. Pospisil, chooses almost entirely to ignore such differences; at least, he suggests that the differences within each category might be as fundamental as the differences between them (Pospisil, 1963, pp. 399-405). This all arises out of his study of the Kapauku Papuans. Pospisil notes that the economy of these people has a number of characteristics which are similar to those of capitalist societies. There is a powerful motive to accumulate wealth, for success brings prestige and power. Prestige comes not from patterns of consumption but from power, through the extension of credit. Men who are successful at growing and selling sweet potatoes buy pigs, which are also needed to acquire wives. Wives give children, or manpower, to increase the production of potatoes. Some men succeed in becoming rich and no longer have the manpower to manage increased pig-breeding; they therefore contract this out to others. They also make loans to men who wish to buy pigs for breeding or to acquire wives. Loans bear interest which, according to Pospisil, is compensation for risk of default, not for loss of liquidity; for the return of loans is not judicially enforceable and rich men make them to those whom they can trust (ibid., p. 312). The Kapauku Papuans engage in widespread trade, both internal and external; and for this purpose they use shell-money in several denominations. The prices of goods fluctuate, sometimes as a result of real changes in the conditions of supply and demand, sometimes as a result of 'manipulations' on the part of 'big men'. Different prices are found in different regions; but the 'circuits' are not closed; men buy in cheap markets to sell in dear ones. Values are fiercely individualistic; for example, strips of fence and drainage ditches

are owned and maintained privately; and gift-giving is not
common.

It is hardly surprising that Pospisil sees this economy as
American capitalism in miniature. Nor is it surprising that he
rejects the hypothesis of primitive communism; although it is
surprising that he still considers it necessary to refute this
doctrine. He argues convincingly that the analysis of this
society requires the use of some elementary principles of
economics. But he overlooks certain important differences
between this economy and that of capitalism, and confuses
similarities in values with similarities of structure.

Sahlins, the most recent contributor to this debate, is quite
explicitly polemical: he denies the applicability of economic
theory to the study of primitive society, rejects the definition of
economic conduct given by Lionel Robbins and accepted by
Firth, which emphasizes the process of allocation of scarce
means to alternate uses, and opts for the view that the study of
the economy is the study of how men 'provision' their society
(Sahlins, 1965). As part of his discussion, which is concerned
with the nature of primitive exchange, Sahlins distinguishes
three forms of reciprocity: 'generalized', 'balanced', and 'negative'. The first exists where goods and services are given by one
party to another without any demand for a return at a specified
time or of a specified kind; the prototype of this is the nurturant
relationship between mother and child. The second exists where
a return is made which is recognized by both parties as the
equivalent of what is given; custom or moral principle defines
such equivalence and is unquestioned. The third exists where
there is bargaining; no party is morally inhibited from seeking
gain at the other's expense; and, in many cases, there is no
restraint on the use of persuasion or even chicanery in obtaining
the most favourable terms of exchange. All three types are
found in most societies, though the third is very rare in the
simpler types of primitive society. Sahlins suggests that in all
societies 'generalized reciprocity' is the norm within the family,
but that in modern industrial societies 'negative reciprocity'
might predominate in many relationships outside of the family.
In primitive societies there is a movement towards 'balanced'
reciprocity in those relationships which lie outside of the closest

ties of kinship and vicinity, and the practice of 'negative' reciprocity is found almost entirely outside of the moral community. In short, Sahlins proposes a correlation between type of reciprocity and degree of social distance. He is aware that this correlation does not occur perfectly in concrete cases, and suggests a number of models in which the operations of other factors are introduced. Sahlins thinks that economic theory can only explain conduct which is based on the principle of 'negative reciprocity', and therefore agrees with Polanyi and Dalton that the study of other types of economic conduct calls for different principles of analysis (ibid., p. 186). Sahlins has made an important contribution to the comparative sociological study of primitive exchange. However, he adopts too extreme a position on the question of economic analysis. I think that his, and some other, arguments on this matter result partly from a confusion in the use of the term, and partly from a misunderstanding of economic analysis.

TYPES OF ECONOMIC ANALYSIS

One of the main reasons why it is so difficult to assess arguments for and against the wider applicability of economic analysis lies in the fact that the term is used to mean three, or even more, different things, or to refer to three different types of economic analysis. The first type, which until the recent past was thought of as the main substance of economic science, is supply and demand analysis and its many applications; these applications can themselves be classified as micro-economic and macro-economic. The second type, which some economists now consider the basic method of their science, consists in the application of the principle of economic rationality, or the formulation and use of the 'pure logic of choice' (cf. Hayek, 1949, pp. 33-56). The third type consists in the analysis of those institutions and, more importantly, those processes which organize productive, distributive, and exchange activities. A variant of the third type is the analysis of any social structure in terms of the relationship between economic and non-economic factors. These three types are not, of course, mutually exclusive: the first usually involves the use of the second, whether explicitly or not; but the second

99

Percy S. Cohen

can be used without the first; and the third may make use of the second and, possibly, of the first also.

The first type originated in antiquity; but it was only in the eighteenth century that it became a fully recognizable scientific activity (cf. Roll, 1942). The central issue with which the so-called classical economists of the eighteenth and nineteenth century were concerned was that of free trade; and it was this concern which gave rise to a system of thought which formed the basis of economic science for nearly two hundred years.

For the classical economists there was something almost natural about free trade which, while allowing for the full expression of self-interest, unhampered by custom or moral or physical coercion, produced an orderly arrangement which promoted the benefit of all. But the very existence of such an arrangement, undirected by anything but the 'invisible hand', was very puzzling. It was this puzzlement which gave rise to speculation about the nature of this system.

What *was* puzzling was the very fact that order could result as the unintended consequence of the intentional acts of many separate individuals, each one totally unconcerned with the welfare of anyone but himself and his immediate family. Had the economic order been governed by custom, there would have been no puzzle: men would have acted the way they did because they had always done so; and orderliness would have resulted from the fact that they did exactly what was expected of them. Had the economic order been governed by coercion, whether moral or physical, there would equally have been no problem to solve. But had the economy been governed by these other forces it could not have conferred the benefits that it did. There must be some other mechanism, far more subtle and unobserved in its workings than the obvious ones of custom and coercion, which ensured that the pure pursuit of self-interest did produce this superior effect.

The great achievement of the classical economists was to show how the mechanism of supply and demand did produce this effect. But it went a good deal further than the simple enunciation of the laws themselves. It consisted not only in the application of a principle, which was already known in its crude form, but far more in the construction of a model of a self-regulating system, in which seemingly separate spheres of supply and demand were brought into relation with one another. This model has been appropriately described as the 'concept of the economic machine' (see Meek, 1965); for it is obviously similar in form to the models of classical mechanics.

It would be argued – indeed, it has been – that classical economics was simply part of an ideology to defend free trade, and that its contents are therefore explicable in terms of the interests of the new entrepreneurial class. There is, of course, some truth in this: the 'subsistence' or 'iron law' theory of wages was based on demographic assumptions for which there was not a scrap of evidence; but, as a theory it suited, or seemed to suit, a policy of low wages and high profits.[2] Similarly, Ricardo's theory of rent looks as though it reflected class interests.[3] It could also be argued that, in glorifying the self-regulating mechanism of the system, the classical economists were simply giving merchants and industrialists *carte blanche* to ignore the interests of other sections of society. However, it would be a gross injustice to the classical economists to dismiss all their efforts in this way. For, however mistaken or misleading their model may have been, its assumptions did reflect a very significant trend in social life: the gradual disengagement of economic relations from the interpersonal bonds which were governed by custom and moral influence and, equally, from the constraints of centralized authority.

The particular macro-economic model which the classical economists constructed reflected the increasing interdependence of economic variables which resulted from the increasing interdependence of occupational roles. There is a curious 'paradox' here. While the economy itself became increasingly autonomous with respect to other processes in the society, different areas of economic activity lost their relative autonomy: for example, particular wage-rates or interest rates, which might formerly have been determined by specifically local conditions, were now affected by the market conditions of the wider society; and all the market conditions within a particular society – or national state – were affected increasingly by international trade and, therefore, by conditions in other societies.

Now, this growing interdependence of economic variables, which had themselves become increasingly independent of the controlling, stabilizing influences of custom and coercion, made for a greater complexity in economic life; it became more difficult for individuals, particularly entrepreneurs, to predict events in order to make their decisions. But it was just this very decline in predictability which stimulated the attempt to predict, or at least to explain and understand, the workings of the economy. In a sense, the conditions which promoted speculation *within* the economy also stimulated speculation *about* the economy. The concerns of the classical economists reflected important developments in the social structure: the growing domination of an impersonal market mechanism; the growing autonomy of economic conduct; and the increasing complexity of economic life.

The particular assumptions of the classical economists, and the models which they used, have all been considerably refined and modified, particularly in the last fifty years. These changes reflect not only a different reality but also different thinking. The assumption of near-perfect self-regulation was discarded as part of the 'Keynesian revolution': supply, Keynes argued, does not create its own demand, as Say, and others following him, had thought (Keynes, 1946, pp. 18-22). Other modifications have brought the model of the economy more into line with broader aspects of social reality. It is now recognized that the decisions of firms are not governed solely by precise estimates of short-term or even long-term rates of profit, but are also affected by assessments of the needs of organization and the goals of expansion and survival which are not necessarily measurable in purely monetary terms (see, for example, Papendreou, 1952). More recent conceptions of capitalist economies take account of the factors of power and coercion which were long neglected, if not ignored, by 'respectable' economists, though not, of course, by Marxists (see Galbraith, 1963). Even custom or convention must be allowed back into the economists' system of ideas: it is generally recognized that, although economic analysis can usually explain changes in certain values, such as wage-rates, it can explain neither the actual values themselves nor, therefore, why some values are much lower than others, since these have their origins in certain customary arrangements of the past.

These departures from earlier assumptions bring economic analysis closer to economic anthropology, which has always taken full account of the requirements of organization, the exercise of power, the ,dictates of custom, and the influence of morality. But there is an important difference between the economists' recognition of these factors and the anthropologists' emphasis on them: the economist introduces them into his assumptions so that they describe the conditions of supply and demand; the anthropologist may introduce considerations of supply and demand into his analysis of customary obligation, but is unlikely to make this the main focus of his attention.

How far this first type of economic analysis can be taken, and how much of it can be used, depends entirely on the type of society being studied by the anthropologist. Keynesian economics, for example, has little relevance for the study of traditional peasant economies for it was designed to explain phenomena, such as involuntary unemployment, which do not usually occur outside of capitalist societies. In fact, most economic analysis of this kind has been devised to solve certain intellectual puzzles or practical problems which do not arise for the anthropologist. This does not mean that anthropologists never use this type of analysis at all; they do, but in a relatively simple way. For example, if one is studying the payment of tribute in a tribal society, one will ask the following type of question: who pays the tribute? how much does each person or group pay? in what form is it paid? how does the payment of tribute and the uses to which it is put affect the distribution of wealth? and so on. In answering such questions the anthropologist may make some use of supply and demand analysis; he may show that one effect of a levy is an increase in production of the commodities to be paid, with a subsequent fall in production of other commodities, which become relatively scarce and more highly valued. But if an *economist* were studying the effects of a new tax he would have to make much greater use of a complicated apparatus of economic analysis: he might have to consider, for example, the marginal propensity to consume, the marginal efficiency of capital, the structure of the capital market, and so on. In dealing with these variables the economist may also find it necessary to introduce others, of a 'non-economic' kind: for example, he may take account of the effect of social status on the propensity to consume (see Duesenberry, 1949). But his main task would lie in his specialized handling of the economic assumptions.

In short, supply and demand analysis may well be applicable, at least for some purposes, to many types of society studied by anthropologists. It is often the difficult task of the anthropologist to identify the processes which should be examined in this way. But the more complex economic models, which make use of supply and demand analysis, are largely irrelevant to the study of primitive and most peasant societies. These models deal with a particular form of interdependence of economic variables which occurs only with the decline of the subsistence economy.

The principle of economic rationality, whose application constitutes the second type of economic analysis, is, in fact, a combination of three assumptions. The first of these is the law of diminishing marginal utility, which is now better known as the theory of indifference. It states, in effect, that at any particular point in time the more one has of one commodity the less one is prepared to give, in money or in kind, for one more unit of it (cf. Stigler, 1947, pp. 67-76). The second assumption, the law of diminishing returns, states in effect that one factor of production is an imperfect substitute for another (ibid., pp. 116-123). The third assumption states that, given enough information, men will act in accordance with the first two laws: that is, they will seek to maximize their gains by obtaining the highest possible return for any given resources, or that they will seek to use the smallest quantity of resources to obtain a given return.

It is probably this type of analysis which Firth, Burling, and LeClair have in mind. However, one should note a number of difficulties in the assumptions themselves, before considering their application.

The first assumption, the theory of indifference, has, in fact, been applied by economists to just the sort of situation which anthropologists might meet: the case of barter between two (or more) individuals, each of whom has one commodity to exchange (ibid., pp. 79-81). What the economists do is to juxtapose the indifference schedules of the two parties so as to show how the rate of exchange is determined. But the conclusion which they reach is that the indifference schedules only set limits between which the rate of exchange is determined. For even if the process of barter is governed solely by the motive to maximize gain, and is not affected by custom, moral constraint, or force, the final rate of exchange will be determined by the bargaining skills of the two parties, within the limits set by their indifference schedules (loc. cit.). The anthropologist does not need to be told that exchange rates which are not determined by custom or force are determined by bargaining skills. It would seem, then, that the economist's contribution to his stock of analytic devices consists of the theory of indifference itself. But how useful is it to an ethnographer? Can he, in fact, construct indifference schedules either before or after the act of exchange?[4]

Of course, the economists are right. If exchange is left to the 'maximization process', and if relative bargaining skills could be observed, then it should be at least possible, *ex post facto*, to explain why exchange occurred at a particular rate. (This type of observation is graphically presented by Firth (1946, p. 202).) Moreover, it should be possible to explain an average rate for a population in terms of relative scarcity, assuming that bargaining skills and personal preferences are randomly distributed. But all this assumes that what is being maximized is simply the satisfaction of having more of one commodity than of another. And this assumption may be unwarranted.

The application of the second law, that of diminishing returns, presents other difficulties. It assumes that men in primitive and peasant societies can and do calculate the marginal productivity of each factor, and that if they could they would make use of the information. But to make such calculations men have to experiment with different factor combinations and estimate the opportunity costs of withdrawing factors from one use for another. While it is possible for tribesmen and peasants to experiment in this way, it is difficult to know how they could anyway measure certain opportunity costs in a non-monetary economy. If one withdraws productive factors from fishing to expand agriculture, it is safe to say that one prefers more agricultural produce to more fish: but is it possible to translate the additional *value* of agricultural produce into fish to show that the increased production of one justifies the transfer of labour and capital?

Even if such calculations were possible they would not necessarily be made or used; for there are always some 'incalculables'. For example, increasing the labour supply might mean using the labour of women or of other men; but the first may be ruled out by custom and the second by the moral obligation to share with other males whether they contribute efficient labour or not. These norms and values may have their advantages which outweigh those of increasing production; even if, in the absence of money, one cannot easily calculate these advantages, one can indicate a revealed preference for one set of goals rather than another. One can also possibly state the degree of preference in terms of actual alternatives forgone.

The third assumption of the principle of economic rationality is, in some ways, the most troublesome of all: for it easily becomes little or nothing more than a self-defeating tautology. Any action can be said to maximize someone's gain; if a man fails to obtain the highest possible price for his goods because of his impatience to quit the market, then he could be said to have maximized his gain, since the prospect of additional monetary gain is inadequate to outweigh some other advantage, such as attending a ceremony. But if the same man remains in the market and forgoes some other pleasure, thereby obtaining a higher price, it could still be said that he has maximized his gain. If a man feeds his kinsmen, regardless of whether they contribute efficient labour or not, he is investing in social solidarity; if he refuses to feed them, then he is placing his material gain above that of solidarity. Since he is maximizing his gain *whatever* he does, the concept can hardly have explanatory value. (This difficulty has been noted by Firth, 1939, pp. 25-29.)

In all societies there are intangible benefits, such as those of not offending against authority or against the moral code, or not alienating friends or kinsmen, which can be weighed against the benefits of material gain; for example, many industrialists find

106

that they can afford a few 'nepots' in their organizations (but not too many). In fully monetized economies many such benefits can be measured against material gain or even against other intangibles. For example, the aesthetic or prestige rewards of shopping in an upper-class ambience can be measured in terms of the higher prices which the consumer is willing to pay. In non-monetized economies one can measure the cost of intangibles in terms of any material object: for example, one can measure the value of social solidarity in terms of the additional output which is sacrificed by employing the labour of kinsmen instead of that of strangers. But one cannot measure a material gain in terms of an intangible: for example, one cannot measure the value of additional food supply, or the prestige which it brings, in terms of the amount of kinship solidarity which is sacrificed to produce it. The principle of economic rationality would seem to be applicable, in the study of non-monetized economies, only to the analysis of conduct concerned with the production, distribution, acquisition, or sacrifice of material goods which can be counted, weighed, and measured and their use in the acquisition of services. Even with such a limitation there would still exist the problem of measuring quality as opposed to quantity.

On the whole, this principle does serve a useful purpose when analysing conduct in terms of specific goals, such as profit maximization; but it becomes difficult to apply to conduct involving a conflict of goals. Economists in socialist societies are doubtless acutely aware of this. For example, they can fairly readily apply the principle of economic rationality to the problem of industrial location and make fairly precise estimates in terms of marginal costs which suggest the most suitable location. But they cannot so easily include in their estimates the social costs of spoiling the landscape or of causing population mobility and communal disorganization. (In capitalist societies the first of these costs might be estimable: the spoliation of landscape might be reflected in a fall in value of property for private housing.)

That economic analysis cannot easily cope with conflicts of principle is thus as true of industrial societies as it is of primitive and peasant societies. But there is an important difference: in industrial societies it is possible to make calculations in purely 'economic' terms, and then consider the cost of abandoning pure economic rationality. In non-industrial societies this is more difficult to do. It is not that men are more rational in industrial societies – from many points of view, nothing that tribesmen and peasants do is less rational than much consumer behaviour – but that their social structure and technology enable them to make calculations which would be difficult, if not impossible, in non-industrial societies; and the mechanism of the market to some extent compels or induces them to make such calculations.

All of this implies that it is difficult to use the principle of economic rationality to analyse the conduct of men in non-monetized economies; it does not imply that it is either impossible or undesirable to use it. To grasp the principle of economic rationality is, in effect, to be constantly reminded that men in all societies are faced with the problem of scarcity and allocation, and that their conduct is to be understood – at least *ex post facto* – as an attempt to approximate a rational solution to the problem. However, if the use of economic analysis of this kind is not to produce fatuous 'explanations' it should be confined to certain problems.

The third type of economic analysis is that most commonly used by anthropologists, often in conjunction with the second and even with the first. As a rule it involves the use of categories which are adopted from the study of capitalist and other industrial societies, such as 'capital', 'investment', and 'opportunity cost'. These are not simply labels to differentiate different types of object; their use suggests similarities of function. To use a term like 'capital goods' to refer to canoes and fishing-nets seems innocuous enough: and so it is, if it denotes that these goods are not themselves consumed, but are used to produce other goods which are consumed, that they are made to last, and may therefore embody more labour-time and other scarce resources than goods which are less durable. But the use of such a term can become misleading if it also denotes that the investment in capital goods is calculated to bring in an expected return. Admittedly, tribesmen may discontinue the building of canoes or restrict the amount of labour and materials used in their production, if they expect only a small catch; and they are very likely to do this if there are other ways of using labour and material which will bring more substantial rewards. The anthropologist should certainly be sensitive to such possibilities.

It is easy to slide from a set of similarities, parallels, or analogies to assumptions which are quite unwarranted. This lack of caution is unfortunately shown by Pospisil in his use of the term 'capitalism'. In a capitalist society a fall in the marginal efficiency of capital can lead to involuntary unemployment: this is exactly what is most unlikely to happen in the Kapauku Papuan economy. Furthermore, the structure of power in Kapauku is far closer to that of clientship than to that of capitalist employment.

Economic analysis, of one type or another, can be used far more extensively than it has been in the study of non-industrial economies; and such analysis should be indispensable to any inquiry concerning the processes and possibilities of planned change in the modern world. When confronted with the question of why some societies respond more rapidly and positively to modern influences, there is a great tendency for sociologists and anthropologists to offer explanations in terms of values or even character; there are remarkably few attempts to show that the explanation may lie, at least in part, in the structure of the indigenous economy.[5] No doubt, one of the reasons for this is that anthropologists know so little about the economic systems of the people they study. It is particularly this type of ignorance which has led Firth, and others, again and again to urge anthropologists to think in economic terms.

But if anthropologists have been and still are so shy of genuine economic analysis – particularly of the kind that is necessary for the study of economic development in contemporary conditions – does this not suggest that they simply recognize the limits of their professional competence, and invite economists, particularly agricultural economists, to cooperate with them in their studies? Surely such professional caution is desirable?

It is instructive in this respect to compare economic anthropology with political anthropology. Anthropologists who study political systems make use of certain general principles which they may have learned from political theory or, alternatively, which they may have worked out for themselves, and which are applicable to many types of society. For example, they assume that there is always some process of exchange, whereby those who seek support offer patronage in return; or they assume that those who wish to retain their authority, without having to resort to constant physical coercion, intimidation, or punishment, must seek compromises between their own interests and those of the contending and conflicting groups or sections in the society; or they assume that positions of secular power must obtain legitimation in terms of values and symbols which induce men to obey willingly rather than merely submit to command. In using these assumptions, sometimes implicitly, without even formulating them, anthropologists do not feel the need to consult a specialist or master a special discipline; they are aware that some of them have greater applicability in some cases than in others, and that the transplantation of some can create confusion; but they believe, on the whole, that they can sort these problems out for themselves without going beyond the recognized 'limits of naïvety' (cf. Gluckman, 1964, pp. 13-19, 158-261).

All appears to be different where the study of economic conduct is concerned: anthropologists either confess their ignorance of a special discipline – just as they might confess their ignorance of depth psychology – or express their concern lest they be taken to task by economists. There is, of course, an obvious reason for the difference between the two attitudes: students of politics have not, till now, formulated a set of precise propositions such as those of economics; they have not produced any general principles which cannot, on the whole, be understood by the non-specialist. The anthropologist who does not consider himself incautious in using the ideas of political science because they are imprecise, non-mathematical, and expressions of 'commonsense', will therefore plead modesty and professional incompetence when faced with the prospect of economic analysis. What he overlooks is that the only economic principles he can effectively use are in some ways easier to grasp, though more precisely formulated, than those ideas which he *is* willing to appropriate from other special disciplines. This does not mean that the study of the economy in primitive and peasant societies is a simple matter, any more than the study of politics in such societies is a simple matter. The complexity lies not in the use of the rather trivial assumptions of economic rationality, but in the substantive analysis of social process itself.

ECONOMIC MAN AND THE SOCIAL SYSTEM

Those who deny the wider applicability of economic principles seem also to endorse the view that there are fundamental, qualitative differences between primitive and peasant societies, on the one hand, and industrial societies, on the other. This view is consistent with, and possibly influenced by, a doctrine which has achieved the status of received wisdom and which derives from the classical writings of Maine, Tönnies, Durkheim, Simmel, and Weber, and which has more recently been revived by Parsons (see Maine, 1861; Tönnies, 1963; Durkheim, 1947; Parsons, 1951). This doctrine asserts, in its most general form, that the development of society from simpler to more complex forms has been associated also with a fundamental change in the quality of social relationships and action and in the character of social persons.

A case could be made in support of this view by synthesizing separate doctrines, taking the most plausible elements from each, and creating the strongest possible version of this received wisdom. This involves, at the outset, constructing ideal types of simple and of complex society.

The characteristics of the simplest society are as follows. There is a domestic technology which does not change from one generation to another and which supports a subsistence economy of each household, domestic group, or band. The whole society consists of a number of such domestic groups or local bands linked together by cross-cutting ties of kinship and affinity, and is internally differentiated largely by age and sex. (In such societies ties of affinity may also be those of kinship.) For each individual member, the society consists of a number of categories of kinsmen. This network of kinship ties provides almost the sole framework of social action, within which a variety of

111

activities are performed. Everyone of the same age-group and sex participates in the total range of activities. Different activities are governed by different norms. Everyone (of the same sex, at least) will, during the course of his life, internalize the whole range of norms; and this will provide one set of conditions for making the norms mutually consistent with one another. In addition, each member of society interacts with a large proportion of the total society; in this way norms are reinforced and, at the same time, the pattern of normative consistency is maintained. Thus, one aspect of this is a state of intense social cohesion: for all social relationships are governed by a number of different norms and interests; powerful forces of social control are therefore inherent in interpersonal relations. Furthermore, in such societies there is a high degree of circulation of personnel, largely through marriage; this promotes cultural uniformity and serves to narrow the range of individuality. In such societies the level of technology sets narrow limits to the choice of means adopted to the attainment of certain goals; but within these limits rational action is 'hemmed in' by the social prescription of means and ends; economic rationality is severely limited. The norms of economic conduct are embedded in a total set of norms; there is relatively little autonomy for economic criteria of evaluation.

In the most complex form of society there is a reversal of most of these characteristics. There is a machine technology which is continuously changing, partly as a result of the organization of science and partly as a result of pressures within the economy itself. The division of labour, a necessary concomitant of this technology, cuts across domestic groupings and, indeed, most other ties in the society. Each individual is involved in many networks of interpersonal and impersonal relationships, which are governed by different and specific norms and interests. No one participates in all or even most social activities, and participation in any social activity is frequently partial. Consequently, different individuals, groups, or categories of people internalize different norms and different sets of norms. Even if each individual personality is under some pressure to produce some consistency between the different norms, the patterns of normative consistency will themselves vary. Thus there will be a low degree of normative integration for the society as a whole though there may be a higher degree for different sections of it, such as social classes, regional groups, local communities, ethnic groups. . . . In view of their size and because many social relationships are based on single interests and specific norms, complex societies have a low degree of social cohesion. These various characteristics strengthen one another. Unity and order in such societies are maintained largely by economic interdependence, by the efforts of a central administration, and by the acceptance of certain diffuse values and identification with common symbols. Economic interdependence encourages an instrumental approach to others. Large-scale pervasive bureaucracy encourages depersonalized application of norms. And common values and symbols are of such a nature as to leave everyday activities relatively unaffected. There is a high degree of autonomy of different institutional sectors; and although a powerful central authority can attempt some coordination of these, it is severely limited in this by the scope and variety of social activities. Rationality is less 'hampered' by the immediacy of social relationships, and economic rationality, in particular, is allowed considerable scope for expression.

If one accepts this characterization of extreme simplicity and extreme complexity of social structure, one will tend to agree that there is a seemingly fundamental, qualitative difference between the two types of society. But these are not descriptions of real polar types. This suggests the possibility that all real societies can be placed on an evolutionary scale between the two 'Utopian' poles, and that they will represent degrees of 'disengagement' of the economy from the social structure. At one extreme economic analysis will have least applicability and at the other extreme most.

That there is a continuum of this kind is suggested by a number of writers on economic anthropology, particularly by Bohannan and Dalton with their threefold classification of 'marketless economies', 'economies with peripheral markets', and 'market economies'. This kind of continuum can also be read into Sahlins's typology: as society becomes more complex, 'generalized reciprocity' gives way to 'balanced reciprocity', which is succeeded in turn by 'negative reciprocity'. Of course, there is no need to stop at threefold classifications; one can place every known society or group of societies somewhere along the line of development. For example, the case of pre-industrial China would lie somewhere between 'peripheral' market economies and full market economies. Skinner has shown that in China there was a complex hierarchy of markets. The lowest type was the 'minor' market, which catered for a small number of villages; in these, the volume of trade was small and 'horizontal' – that is, goods originated within the market area and were consumed within it – and relations of familiarity dominated. The second type was the 'standard' market town, which was used regularly by a fixed number of surrounding clusters of villages; here the volume of trade was bigger and largely, but not entirely, 'horizontal'. These market towns were also the starting-point of the upward flow of goods to other market areas or metropolitan centres, and did receive some 'exotic' goods. In the third type, the 'higher-level' markets, there was also large-scale trading which made use of agents and intermediaries and in which the impersonal element was marked (Skinner, 1964).

The possibility of constructing a continuum of this kind seems to undermine the argument that there is a sudden 'quantum jump' from the pre-industrial to the industrial market economy. One would have thought that the history of European economic development could provide such a scale, or part of one, showing the gradual process whereby the market mechanism increasingly pervades the economy.

It would be comforting to leave the argument here. But unfortunately the problem is not solved by accepting the evolutionist position and simply modifying it in some respects to convert simple typologies into continuous scales. For that would be to assume the truth of the conventional wisdom that there is such an evolutionary process and that it occurs 'on all fronts' of the social system and culture. This, however, is pure assumption, and some of the evidence would seem to refute it: in some respects Pospisil *is* right in suggesting that the characteristics of Kapauku Papuan society have more in common with some highly complex societies than with others which are as simple as it is – measuring simplicity in terms of technology and scale of social relationships.

In any case, many comparisons of non-market and market economies are based on a rather idealized version of the market economy itself. As Joan Robinson has pointed out – to take only one example – it is rather fanciful to assume that entrepreneurs in capitalist societies are, or ever were, fully committed to the goal of profit maximization. To attain this goal they would have to experiment with prices and outputs in order to test elasticities of demand for their products. This they are unwilling to do because such manipulation in itself could affect the elasticity of demand; they therefore accept less than the maximum possible gain in return for security; they settle for what is called a 'normal return', which is very much a customary conception (Robinson, 1942, p. 94).

Furthermore, in most capitalist societies there has been a reduction in the autonomy of the market principle: rates of interest, levels of employment, and income levels and differentials are all subject to State interference and affected by considerations that are not purely economic. On the other hand, socialist societies are becoming increasingly affected by the market principle. This means that in all complex societies there must be some process whereby the economic and non-economic spheres are brought into relation with one another while allowing some autonomy for economic criteria of evaluation. It could be argued that with this development pure economic analysis must be supplemented increasingly by institutional analysis (cf. Nove, 1961). It could also be argued that this conception of industrial society brings it nearer to the anthropologists' conception of primitive and peasant societies. However, an important difference should not be overlooked: in industrial society the integration of economy and society, in so far as there is integration, is achieved increasingly by bureaucratic administration; in non-industrial societies it inheres far more in the nature of interpersonal relationships.

CONCLUSION

The purpose of this essay has been twofold: first, to show that the debate concerning the wider applicability of economic analysis is misconceived and derives largely from ambiguity in the use of the term 'economic analysis' or else from a fundamental misunderstanding of economic problems: second, to show that this debate is linked with another one concerning the nature of differences between types of society and of the relations between society and economy.

In discussing these matters, I have suggested some criticism of the conventional wisdom concerning the difference between simple and complex societies. I do not, however, deny the value of the fundamental insights of Maine, Tönnies, Durkheim, and others. I suggest, rather, that these insights should be treated as hypotheses, rather than as self-evident truths to be applied unquestioningly to the analysis of societies. A good way of testing these hypotheses would be to analyse systems into a number of elements and to construct models to represent levels of social complexity, by using a few elements at a time. With this method it might then be possible to propose generalizations that state the connections between structural complexity, in its *various* dimensions, and the forms of economic relationship and conduct.

NOTES

1. An earlier version of this essay was presented as a paper to the A.S.A. Conference and was also read to the Sociology staff seminar in the London School of Economics. I am very grateful to numerous colleagues and, in particular, to Dr A. Cohen, to Professor Max Gluckman, to Mr L. Joy, and to Dr S. Ortiz for their comments. I owe a very special debt of gratitude to Professor Raymond Firth, not only for suggestions and comments but also for introducing me to the problems of economic anthropology.
2. The 'iron law of wages' stated, in effect, that the real wages of labourers could not rise (or fall) in the long run. If real wages rose, in the short run, then the labouring population would increase in size, so that a larger number of people would have to share the same wages fund; if it fell, in the short run, the size of the labouring population would fall, so that a smaller number of people would then share the same wages fund.
3. Ricardo's theory of rent explained rent as a surplus which accrued to landowners purely as a result of natural differences in the fertility of land. While wages were the reward for labour, and profits the reward for risk and entrepreneurial skill, rent accrued to the landowner without effort or skill on his part.
4. It might be thought that the anthropologist could solve the problem of explaining exchange rates by substituting the labour-cost theory for the theory of indifference. But the labour-cost theory is of little help to him. If A wants one unit of B's product more than B wants one unit of A's, then A must give

116

more than one unit of his product for one unit of B's, even if A has expended the same amount of labour time on the production of one unit of his commodity as B has on one unit of his. One of the reasons for this may be that B's labour skill is more scarce than A's, so that the value of a unit of B's labourtime will be greater than the value of a unit of A's. These relative values would have to be measured in order to begin to apply any kind of labour-cost theory. 5. A beginning has been made in this kind of inquiry in Firth and Yamey (1964).

REFERENCES

ALTMANN, S. P. 1903. Simmel's Philosophy of Money. *American Journal of Sociology* 9: 46-68.

BOHANNAN, PAUL & DALTON, GEORGE (eds.). 1962. *Markets in Africa*. Evanston, Ill.: Northwestern University Press.

BURLING, ROBBINS. 1962. Maximization Theories and the Study of Economic Anthropology. *American Anthropologist* 64: 802-821.

DALTON, GEORGE. 1961. Economic Theory and Primitive Society. *American Anthropologist* 63: 1-25.

DEWEY, ALICE G. 1962. *Peasant Marketing in Java*. New York: Free Press of Glencoe.

DUESENBERRY, JAMES. 1949. *Income, Savings and the Theory of Consumer Behavior*. Cambridge, Mass.: Harvard University Press.

DURKHEIM, EMILE. 1947. *The Division of Labour in Society* (trans. George Simpson). Glencoe, Ill.: Free Press.

FIRTH, RAYMOND. 1939. *Primitive Polynesian Economy*. London: George Routledge.

—— 1946. *Malay Fishermen*. London: Kegan Paul, Trench, Trubner.

—— 1951. *Elements of Social Organization*. London: Watts.

—— 1957. The Place of Malinowski in the History of Economic Anthropology. In R. Firth (ed.), *Man and Culture: An Evaluation of the Work of Bronislaw Malinowski*, pp. 209-227. London: Routledge & Kegan Paul.

FIRTH, RAYMOND & YAMEY, B. S. (eds.). 1964. *Capital, Saving and Credit in Peasant Societies*. London: Allen & Unwin.

GALBRAITH, J. K. 1963. *American Capitalism: The Concept of Countervailing Power*. Harmondsworth: Penguin Books.

GLUCKMAN, MAX. 1955. *The Judicial Process Among the Barotse of Northern Rhodesia*. Manchester: Manchester University Press.

—— (ed.). 1964. *Closed Systems and Open Minds: The Limits of Naïvety in Social Anthropology*. Edinburgh and London: Oliver & Boyd.

HAYEK, FRIEDRICH A. 1949. *Individualism and Economic Order.* London: Routledge & Kegan Paul.

KEYNES, J. M. 1946. *The General Theory of Employment, Interest and Money.* London: Macmillan.

LECLAIR, EDWARD E., Jr. 1962. Economic Theory and Economic Anthropology. *American Anthropologist* **64**: 1179-1203.

MAINE, H. S. 1861. *Ancient Law.* London: Murray.

MALINOWSKI, B. 1922. *Argonauts of the Western Pacific.* London: George Routledge.

MEEK, RONALD. 1965. *The Rise and Fall of the Concept of the Economic Machine.* Leicester: Leicester University Press.

NOVE, ALEC. 1961. *The Soviet Economy.* London: Allen & Unwin.

PAPENDREOU, ANDREAS G. 1952. Some Basic Problems in the Theory of the Firm. In Bernard F. Haley (ed.), *A Survey of Contemporary Economics*, Vol. **2**. Homewood, Ill.: Irwin.

PARSONS, TALCOTT. 1951. *The Social System.* Glencoe, Ill.: Free Press; London: Tavistock/Routledge.

POLANYI, K., ARENSBERG, C. & PEARSON, HARRY W. (eds.). 1957. *Trade and Market in the Early Empires.* Glencoe, Ill.: Free Press.

POSPISIL, LEOPOLD. 1963. *Kapauku Papuan Economy.* Yale University Publications in Anthropology **67**.

ROBBINS, LIONEL. 1932. *An Essay on the Nature and Significance of Economic Science.* London: Macmillan.

ROBINSON, JOAN. 1942. *An Essay on Marxian Economics.* London: Macmillan.

ROLL, ERIC. 1942. *A History of Economic Thought.* New York: Prentice-Hall.

SAHLINS, MARSHALL D. 1965. On the Sociology of Primitive Exchange. In M. Banton (ed.), *The Relevance of Models for Social Anthropology.* A.S.A. Monographs, 1, pp. 139-236. London: Tavistock Publications.

SKINNER, G. W. 1964. Marketing and Social Structure in Rural China, Part I. *Journal of Asian Studies* **24**: 3-43.

STIGLER, GEORGE J. 1947. *The Theory of Price.* New York: Macmillan.

TÖNNIES, FERDINAND. 1963. *Community and Society* (trans. & ed. Charles P. Loomis). New York, Evanston and London; Harper & Row.

WEBER, MAX. 1947. *The Theory of Social and Economic Organization* (trans. A. R. Henderson and Talcott Parsons). London: William Hodge.

Mary Douglas

Primitive Rationing

A Study in Controlled Exchange

If we contrast primitive money with modern money issued by a
single national authority one difference is striking. Primitive
money is restricted in its flow, there are ranges of goods it cannot
buy or persons to whom it cannot be transferred. By contrast,
modern money flows freely. In this perspective primitive money
is evidently a very imperfect form of money. But I suggest that
it is the wrong perspective for a useful comparison between
primitive and modern money. There are many situations in
which modern money is restricted, particularly at the international and at the purely personal levels. In these fields there
are sharp discontinuities in demand that are expressed by
control devices such as rationing. Therefore I argue that it is
enlightening to approach money, both primitive and modern,
through the idea of rationing and control.

This idea came to me from two sources. The first in time was
from field research among the Lele of the Kasai region of the
Congo. I do not regard the units of raffia cloth with which they
paid fees and fines and tribute as money, since the raffia units
did not normally circulate in a market context. Very clearly,
they were standardized entitlements to a series of social pre-
rogatives – a kind of coupon. This in itself would not have led me
to generalize more widely about primitive coupons were it not
for introspection on my own personal experience with money.
Menger's account of the origin of money, which I quote below,
arouses a deep personal response in me. As he puts it, money is
essentially something which permeates and flows. As I know it,
money's tendency to flow continually threatens to destroy the
ordered pattern of my wants. So I am always involved in the
attempt to reduce liquidity by blocking, earmarking, and fund-
ing it in various ways. My friends also try to impose crude
controls on their own use of money, and these restraints resemble

strangely those restraints on the use of some primitive moneys reported by anthropologists (see Firth, 1938, p. 95).

It is well known that there are so-called primitive moneys which are rarely used as media of exchange, which are accepted for only a limited range of services and commodities and are transferable only to a limited range of persons. Their rates of exchange do not express a price system – or if there is one it is very insensitive. If these are money they do not expedite the transfer of goods and services as our money does. Many writers find difficulty in admitting that they are to be classed as money at all (Firth, *op. cit.*; Einzig, 1948, p. 328). I should like to agree with them and take the narrow, conventional view of primitive money, counting it as money only when the medium of exchange function is well developed. So-called primitive money that is used only as a means of ceremonial payment I should consider as coupons or licences in a system of control. But it is pedantic to worry too much about terms. In many cases both the coupon function and the medium-of-exchange function are performed by the same units. Moreover, the analogy either with modern money or with modern coupon systems only applies in a very broad and general sense. Modern money and modern coupons are highly specialized instruments functioning in highly differentiated economies. We can make worthwhile comparisons by looking for similar functions and not by looking for similar formal characteristics.

As I see it, money in its nature is essentially an instrument of freedom, rationing in its nature an instrument of control. Money represents general purchasing power over all marketed goods; coupons restrict and channel the purchasing power of money. Money emerges as a spontaneous solution to the need for easier trading conditions; it represents the opening of opportunities. It develops its uses with the development of the market. Restrictions on trade restrict the use of money. Protective legislation sets up barriers to its free flow. By contrast, coupons are essentially instruments of control. In so far as they seek to contain and bar the use of money they are anti-market in intent, the tools of restriction, of closing of opportunities. Money and coupons could hardly be more opposite in their beginnings and in their purposes. Money starts as a set of open possibilities of acquisition, while coupons start within the context of restraint. It is in the nature of money to flow freely, to be like water, to permeate. By their nature coupons represent closed doors, restriction, and control. In a sense they represent form and rational order, for they express society's overriding purposes which curb the drive of individuals. But confusingly this opposition of money and coupons in their basic nature is lost in their actual functioning at any time. For money can be used as an instrument of control, closing doors and blocking outlets for individual energies, while coupons can easily come to represent purchasing power and become barely distinguishable from money. Hence the confusion of the two in the field is very understandable. We have to recognize both the basis of the distinction between money and coupons and their close similarity before we approach the study of primitive distributive systems.

Money may sometimes have emerged from the barter situation which is described in the first page of textbooks on money. On this familiar argument, the inconvenience of barter and the difficulty of arranging credit lead to the adoption of a medium of exchange. The only objection to this supposed historical sequence is that credit is never difficult in a primitive economy; credit exists before market, and Adam Smith's tailor who wants to buy bread for his children should have no difficulty in arranging long-term credits with the baker for whom he has made a suit. In practice, while I readily admit that money can arise in these circumstances of inhibited barter, the evidence for primitive money suggests that this is rare, while the origin of money in a type of primitive rationing system seems likely to be more widespread. I shall develop my argument by distinguishing medium-of-exchange money from coupon money in primitive economies, and start by considering the conditions in which real money is likely to emerge. Karl Menger said that where barter is going on the commodity which is the relatively most saleable will tend to be used as a primitive medium of exchange.

'Their superior saleableness depends only on the relatively inferior saleableness of any other kind of commodity, by which alone they have been able to become *generally* acceptable media of exchange . . . when the relatively most saleable commodities have become "money" the event has in the first place the effect of substantially increasing their originally high saleableness. Every economic subject bringing less saleable wares to market to acquire goods of another sort has therefore a stronger interest in converting what he has in the first instance into the wares which have become money. . . . The effect produced by such goods as are relatively most saleable becoming money is an increasing differentiation between their degree of saleableness and that of all other goods. And this difference in saleableness ceases altogether to be gradual, and must be regarded in a certain aspect as something absolute. . . .' (1892, pp. 249-250.)

On this account, money emerges as the market develops. All the emphasis is laid (and surely rightly) on the medium-of-exchange function of money. It implies that perfect money would be completely able to permeate any situation, flow freely, be interchangeable with everything else, be more widely acceptable than anything else. There are a few examples of primitive currencies whose purchasing power is so unrestricted. But in general primitive currencies do not flow freely, they are acceptable in only limited situations, they are not highly saleable. Very often several currencies operate side by side in the same economy. Thus we arrive at the traditional idea of primitive money as imperfect money. But to stay with this approach is, as I have said, to overlook the rationing and licensing functions for which many kinds of primitive money appear to be well-adapted instruments.

CONTROLLED AND COMPETITIVE ECONOMIES

Modern economic systems are often classed as planned, unplanned, or mixed. These classifications are very broad. In the same way we can distinguish three types of primitive economy: controlled, freely competitive, and mixed, that is, with a certain degree of control over certain areas. My argument is that primitive currencies which are found in the more controlled economies are more like coupons than money, while true primitive money only flourishes in the freely competitive economies. The latter are relatively rare. There are instances of small-scale primitive societies whose internal economies are largely organized by market principles and which clearly make use of money in the full medium-of-exchange sense. I shall discuss these first, partly because (as Pospisil points out (1963, p. 400 *et seq.*)) their existence is often overlooked in general statements about the characteristics of primitive economies, and partly because they are less interesting to my general thesis.

The Reverend Benjamin Danks, a well-known missionary writing at the end of the last century, described (1888, 1892) what he called a type of 'commercial savagery' in New Britain in Melanesia. Here shell-money (*tambu*) was needed for ceremonial payments, blood compensation, marriage dues, funeral gifts, and for burial with the dead. If it had been required only for these purposes we would not account it as money. But it was also used extensively for purchase, and he gives a long list of everyday utensils and foods and their prices in lengths of *tambu*. He mentions that purchase and barter had two distinct words in the language, and that some things had fixed prices while for others the price varied according to the demand and state of supply. For instance, taro and yam prices varied according to the seasonal supply. Furthermore, he clearly describes how the money circulated in the economy. It was acquired directly by trade. Fishermen and farmers sold fish and agricultural products; bananas, coconuts, breadfruit, and fishing-gear fetched good prices. He praises the all-pervasive power of commerce for making the people energetic and industrious. He describes the credit arrangements by which money was lent at ten per cent, or deposited with a banker; the latter had to be in a position to defend the stores of money in his house and by that very fact became a political leader, since his clients could be relied on to rally round him if he was attacked and their wealth endangered. This shrewd observer also noted how the market economy provided the framework of the political system, since, apart from the *de facto* power of bankers, brokers, and creditors, there was no constituted authority and little control over their behaviour other than that provided by the need to maintain confidence in their future dealings. By their control of Duk Duk, a secret society, these same rich men seem to have been able to terrorize the neighbourhood.

Such a circumstantial and intelligent account leaves one in no doubt that New Britain in the nineteenth century had a true monetary economy (see also Epstein, S., 1964, p. 56), for modern confirmation of Danks's view). There are other modern accounts as convincing, of which I cite only two. By Oliver's description (1955), Siuai, on the south shore of Bougainville, in the Solomon Islands, evidently had a well-developed monetary sector which was geared to the provision of utensils, containers, and luxury foods for feasts. Oliver's fieldwork was in 1938. A more recent report is Pospisil's account of Kapauku economy. Considering that Danks had already described the New Britain economy, and that Oliver had analysed his Solomon Island society as an 'exchange economy', and that Mead (1937, pp. 215-218) had described financial transactions as dominating the social life of the Admiralty Islands, Pospisil seems unduly surprised by his own discovery of thorough-going commercialism in a New Guinea island, but he also is very convincing and circumstantial in his documentation (1963, p. 402 *et seq.*).

'Kapauku economy is a true money economy. The cowrie shell and the *dedege* and *pagadan* necklaces function in Kapauku society as true money is expected to do. They represent a common measure of value of commodities and are a general medium of exchange. Sale is the most important form of exchange. . . . Except for human beings everything can be bought in this society for the shell currency. . . . With the emphasis on wealth, money and trade, Kapauku combine a strong version of individualism which, I dare say, could hardly be surpassed in our capitalistic society.''

We can abstract from these accounts the following general characteristics of primitive monetary systems: First, there is evidence of a price function which relates supply and demand and responds to seasonal changes in output. This is the proof that in these economies what seems to be money is really performing an authentic monetary function. Second, the institutions of market are well developed: a wide range of goods can be bought and sold, the role of entrepreneur is recognized, and his success is rewarded. Third, credit is available for the promising entrepreneur, and part of his success lies in knowing how to attract credit and use it to the best advantage. In each case leadership and the political structure of groups are not set apart from the sphere of commerce; the rewards of the successful entrepreneur are the highest rewards of power and prestige which the society has to offer; he cannot dominate the political situation without first dominating the market. Since the native ability to do this is unevenly distributed, and since in competitive conditions the entrepreneur risks ups and downs in his career and decline as he ages, in such systems leadership is open to challenge and change and the political structure is unstable. This kind of fluidity is not a matter of individuals' moving up and down rapidly from one recognized position to another. It is much more an instability in the relation of actual positions, since each outstanding individual creates his own leadership, and when he declines his position lapses and produces changes in the total social pattern. Margaret Mead describes this characteristic formation in Manus as

'an uneven skyline, a few leaders standing out against the sky and giving form and definition to the immediate situation. The position of each leader is dependent upon the number of other leaders in the community. If the standard is high, his standard must be higher. Thus each leader goads each other leader, both as his partner in economic transactions and as a measure of his own success. No one is primarily interested in humiliating others, but only in maintaining his own position. . . . So each man is matched against the *pace* of the group; his position is a function of it' (1937, pp. 218-219).

Her image of a changing skyline closely corresponds with descriptions of the status pattern in Siuai by Oliver, in Kapauku by Pospisil, and in New Britain by Danks and Epstein. In general, it seems that the more that entrepreneurship, credit, and market principles govern social life in the conditions of a primitive economy, the more the pattern of status is likely to be fluid in this sense.

Since the comparison with Western capitalism is tempting (indeed Pospisil makes it implicitly), we should note the essential difference. These primitive economies dominated by production for exchange are as thoroughly commercial as any in Western Europe or the United States. But technologically they are not advanced, institutionally they are not highly differentiated, and above all the productive energies are not directed in any very notable sense to the long-term accumulation of real capital goods. As far as producers' equipment and stores of consumers' goods are concerned they do not produce anything which will yield over a longer time than the life-cycle of a pig. For all their entrepreneurial energy they are not so blessed with capital as any tribe of cattle-herders. Therefore, it is misleading to think of this as a type of primitive capitalism: it is only primitive commerce. If there was real capital being built up and conserved from generation to generation, the profile of status would be steadied by reference to valuable material assets. As it is, the changing skyline is typical of the status pattern in primitive societies using true money.

Much more common is the mixed economy in which some measure of control is exercised over certain key transactions. Then we find large areas of social life are protected from the challenge of free competition. Institutions of credit and the rewards of entrepreneurship are arranged so that productive effort supports and does not undermine the traditional forms of society. For a fixed pattern of status to survive at all, social policy must override divergent private concerns. This type of social system, status-oriented and therefore conservative, is so much more common in primitive conditions that it is understandable why Pospisil, describing the competitive commercial atmosphere of Kapauku life, felt that he was challenging all the established assumptions of anthropologists about the nature of primitive economy. In this he was exaggerating, perhaps. But he was right to the extent that his picture of the primitive commercial society is relatively rare, and that the other, non-commercial type predominates in the records of anthropologists. It is in the latter status-governed type that I propose that we should reconsider the functions of what has been previously regarded as a form of primitive money.

There are many different ways of channelling distribution and of making sure that access to scarce resources is under the

control of those in authority. Which method is developed
depends partly on scale. In a very small community consensus
on ends and means may be so complete that no specialized
institutions may be required. Again, scale may not be so relevant
here as the sense of distributive justice. If the pattern of social
rewards seems manifestly equitable it may be maintained
without a special manipulation of the economy. I would
expect primitive coupon systems to emerge where there is some
danger that the effective demand for scarce resources may so
disturb the pattern of distribution as to threaten a given social
order.

PRIMITIVE COUPON SYSTEMS

The object of rationing is to ensure a fair distribution of necessities, necessities being a culturally defined concept meaning
goods which ought to be and usually are freely available.
Rationing is applied when something restricts the supply of
necessities, so we have bread and meat rationing in the wartime
economy. The idea of necessities also includes things which it is
held ought to be freely available, even though they may in
practice never have been. Education or petrol, for example, may
be regarded as such a necessity in our own society, water in an
arid country. If we define necessities as those things which ought
to be available to all, there are some societies in which it is
thought that certain minimum forms of prestige and civic
status ought to be available to all members of the community
and should be recognized as necessities. In such societies rationing is an appropriate model for interpreting institutions which
seek to ensure an equal distribution of high status. For example,
the Lele social system lopsidedly reserves most prestige to old
men, and keeps their young men in a deprived status. Yet their
gerontology is inspired by a basically egalitarian principle. It is
not birth or achievement or the unequal endowments of nature
which, under this dispensation, will bring one man more prestige
than his neighbour. But mere seniority, relatively greater age, in
the due course of time is expected to make up to each deprived
junior for the privileges forgone in his youth. In the interests of
this principle of distribution, the Lele put wives and the means

of procuring wives under rationing control. In seeing their bride-wealth as a system for rationing women, I am closely following Lévi-Strauss. Taking the case of petrol rationing, he says:

'Certaines formes de rationnement sont nouvelles pour notre société, et créent une impression de surprise dans des esprits formés aux traditions de libéralisme économique. Ainsi sommes-nous portés à voir dans l'intervention collective, se manifestant à l'endroit de commodités qui jouent un rôle essentiel dans le genre de vie propre à notre culture, une innovation hardie et quelque peu scandaleuse. Parce que le contrôle de la répartition et de la consommation porte sur l'essence minérale, nous croyons volontiers que sa formule peut tout juste être contemporaine de l'automobile. Il n'en est rien cependant: le "régime du produit raréfié" constitue un modèle d'une extrême généralité. Dans ce cas comme dans beaucoup d'autres, les périodes de crise auxquelles notre société était, jusqu'à une date récente, si peu habituée à faire face, restaurent seulement, sous une forme critique, un état de choses que la société primitive considère plus ou moins comme normal. Ainsi le "régime du produit raréfié", tel qu'il s'exprime dans les mesures de contrôle collectif, est beaucoup moins une innovation due aux conditions de la guerre moderne et au caractère mondial de notre économie, que la résurgence d'un ensemble de procédés familiers aux sociétés primitives, et sans lesquels la cohérence du groupe serait à chaque instant compromise' (1949, pp. 39-40).

In his succeeding analysis of the controlled distribution of wives, Lévi-Strauss restricts himself to 'elementary structures', that is, structures which positively prescribe permitted classes of spouses. He does not apply the rationing model to more complex structures in which the rules of sharing are negatives which merely limit the range of possible spouses by forbidding certain categories. Yet it is in this range of kinship structures that the analogy with petrol coupons applies most fully. The man equipped with the right number of raffia cloths, spears, cattle, or whatever is the accepted commodity, can use them with a certain freedom, other things being equal, to acquire the bride of his choice. In a sense his use of the bridewealth coupon is very like the use of money. But this is the case with any coupon: it is a supplementary means of purchase, it makes purchasing power effective. What makes the situation more like rationing than like money is not the use to which the coupons are put but the conditions by which their acquisition is controlled. The essence of money is to be transferable. It circulates, but coupons when spent return to an issuing point and their acquisition is continually under survey and control. Admittedly, there is a big difference between modern and primitive coupons. In a modern economy paper coupons once spent are returned to the office of issue, counted, and destroyed. But primitive commodity coupons simply return at each transfer into the hands of the senior members of the community who become by this fact to all intents and purposes the issuing authority. This makes it almost impossible to acquire coupons without being acceptable to the senior old men who hold them. Coupons do not circulate; they are continually issued and returned and re-issued. The dynamics of this movement I shall discuss later.

We should first consider further some characteristics of modern rationing systems. Coupons can be combined with the use of money in various ways. They can even be substituted altogether for money. At the beginning of the war Colin Clark published a scheme by which the whole of the Australian economy could have been organized by means of coupons, which would have replaced money for the duration (*Sydney Daily Telegraph*, 18.3.1942). Such a scheme was never applied, but instead belligerent countries used money and coupons as two kinds of entitlement to purchasing power which had to be combined in the specified units for acquiring rationed goods. De Scitovsky (1942) distinguishes three methods of rationing: specific rationing, in which a specific coupon has to be tendered for a specified commodity; group rationing; and value rationing. In group rationing a class of goods which are in consumer's practice generally substitutable are grouped together and acquired by means of a transferable coupon. Thus the consumer's choice within a certain range of behaviour is not limited, and no minimum expenditure on any specific item in the group is anticipated. So there would be not hat or coat coupons but clothing coupons; edible fats fell into one such group and nonalcoholic beverages into another. The idea of group rationing, by which the coupons are freely transferable between different items in the group, can be reversed to make it applicable to certain primitive conditions. In many primitive economies it would seem that any of a specified group of valuables can serve as a coupon for obtaining a specified status. For example, the Yurok of Northern California, who import so-called shell-money, used standard lengths for settling claims against one another: damages for adultery or insult, marriage gifts, fees for initiations or medical aid. I argue that it is a distortion to consider the medium used for these payments as money, since it did not perform the medium-of-exchange function. It was much more a coupon or ticket for acquiring or amending status. But the coupon consisting of a standard string of shells had a fixed value in terms of certain other commodities, for example, heads of rare birds, rare pelts, obsidian blades (Kroeber, 1925, pp. 26-27). These fixed values introduce the same flexibility into the system of payments that group rationing does in the wartime economy. What appear to be prices are not exchange values; there seems to have been no real internal market in which pelts or knives were bought and sold for shells. They merely were rates of sub-stitution by which a coupon of one kind was equivalent to a coupon of another kind in the rationing system. Instead of a grouping of consumer commodities there was a grouping of commodities serving as coupons.

Value rationing is used when the amount of the scarce com-modity which anyone is allowed to acquire is controlled simply by setting a limit on the expenditure of money. Thus, instead of the impossible task of deciding how many stews, joints, or cutlets of meat a family was entitled to per week, the meat rationing left the choice of prime or cheap cuts of meat free, and rationed it by a restriction on overall weekly expenditure. Here the rationers used the monetary system as part of the system of control. When we read of economists' elaborate calculations of the effect of rationing on prices (Hugh-Jones, 1950), discussions which consider the coupons as a kind of second currency, we are close to the cruder reality of primitive money in which multiple currencies operate side by side in not completely distinct spheres of exchange. The Kapauku have several cowrie and bead currencies circulating simultaneously which are fully interchangeable at known rates. Since theirs is a commercial economy, their various shells function more like coins of different denominations. Thus they differ essentially from the multiple currencies of some primitive economies. In these, each type of currency is acceptable only for a limited range of goods or services. One of the most famous examples are the currencies of Rossel Island, of which the most valuable units are reserved exclusively for the use of men.

Some primitive currencies are perhaps more like systems of licensing than like rationing, and it is as well to be clear about the difference here too. Both are instruments of social policy, but whereas rationing is egalitarian in intent, licensing is not. The object of licensing is protective, and to promote responsible administration. The object of rationing is to ensure equal distribution of scarce necessities. One of the objects of licensing is to ensure responsible use of possibly dangerous powers, so we have licensing of guns and liquor sales. Licensing pins responsibility, so we have marriage licences and pet licences. Licensing protects vulnerable areas of the economy, so we have import licensing, and so on.

An important side-effect of licensing is to create monopoly advantages for those who issue licences and for those who receive them. Both parties become bound in a patron-client relation sustained by the strong interests of each in the continuance of the system. Modern rationing does not have this effect so strongly, though it sometimes ties groups of consumers to particular retailers. The emergence of patron-client groups around a licensing system recalls the groups which crystallize round the issuing of primitive coupons. I have mentioned the Lele bridewealth in raffia cloth as an example of primitive rationing of women in the interests of an equal distribution to all who reach a certain age. The raffia cloth units are hand-woven by the men of the tribe. Thus in a sense it is possible for every man to issue his own coupons to himself. This, of course, no more makes nonsense of the rationing analogy than it makes nonsense to speak of money when the unit of currency is freely produced and marketed. The cost of production merely affects the price of money and equally the cost of production limits the possibility of flooding the rationing system with new coupons. In practice the demand for raffia cloths at every turn of his career and every step in status so overwhelmed a young Lele man that he could not expect to produce raffia for all his own needs. He turned for contributions to the men who were on the receiving end of the system. These old men had themselves passed through all the stages of payment and could now reckon to receive levies of raffia cloth in large amounts. These senior men thus found themselves at the issue-desk, as it were, and did not fail to take full advantage of the patron-client opportunities of their situation. I have described in *The Lele of the Kasai* (see especially Chapters III, V, and VIII) how the effective kin groups of adult men were activated in this way, and also the dynamics of the movement of raffia from old men to young men and back again.

Having distinguished rationing from licensing as found in our own society, I am no longer concerned to maintain the distinction in primitive societies. For it is academic whether we consider a revolving fund of bridewealth, cattle, or spears as a set of coupons controlling distribution of wives or as a set of licences creating a strong patron-client interest. In the primitive social system these functions remain in an unspecialized matrix.

Primitive coupon systems can be recognized by the following characteristics:

(i) The coupons do not represent general purchasing power in the internal economy. Indeed, market conditions are very limited, if they exist at all, within these economies. The powers of acquisition which the coupons represent are highly specific.

(ii) Their distribution is controlled in various ways. For example, in the Southern Bantu tribes, cattle are transferred in bridewealth payments, and this function is so dominant that it is hardly possible for a young man seeking to marry to acquire cattle except through the marriage of his sister. Since cattle paid for her have passed into the hands of his father, their allocation to him for his marriage is in every sense a restricted permission or licence.

(iii) The conditions which govern their issue create a patron-

132

client set of relationships. Those seeking coupons must first acquire the favour of those who control the allocation; thus arises a focus of social control.

(iv) Their main function is to provide the necessary condition for entry to high-status positions, or for maintaining rank, or for countering attacks on status.

(va) In general, neither the economy nor the social system in which coupon systems operate is competitive. The coupons function to reduce or eliminate competition in the interests of a fixed pattern of status. The coupons ensure that the distributive system of the economy will not bring about a pattern of control over goods and services which is at variance with the pattern of ascribed status. I will say more about this below. But first I need to note an apparent exception.

(vb) It is possible for coupons to be working in a system which shows the characteristics mentioned above in every respect except that their distribution is not under firm control. Something like a black market in status then develops: the weakest to the wall, and the highest status to the strongest operator. In such a case, so far from being non-competitive and working in the interests of a fixed status pattern, the coupon system itself is open to fierce competition.

This is how I see the use of Yurok shell-money and the shell-money of the Tolowa-Tututni peoples, their cultural neighbours on the Pacific coast of America. Cora Du Bois in her perceptive economic analysis of these latter (1936) points out that in so far as daily subsistence is concerned, there is no competition. Rules of neighbourly sharing and hospitality spread the risks in the way that is common in small-scale non-commercial economies. But the acquisition of prestige is ruthlessly competitive. Men demand compensation for every insult and are trained from childhood to be extremely sensitive in recognizing insults. They pursue their claims for debts, fees, and fines with complete single-mindedness and only respect a man who is rich and has followers who will back him in a show of force. The patron-client relation is highly developed and, though fluid, it is the only effective political grouping in the society. The system of debt collection is tilted so that the rich man who has adherents can exact more for injuries to himself than can his followers in the claims which they would have no chance of collecting if he did not back them. Shell-money changes hands frequently, yet without buying and selling.

The one respect in which this case does not show all the characteristics I have listed above for primitive coupon systems is that here there is nothing analogous to controlled distribution. Anyone can challenge anyone else, claim to have been insulted, and demand compensation. This important difference makes the Yurok and Tolowa-Tututni type of economy a hybrid case, for their political system, focused on the strong man and his followers, is very similar to the focusing on the banker-creditor in primitive monetary systems I have described. The only difference is that such advantages accrue to the man who starts with a lot of shell-coupons and men in his control that a fairly rigid distinction between rich and poor classes develops. It is difficult for the poor man to become rich, and in this sense it could be said that, in spite of the individualistic and competitive atmosphere, the coupon system upholds a steady status pattern as it does so much more obviously in other cases.

Like most other anthropologists I have been intrigued and baffled by Armstrong's account of Rossel Island currency, and pored over the ranked series of shell coins to which Armstrong gives numerical value. Lorraine Barić in a very stimulating essay starts from the fact that, though some of the shells can be used for day-to-day purchases and so have normal monetary functions, for the most part each type of currency is reserved for a special transfer which has essentially to do with ceremonial and status (marriage gifts, blood compensation, feasting, and so on). Borrowing was a constant necessity for Rossel Islanders to fulfil their social commitments. Loans had to be repaid according to rules which prevented a simple return of the original loan. Either a higher-ranking coin was due or a coin of the same rank as the original one borrowed had to be supplemented by another lower-ranking coin. Old men argued keenly about what return was appropriate for a loan of given length of time, and in the system there seems to be a general idea of interest being paid for use over time. But Lorraine Barić denies the possibility of equating the values of the different series of coins. She emphasizes instead

'The uncertainty of interest, the impossibility of expressing interest as an exact ratio of the principle, the impossibility of aggregating coins of different categories as equivalent to one of a higher rank, the impossibility of saying that one category of coins was in any way a multiple or proportion of any other category' (1964, p. 47).

Since the economic background seems not to have been dominated by market forces, she is clearly justified in claiming that these coins are not money in any strict sense: a view in harmony with Raymond Firth's treatment (1938, pp. 95-6). More interesting to me is her implied suggestion that Rossel Island might have much in common with other non-monetary systems of creating solidarity through indebtedness. Thurnwald already gave this insight in his perceptive account of shell and pig transfers in Buin:

'The process of converting one kind of object of value into another, of pigs into *abuta* and *vice versa*, upon the basis of reciprocity is a means of intensifying and adding complexity to the social texture of the community and the intercommunal life' (1934-1935, p. 140).

This was a very far-seeing reflection, but until Lévi-Strauss had analysed elementary structures of kinship as artificial techniques for elaborating reciprocity, it was not possible to take the next step and see primitive currencies performing not a specialized economic function but a generalized social function. We can now more easily recognize the advantage to solidarity gained by a system of universal mutual indebtedness.

If we interpret the independent series of Rossel Island coins as coupon-licences we can learn more about primitive money in general. Imagine our English experience of wartime rationing and our present experience of licensing enormously extended. Recall that rationing and licensing are limited and specific permissions to do or obtain certain things. Since they are specific, a gun licence is no good to a man who is seeking a liquor licence, and a TV licence is no good to one who wants to sell tobacco or to buy a watchdog. To cope with this extended system of licensing one might decide to make licences transferable, thus making them rather more like money than like coupons. Exchanges could be arranged on a modified group-rationing system. For example, there could be a series of pet licences, weapon licences, work licences, and there could easily grow up a system of swopping between holders of licences in the same category, with a scale of compensation for those who accept obviously smaller licences in exchange for more substantial ones, and obvious difficulties for swopping between categories. How many gun licences would be worth one marriage licence or vice versa? One solution would be for the acceptor of a marriage licence to accept the obligation to return a marriage licence to his creditor when need arises. Another would be to develop a system of brokerage with commission. Both of these solutions were adopted on Rossel Island.

DISCONTINUITY IN THE DEMAND FUNCTION

If an imaginary Kafka-like outbreak of bureaucracy in England helps to interpret Rossel Island currency, it also raises another question about primitive coupon systems. In our experience controls are imposed by a central authority: rationing and licensing may seem to be far-fetched as analogies for a system that arises spontaneously without central direction. I have therefore to explain how it can happen that people, while independently pursuing their own ends, can take private decisions which have the effect of creating a controlled economy. In order to do this we should recall first the common tendency of non-monetary economies to have distinct, impermeable, ranked spheres of exchange.

Hoyt describes this (mistakenly) as a characteristic of primitive economies in general. She lists examples of the custom

'by which certain things must always be exchanged for certain other things. For instance the Marindanim of Dutch South New Guinea will exchange articles of need only for articles of need, food for food. . . . In the Solomon Islands and Bismarck

Archipelago, likewise, similar things must always be exchanged for each other: necessaries for necessaries; iron hatchets for stone hatchets; taro for tobacco. The famous traveller of the 17th century, Peter Mundy, was unable to buy cattle in St. Lawrence, Madagascar because the people would exchange them only for large cornelian beads, though sheep, hens, fish, milk and oranges could be bought with various trade articles' (1926, p. 84).

Many anthropologists have borne witness to similar restrictions on exchange (see Firth, 1959, p. 36). The best account is Bohannan's analysis of the pre-colonial Tiv economy in which he discerned three distinct spheres of exchange. In the domestic sphere chickens, baskets, and food crops could be exchanged. This sphere ranked lower in esteem than the trade and war sphere in which guns, metal rods, trade cloth, and slaves were exchangeable. And this ranked below the sphere in which men competed for rights to acquire wives. In the old days a man could not get a wife without being allowed by the lineage head to offer one of the lineage girls as an exchange. Each sphere was impenetrable from a lower sphere save in exceptional circumstances. Any man would be delighted to make a deal offering subsistence goods for trade goods, but what man in his senses would be so foolish as to 'convert down', as Bohannan puts it, and give up goods held in the high-prestige trade sphere in exchange for subsistence goods? Conversion was only likely to happen if one party was desperate, say, to feed his starving family in a famine. The Tiv case is instructive, for the breaks in continuity in the distributive system correspond to breaks in the status system. The path to high status was not based on economic achievement so much as on a shrewd manipulation of esoteric knowledge of genealogy, ritual, and law. In the days when the Tiv system flourished, a wife was a necessary condition of lineage status, but while old men were polygamists, young men were bachelors. The age of marriage for men was late and many men probably did not make marriages at all (Abraham, 1933, p. 145; East, 1939, pp. 109-110). If coupons for the acquisition of wives had been available to any industrious young man who did well in trade, the whole status system would have tottered – as indeed it did under the combined impact of colonial government and commerce (Bohannan, 1955). It seems only reasonable to expect to find restricted, ranked spheres of exchange in societies with restricted, ranked spheres of status. In the terms of our analogy with a modern rationing system, the restricted spheres of exchange result from individual refusals to do deals which will result in giving up a coupon valid for a low-ranking position. The restricted spheres emerge in the struggle of those in privileged positions to keep control of the issue-desk. As soon as the restricted spheres of exchange are allowed to interpenetrate, the structure of privileges must collapse. No official regulation is necessary to impose these restrictions on the free working of the economy. They develop out of each man's sound perception of where his own interests lie.

The existence of separate, ranked spheres of exchange within a primitive economy is the clue to the development of multiple currencies in some of these economies, and I find it helpful to compare them with the development of hard and soft currency areas in modern international money. Disequilibrium in trading accounts may lead to some countries having overall deficits and others overall surpluses. The old Tiv lineage head, well-endowed with wives and daughters, and with guns, slaves, rods, and cloth, is like a hard-currency area which demands that its claims shall be settled only in its own currency. He will not give up a daughter except in exchange for a wife, and nothing would induce him to give up guns or slaves for chickens in any quantity, since he has plenty of these in his own compound.

CONTROLLED EXCHANGE

At this point I must temporarily drop the distinction I have been at pains to draw between primitive money and primitive coupons. By comparing international exchange and also our own intimate treatment of our money incomes, I hope to explain the bizarre aspects of primitive distribution systems by quirks in our own experience of money. So long as it is circulating within the control of a sovereign authority, modern money is nearly perfect in Menger's sense. It can permeate almost any situation. It is almost completely buyable and saleable, its flow is unrestricted. But in dealings between two or more sovereign authorities this is no longer so true. Political considerations intervene, social policy demands protective measures for vulnerable areas of each economy: the free flow of money is not allowed to go unchecked. In a true sense, money in the international economy is very like money in the primitive economy where no sovereign authority is in control. In its international aspect modern money is hardly more freely saleable and unrestricted than the most primitive coupon/money we know. And here the distinction between coupons and money for obvious reasons is no longer interesting. I shall develop the analogy with reference to international blocked currencies and double exchange rates. But first let me try to fill in a gap in my argument.

If we admit that we ourselves as private individuals living in a modern monetary economy try to restrict the free flow of money by earmarking, blocking, and hoarding, then it becomes plausible to argue that in primitive conditions individuals do much the same. This capacity that money has for flowing freely in all directions can be a great nuisance. There are some who read their bank statement without astonishment, but they must be exceptions. It is more realistic to suppose that failure in 'controlling and structuring the future in long-run consumption' is the usual case (Reuben Hill, 1961, p. 70). Many of us try to primitivize our money as soon as we get it, by placing restrictions at source, by earmarking monetary instruments of certain kinds for certain purposes, by only allowing ourselves or our wives certain limited freedoms in the disposal of money. Some people hate to pay cheques, thinking that money disappears too easily that way. For others cheques are the preferred means of settlement just because they offer a means of control. Money from different sources is sometimes personalized and attracts distinctive feelings which dictate the character of its spending. For example, a friend whose main income derives from investments also earns irregular amounts by writing. The income which comes from this voluntary, private, and creative activity she refuses to spend on what is compulsory, public, and routine. So she tries never to pay rates and taxes with the earned income. Another friend artificially creates windfalls for herself by putting aside 3d. bits. In this way she has a fund for what she regards as luxury purchases. All these practices are but clumsy attempts to control the all too liquid state of money.

In accounts of primitive economies we find many parallels. Danks said that the entrepreneurs of New Britain hated to break into a big coil of *tambu* which represented a capital sum. Rather than change it, they would pledge it and pay interest on the loan of the required small sum. This would almost be like our being prepared to lose something for the sake of having a sum held in an illiquid and untouchable form. Considering that the secular decline in the value of money threatens to cancel the increase in the value of Post Office Savings Certificates, I feel that the continued attraction of this kind of holding is very like the big coil of *tambu*. The fight to control the liquidity of money is the reason why the pastoral Massa of the Cameroons constantly seek to put their cash into 100 F. notes, a form which is more solid and resistant to petty inroads (De Garine, 1964, p. 122). The Kapauku, who are cursed (or blessed) with almost completely saleable-buyable money, when they want to put aside a sum for their sons to inherit are never sure that they can resist touching it. So the would-be saver places a terrible curse on himself should he ever break into his pile. How difficult it is to keep under review the hierarchy of our wants, and to impose a rational pattern on our spending. It would be easier if money came in vouchers tailored to our various purposes. If a husband wanting to stop his wife from spending housekeeping money on clothes or cigarettes could issue her with vouchers for these items then he could successfully enforce his budget policy. The Rossel Islanders actually have a series of high-value coins which women are prohibited from using. This certainly suggests that primitive money may not be an ineffective means of fulfilling particular economic policies. I hope that I can take it as established that exchange controls can arise very spontaneously, and that we need not be surprised to find something like hard and soft exchange areas appearing within a primitive economy.

To return to the international exchange analogy, travellers have often been surprised to find a low official rate of exchange (whether for native and modern money or for barter goods) existing side by side with a much higher unofficial rate. The official rate is not necessarily very widely applied in the internal economy. It is often a mere standard of value against which other goods are measured. For example, among the Lele in the Kasai in the nineteen-fifties a big store basket was worth 40 Belgian Congo francs or 4 raffia cloths. This did not mean that 10 Congo francs could buy one raffia cloth. I have described elsewhere (1963, pp. 59-67) the absence of a free market for raffia cloth. The official rate for raffia, though it gained steadily between 1924 and 1953 in relation to Congo francs, was applied only when using raffia as a standard measure for barter. The 'unofficial' rate was not applied in exchanges of raffia for other commodities, but was quoted only when the equivalent values were being worked out for other goods. For example, one cam-wood bar of a certain height, valued at 200 raffia units, could be exchanged for one female goat. If in these exchanges anyone came forward with raffia cloth instead of any of the goods valued in terms of raffia, the rate for settling in raffia was automatically lowered by 10 per cent (and sometimes even by 20 per cent) so that 9 raffia cloths were accepted in exchange for an object valued at 10 raffia cloths, 90 for an object valued at 100, and so on. The same practice was reported independently by Luc de Heusch (1955) working among the Songo, hundreds of miles north and west of the Lele.

On the other side of the Kasai river, the Bushong tribe seem to have had a similar convention. I surmise that the strip of raffia on which 320 cowries were sewn and which was a standard unit of money (Vansina, 1964, p. 23) was probably reckoned at 400 cowries, 20 per cent being discounted. This is not just a matter of giving a 10 per cent or 20 per cent discount for cash down or for the less liquid form of money, though I think these considerations are present. The main reason for the double exchange rate is to protect the pattern of wealth-holding within the economy. The old Lele men who held most of the rights in raffia would be foolish to sell these rights for Belgian Congo francs, which only the young men were in a position to earn. No one would convert raffia into francs unless he were forced to do so. The soaring price of raffia (in terms of francs) represented the blocking of one area of the economy and of the social system; an attempt to freeze a pattern of social relations.

I would now like to use the foregoing to explain two characteristics of primitive economies. One is the unexpected tenacity of primitive currency in the face of European money with greater purchasing power. The other is the reported inelasticity of prices in many primitive economies.

It seems on the face of it surprising that *tambu*, described in the nineteenth century, should be a medium of exchange circulating alongside European shillings in New Britain, and that manillas should have been forcibly suppressed in Nigeria only in the late nineteen-forties after many centuries of trade with Europe. My answer is that those types of primitive money which display vitality are those which have a coupon function in controlling status in the social system. Their medium-of-exchange function is easily displaced, and there are indeed many currencies used specifically for trade which have disappeared. To take *tambu* first, A. L. Epstein describes it as the linch-pin of the social order in New Britain. Wages there are paid in Australian currency, and no European or Chinese store accepts payment in shell-money. For paying bridewealth and other ceremonial dues only *tambu* is acceptable. Between the two extremes there is an area within which cash and shell serve as alternative media of exchange. There is no fixed conversion rate between the two currencies, cash and shell. *Tambu* cannot be bought in cash.

'Cash and *tambu* operate in an area of overlap but they relate essentially to different sets of social values, each of which is recognized as valid in its own sphere. Those who would like to see *tambu* replaced by cash seem to be those with least stake in the perpetuation of the old social system, that is, younger and more educated men, and urban workers' (Epstein, 1963, pp. 28-32).

In the Cross River area of Nigeria a similar situation maintained the value of manillas in spite of disturbing fluctuations in price. Exchange rates between manillas and West African shillings fluctuated according to seasonal booms in the palm-oil trade and on the long secular trend manillas increased in value in relation to shillings. Speculative hoarding increased still more the relative scarcity of manillas, which was mainly due to the increase in shillings in circulation as opportunities for employment went up. The government recognized that hardship resulted from a coinage with marked fluctuations in value, but its first attempt to suppress manillas failed. This was an attempt to buy them up, but I suspect that holders of manillas were not willing to part with them at prices which the government thought it reasonable to offer. Finally, the manilla problem was solved by legislation restricting its use in trade. It is hardly necessary to add that manillas were used in Cross River societies as coupons for bridewealth and so were more than mere media of commercial exchange.

We can also look at one of the many cases on record in which Europeans have gained access to large quantities of the local coinage. Inflation inevitably results and inevitably the primitive currency soon loses its purchasing power. Einzig (1948, p. 162) cites a case in which iron-bar currency in the Congo, thus inflated by Europeans importing it to pay their way, devalued to such an extent that it defeated the travellers' intention. The point was reached at which the amount that a man could carry was not valuable enough to pay his wages for carrying it. In Mt Hagen, in New Guinea, the Europeans brought in large quantities of gold lip shell, the most esteemed currency, in order to pay for pigs and for labour. Inflation worked against them so that the size of pig a gold lip shell could buy became smaller and smaller, while the Mt Hagen natives fully exploited their position in inter-tribal trade and acquired foreign wives and pigs in large number. But although thousands of gold lip shells were now circulating and seeping out of Mt Hagen in inter-tribal trade, when the Europeans tried to buy gold lip shells for money, they could only do so at 'exorbitant prices' (Gitlow, 1947). So even severe inflation did not alter the situation which tends to govern the relations between primitive and modern currencies when the former have a coupon function.

I now turn to the reported inelasticity of prices in primitive economies. Basil Yamey invites anthropologists to make suggestions about this:

'There are references in the literature on peasant economies suggesting that there is a long-term stability in the values of such economic variables as the prices of particular goods or

services, or the rate of interest in particular classes of transaction. It seems as if for long periods particular prices, wage-
rates or rates of interest remain unchanged, despite other
changes in the peasant economy at large. The economist, with
his firmly entrenched idea that changes in prices both reflect
changes in economic conditions and also bring about adapta-
tion to the changes, is perhaps somewhat suspicious of the
reality of such inflexibilities' (1964, p. 383).

Equally puzzling reports about prices that are insensitive to
changes in supply and demand are made about the primitive
economies I have discussed here. The explanation of these may
also apply to peasant economies, since the people living in the
latter are often concerned to protect a traditional pattern of
society from change (Wolf, 1955). I would seek the answer in the
analogy with coupons, on the one hand, and with international
exchange, on the other. To suppose that prices should be highly
responsive to supply and demand is to assume that they are
operating in a free and perfect market. But such markets are
rare in primitive conditions. To understand the slow movement
of prices in some sectors of primitive economies we should recall
that the rates at which coupons and licences are exchangeable
for goods or money are inelastic even in our own modern
economy. The price of gun licences and pet licences is not closely
related to conditions of supply and demand, nor are legal
penalties for that matter. These rates tend to change only infrequently, and to move with big steps when they do move.
Where the patterns of obligation and privilege are governed by
ascribed status we should expect to find that certain prices tend
to be controlled, either by discontinuities in the internal distributive system or by discontinuities in the demand for foreign
currency. In either case, issues of social policy restrict the freedom of the market. The Lele operated three exchange rates for
raffia: one applied to internal transactions when raffia was the
standard of value but did not actually intervene; another rate,
10-20 per cent higher, was applied internally when raffia was
used in settlement; a third was used when anyone sought to buy
raffia with francs, but it was prohibitively high. Thus they kept
internal prices in terms of raffia low and discriminated against

Primitive Rationing

Belgian Congo francs so as to prevent francs displacing raffia. In such transactions there is an appearance of centrally imposed control, but it is deceptive. No central governing body imposes the rates of exchange. The exchange control emerges by the decisions of individuals striving to hold to their position of advantage in a particular social structure.

REFERENCES

ABRAHAM, R. C. 1933. *The Tiv People*. Lagos: Government Printer.

ANONYMOUS. 1949. The Manilla Problem. *Statistical and Economic Review* **3**: 44-56.

ARMSTRONG, W. E. 1928. *Rossel Island: An Ethnological Study.* Cambridge: Cambridge University Press.

BARIĆ, LORRAINE. 1964. Some aspects of Credit, Saving and Investment in a 'Non-Monetary Economy' (Rossel Island). In Firth and Yamey, 1964, pp. 35-52.

BOHANNAN, P. 1955. Some Principles of Exchange and Investment among the Tiv. *American Anthropologist* **57**: 60-70.

BROWN, GEORGE. 1910. *Melanesians and Polynesians.* London: Macmillan.

CLARK, COLIN. 1942. *Daily Telegraph.* Sydney: 18 March.

DANKS, BENJAMIN. 1888. On the Shell Money of New Britain. *Journal of the Anthropological Institute* **17**: 305-317.

—— 1892. Burial Customs of New Britain. *Journal of the Anthropological Institute* **21**: 348 et seq.

DAVIS, JAMES T. 1961. Trade Routes and Economic Exchange among the Indians of California. *Reports of University of California Archeology Survey,* **54**.

DE GARINE, IGOR. 1964. *Les Massa du Cameroun, Vie économique et sociale.* Paris: Presses Universitaires de France.

DE HEUSCH, LUC. 1955. Valeur, monnaies et structuration sociale chez les Nkutshu. *Revue de l'Institut de Sociologie* **55**: 73-89.

DE SCITOVSKY, T. 1942. The Political Economy of Consumer's Rationing. *Review of Economic Statistics* **24**: 114-124.

DOUGLAS, MARY. 1963. *The Lele of the Kasai.* London: Oxford University Press.

DU BOIS, CORA. 1936. The Wealth Concept as an Integrative Factor in Tolowa-Tututni Culture. *Essays in Anthropology Presented to A. L. Kroeber.* Berkeley: University Press of California, pp. 49-65.

EAST, RUPERT. 1939. *Akiga's Story.* London: Oxford University Press.

EINZIG, PAUL. 1948. *Primitive Money.* London: Eyre & Spottiswoode.

EPSTEIN, A. L. 1963. Tambu: a primitive shell money. *Discovery*: December.

EPSTEIN, SCARLETT. 1964. Personal Capital Formation among the Tolai of New Britain. In Firth and Yamey, 1964, pp. 53-68.

FIRTH, RAYMOND. 1938. *Human Types.* London: Thomas Nelson.

—— 1959. *Economics of the New Zealand Maori.* (2nd edn.) Wellington, New Zealand: R. E. Owen, Government Printer.

FIRTH, RAYMOND & YAMEY, B. S. 1964. *Capital, Saving and Credit in Peasant Societies.* London: Allen & Unwin.

GITLOW, ABRAHAM. 1947. *Economics of the Mount Hagen Tribes, New Guinea.* Monographs of the American Ethnological Society, **12**.

HILL, REUBEN. 1961. Patterns of Decision-making and the Accumulation of Family Assets. *Household Decision Making. Consumer Behavior,* **4** (ed. N. N. Foote. New York Press): 57-80.

HOYT, E. 1926. *Primitive Trade.* London: Kegan Paul, Trench, Trubner.

HUGH-JONES, A. M. 1950. Points as Currency. *Economic Journal* **60**: 162-169.

KROEBER, A. L. 1925. *Handbook of the Indians of California.* Washington: Government Printing Office.

LÉVI-STRAUSS, CLAUDE. 1949. *Les Structures élémentaires de la parenté.* Paris: Presses Universitaires de France.

MEAD, MARGARET. 1937. *Co-operation and Competition among Primitive Peoples.* New York: McGraw-Hill.

MENGER, KARL. 1892. On the Origin of Money. *Economic Journal* **2**: 239-477.

OLIVER, D. L. 1955. *A Solomon Island Society.* Cambridge, Mass.: Harvard University Press.

POSPISIL, L. 1963. *Kapauku Papuan Economy.* Yale University Publications in Anthropology **67**.

THURNWALD, R. 1934-1935. Pigs and Currency in Buin. *Oceania* **5**: 119-141.

VANSINA, J. 1964. *Le Royaume Kuba.* Musée Royale de l'Afrique Centrale, *Annales, Sciences Humaines* **49**.

WOLF, E. R. 1955. Types of Latin American Peasantry: A Preliminary Discussion. *American Anthropologist* **57**: 452-471.

YAMEY, B. S. 1964. The Study of Peasant Economic Systems: Some Concluding Comments and Questions. In Firth and Yamey, 1964, pp. 376-386.

ACKNOWLEDGEMENTS

Thanks are due to the authors and publishers concerned for permission to quote from the following works, of which full details are given in the References:

George Allen & Unwin in respect of the chapter by Basil Yamey from *Capital, Saving and Credit in Peasant Societies* edited by Raymond Firth and Basil Yamey; Professor Claude Lévi-Strauss and Presses Universitaires de France in respect of *Les Structures élémentaires de la parenté;* Dr Margaret Mead and Beacon Press in respect of *Co-operation and Competition among Primitive Peoples* (revised paperback edition copyright © 1961 by Margaret Mead); Routledge & Kegan Paul in respect of *Primitive Trade* by E. Hoyt; Yale University Publications in Anthropology in respect of *Kapauku Papuan Economy* by L. Pospisil.

Fredrik Barth

Economic Spheres in Darfur [1]

This paper contains a concrete account of the main structure of the Mountain Fur economy. It also pursues an argument of greater generality concerning the use of the concept of spheres in the analysis of an economic system. Concretely, I try to show in what sense the flow of goods and services is patterned in discrete spheres, and to demonstrate the nature of the unity within, and barriers between, the spheres. I point to the discrepancies of evaluation that are made possible by the existence of barriers between spheres, and to the activities of entrepreneurs in relation to these barriers. To give the material, I also have to give a sketch of some important institutional complexes that constitute especially significant factors in determining the structure of the economy. Basic to the whole analysis is the view that the demarcation of spheres must be made with respect to the total pattern of circulation of value in an economic system, and not merely with reference to the criterion of direct exchangeability.

PHYSICAL BACKGROUND

Jebel Marra is a mountain massif located about 13° N. and 24° E., close to the centre of the African continent. The area is relatively self-contained, and is isolated by deserts to the North and East, arid and sparsely populated plains to the West, and the Bahr el Arab to the South. From a plain of about 2,000 to 3,000 ft in altitude the mountain rises to nearly 10,000 ft and creates an environment rather different from the surrounding savannah belt of the Sudan: despite a dry season from October till May there are perennial streams and stands of large forest. The mountain, particularly on its lower slopes, supports a dense population of Fur-speaking hoe agriculturalists, living in hamlets or villages of up to about 500 habitants (for general background, see Lampen, 1950; Lebon & Robertson, 1961).

149

SUBSISTENCE

The crops cultivated on the Jebel Marra form two agricultural complexes: summer rainland crops, and winter crops on irrigated land. The predominant staple is bullrush millet (*dukhn*) grown on dry terraces and completely dependent on summer rains. Millet fields are prepared and hoed during May-June, the seed is sown as the rains start, and repeated weeding is required until harvest-time in September. The fertility of the soil is prolonged by periodic fallow periods, but extended use leads to impoverishment and final indefinite abandonment to bush.

In rocky fields, and inside the compounds, tomatoes are also grown in the summer, following their introduction by Egyptian troops some hundred years ago. Occasionally, wheat is also cultivated on the dry terraces in the summer, as a final crop before the fields are laid fallow. Low terraces by streams, on the other hand, are artificially irrigated and used for the cultivation of onion, garlic, and wheat in the dry winter season. Whatever manure is available is used on these fields; and they are not normally ever left fallow. In the summer, special crops of chillies, herbs, and potatoes are grown in these fields without irrigation. Scattered among the compounds are also a fair number of cotton bushes. To an increasing extent, irrigated lands are also being developed as orchards, containing limes, lemons, oranges, mangoes, papayas, guava, and bananas.

Of domestic animals, the most important is the donkey, on which the population depends for practically all heavier transport. Pigeons are kept by most families; goats are kept in small numbers for meat, with a negligible yield of milk. Cattle are kept by some, mainly for re-sale; they are not locally bred or milked. Swarming termites, locusts, wild figs, edible grasses, honey, etc. are collected and contribute significantly to subsistence.

INSTITUTIONAL FORMS

Besides this geographical and ecological basis for the Fur economy, there are also some basic institutions in Fur culture which may be regarded as primary, and from which forms in the economy may be derived. These relate to the size and composition of households, the forms of ownership of land, values concerning labour and reciprocal obligations, and the organization of weekly markets.

(*a*) First, the units of management need to be identified – the unit which organizes production and consumption and holds a separate 'purse'. In this respect, Fur society is extreme and simple, in that every individual has his own farm plots, his own grain stores, and his separate budget. Domestic units are not primary economic units; though marriage implies certain reciprocal obligations and services, it does not imply a joint household.

Husband and wife each cultivate separate fields and store their produce in separate, adjoining grain bins in their joint hut. Neither spouse is allowed to take grain from the other's store, nor are they obliged to give any foodstuffs to each other. The economic obligations in a marriage mainly concern services: the wife must provide the husband with female labour, especially for cooking and brewing beer (from the millet he supplies from his stores); the husband in return provides the wife and her issue with clothing – predominantly, and formerly almost exclusively, spun and woven by the man himself. Some spouses elect to work one or several fields jointly, and most do assist each other somewhat in cultivation; but this does not alter their basic independence as units of economic management.

Children are fed by their mother from her stores. Boys remain with their mother till the age of 8-10 years; then they leave their home village to live as wandering scholars, attending the schools of Koranic teachers (*Fakki*) and supporting themselves by begging. After three, four, or five years they pass a religious examination with the last teacher they have been attending, and return to their village, where they start cultivating fields of their own. Until marriage, they depend on a mother or a sister for the female labour of cooking and brewing. The father, and other close relatives, are obliged to assist the boy in providing a bride-price; but he alone is responsible for his own needs. Daughters, on the other hand, remain at home until marriage and, until that time, may either work together with their mother or cultivate separate fields but pool their produce.

In other words, economic activities are characteristically pursued by single individuals, though in a matrix of obligations, mainly of providing labour, to persons in specified kinship positions.

(b) This means that every person must obtain individual access to the basic means of production: land. The rights over land are institutionalized as follows:

Territorial rights are associated with descent groups of a non-unilineal kind – large blocks of kinsmen, with an endogamous tendency, often spoken of as patrilineal in form but in fact of a much looser structure allowing membership 'through our grandmothers'. This looseness in structure is possible only because the groups are non-corporate – their joint rights are vested in a title-holder, who represents the kin group in question and is responsible for its joint estate.

His responsibility consists in essence in allocating usufruct rights to fields. Such rights are given to individuals and are usually retained by them until use of the land is discontinued – i.e. the usufruct rights do not lapse when fields are left fallow in a systematic rotational pattern, only when they are abandoned. However, inside a community, it is regarded as every individual's right to obtain the land necessary for subsistence. When need arises, and when there is no unused land available, usufruct rights may be revoked and some land taken from those who have plenty and given to those who are in need. The title-holder is the person with the power to revoke such rights and redistribute the land of his descent group. Because the argument from relative need is accepted, he will be obliged to allocate fields alike to members and non-members of the 'owning' group; and the distribution of plots shows little correlation with the distribution of the users' descent-group rights.

The rights of the cultivator as *user* as distinct from *owner* are expressed in the symbolic prestation of one pot of beer to the title-holder after each harvest – a custom that is not consistently practised but is universally regarded as correct and proper. No rent in kind or services, or other obligations, are required from the cultivator.

The more shifting nature of cultivation on the unirrigated

lands assures a fair circulation of usufruct rights in the population. There is some tendency for children to take over the dry farms cultivated by their parents, especially for daughters to succeed on the death of their mother; but there does not seem to be any question of the lineal transfer of usufruct rights over several generations. In the case of the irrigated lands, however, no periods of disuse intervene, and usufruct rights come up for redistribution only on the death of the cultivator. The argument of need is used to justify a reallocation of rights to small onion plots, but most of the irrigated land tends to remain in the same hands, and there is an increasing tendency, with the growth of irrigation agriculture, for title-holders to monopolize this resource (see below, p. 170).

None the less, the main picture remains that land, as the main productive resource, is made available to all without any significant rent or other counter-prestation.

(c) With every individual so characteristically constituting a separate unit of management for economic purposes, the predominant pattern of labour tends to be one where every person uses his or her own time to work for the direct satisfaction of his own needs. By Mountain Fur conventions, it is furthermore shameful to work for wages in the local community, though a few men have experience as migrant labour elsewhere. None the less, there are institutionalized opportunities for both symmetrical and asymmetrical transactions involving labour, and there are some kinship and neighbourhood obligations which commit fractions of a person's time and effort.

The Fur institution that facilitates labour exchanges is the beer party. This takes several forms, exemplified by informal reciprocal help, work parties with many participants, and house-building parties. In the simplest form, two or more friends may decide to work together for company, in which case they jointly cultivate each other's field in turn, he whose field is being cultivated providing a pot of beer for their joint consumption. Larger work parties may be arranged in a similar way, but without the obligation of reciprocity: a man will announce his intention a few days in advance, have a large amount of beer prepared, and ask his friends and neighbours to come to the work party. Besides those who are invited, any person who wishes may join the party and drink beer in return for working. In these cases, the beer must be plentiful and is supposed to compensate for the work being expended; when the beer is finished, the work party disperses. Finally, house-building has a communal and reciprocal character; a day is announced for the work – first one for the women, who plaster the hut walls, then for the men, who build the roof and thatch it. On the appointed day, kinsmen and neighbours who have been invited are obliged to come, bringing with them the materials that are needed in the building. Large amounts of beer must again be provided by the host, and other persons may join in the work, in which case they pay a 'fine' of 2 piastres (about fivepence) for not having brought building materials.

Close kin of the house-builders, especially brothers and sisters, also assist by supplying one or several pots of beer at such occasions, as well as by working themselves and egging on the other guests to work well. A person's freedom to allocate his own labour is thus restricted by some commitments; and his opportunities for disposing of it on the Fur labour-for-beer labour market are restricted by the number of occasions offered by work parties in the local or adjoining villages. These are, however, very frequent in the larger communities; and with the above reservations one may say that essentially, a person's time is his own, to use for labour in his own fields or to exchange for beer on a local, relatively open, labour market. The reciprocities that limit a person's freedom on this market derive from obligations of mutual sociability, i.e. they are associated with the 'party' and not the 'work' aspect of the work party. Labour is seen as adequately compensated for in beer, and there is no restriction that each person's input of work and of beer into the system should be equivalent. This fact, together with the considerable degree of freedom allowed persons in choosing partners and occasions for transactions, means that we are dealing with a *market* for the exchange of labour and beer. The fact that persons also enjoy the 'party' aspect of the work party does not affect this argument.

(*d*) Fourthly, the Fur have a well-organized system of market-places, which facilitates a great number of economic exchanges. The medium of exchange used at these markets is, and has for a long time been, money issued in the Nile valley. Previously, cloth may have served as a medium of exchange.

Each market-place is active one day, or in a few cases two days, a week. They are spaced at a distance of 15 to 20 km from each other on the perimeter of the mountain, so that every community is within walking distance of at least one market-place, enabling people to attend the market and return home the same day. Particularly in the slack agricultural seasons, markets are visited by large numbers of people, amounting to several hundred through much of the day.

Villagers bring all varieties of agricultural produce to the market-place, though millet, being very bulky and heavy in proportion to its value, is rarely marketed. Most producers bring only small quantities, since they sell only to obtain cash for specific purchases, though some, anticipating a good price or because of acute need, may also bring larger quantities to sell in bulk. Occasionally, cattle or goats are also brought for sale by their owners. Craftsmen, who form a small, discrete population of male smiths and female potters, also bring their products for sale, and the smith sets up a small anvil for incidental repairs. Finally, travelling pedlars, most of them Arabs but some Fur, set up shops in booths or on mats from which they sell imported industrial consumer goods, particularly cloth, utensils, sugar, etc.

Numerous middlemen appear and mediate the flow of trade while seeking profit, either by speculating in rising prices through the day, or by accumulating products in bulk for transport and re-sale at communication entrepots 50 to 100 km away. Each will specialize in one or two products – garlic, onions, dried tomatoes, or wheat – buying from the individual producers and accumulating for re-sale on the spot, or for transport. Middlemen also buy the livestock, slaughter and partition it, and sell it in small portions to local consumers. Some sales of fresh vegetables, fruits, and other garden produce also take place directly from producer to individual consumer.

Some women also brew beer and bring it for sale in the market-place. Though there is no dearth of buyers, especially as

155

the afternoon wears on, the sale of beer is regarded as immoral and the women who do so are looked upon as immodest. This may be both because the making of beer is an intimate female service appropriate only in a close, domestic context, and because beer, as in a work party, is a festive idiom of cooperation and companionship and not appropriate as an object of commercial bargaining.

In the market-place, then, individual villagers are able to exchange their agricultural products for tools and utensils, cloth, and a variety of other consumer goods which they do not themselves produce. They do so by freely switching between the statuses of buyer and seller, and must deal with factors of supply and demand and with fluctuating prices measured in a monetary currency.

ECONOMIC SPHERES

The facts presented so far invite the use of a concept of economic spheres. They suggest the existence of two discrete spheres of exchange in the Mountain Fur economy: one that embraces a large variety of material items, including also a monetary medium, and is associated with the market-place facilities; and another that exists for the exchange of labour and beer. The two spheres are separated by the sanction of moral reprobation on conversions from labour to cash and from beer to cash. They thus would seem to fit well the definition of spheres given in Bohannan and Dalton (1965, p. 8), i.e. they each constitute a set of freely exchangeable material items and services. They also would seem to exhibit the feature of hierarchical ranking: conversions in the one direction are frowned upon; i.e. the sphere containing labour and beer would be regarded as the higher, that associated with the monetary medium the lower.

However, such a model is inconsistent with some of the empirical material. Thus some highly prestigious items of wealth, such as swords, are obtained in the cash sphere. Furthermore, the bridewealth for a wife is composed predominantly of cash and items from the cash sphere, and this would indicate a high rather than a low rating for the cash sphere.

Nor can one argue that these are the effects of breakdown associated with the introduction of money. Cash had been used in the Fur area long before colonial times, and the system described here is in this sense a traditional and relatively stable one in which cash is an integral part. If a concept of spheres is to be useful for the analysis of this system, the hierarchical assumption is best dismissed.

What is more, it is difficult to relate the labour-beer sphere significantly to the cash sphere by any patterned channels of conversion. On a more fundamental level, I would argue that a separation of spheres based on the criterion of exchangeability alone gives an unnecessarily inadequate representation of the structure of the economy. The concept of spheres has much greater analytic utility if it relates to all forms of circulation and transformation of value, whether by exchange, production, inheritance, or other means.

I shall therefore try to depict all the standard choices of alternative allocations of resources open to the units of management in the Fur economy, and to delimit the significant spheres with respect to the total pattern of circulation or flow of value. The units of management are single individuals, whose basic problem is to transform their own efforts into a range of items that satisfies their own consumption profile. The institutional forms I have described above may be regarded as the main facilities or means at their disposal to achieve this transformation; and the description of the economy is simplified by the fact that persons have approximately equal access to these facilities.[2] It is further simplified by the fact that, as members of a relatively homogeneous society, their habits and appetites are similar, except for the male-female differences which mainly reflect reciprocal obligations in marriage.

An attempt to aggregate the allocations of the whole population of management units, giving a picture of the *village* economy, is therefore unusually simple in this case. In the cash sphere, as long as there is no shortage of land, the village economy can be represented as the *sum* of decisions of management units, since these units do not seriously compete for resources and their activities do not have any great impact on market prices. Aggregating the decisions in the millet-beer-labour sphere is more difficult, since any transformation by a management unit of its beer into labour presupposes the

157

presence of persons willing to exchange their labour for beer. The simplest procedure is to assume a certain supply of labour and beer and to see how the allocation decision of one member unit might affect the availability of these forms of value on the market, and possibly also affect the relative 'price' of each as measured in terms of the other. Some of these problems are taken up below in the section on management and stratification (pp. 165-166) and in connection with new uses of labour and possible responses to this (pp. 167 ff.).

The pattern of standard alternative choices for a Fur management unit can thus be represented as in the diagram. With the reservations noted above, this may simultaneously be regarded as a model of the village economy as a whole. The remainder of this paper is essentially an exposition of this diagram followed by a discussion of its implications.

THE PATTERN OF STANDARD ALTERNATIVE CHOICES FOR A FUR MANAGEMENT UNIT

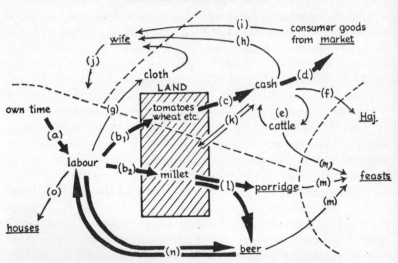

PATTERNS AND ALTERNATIVES OF ALLOCATION

(a) The input into the economic system is the person's own time, used as labour. All self-supporting persons in the

society must and do have the basic skills necessary to cultivate the main varieties of crops, and to trade.

(b) To start production, a person next needs access to land.
This is obtained either from a parent or close relative with
plenty, or from one of the title-holders in the village. Every
individual needs to obtain plots of several kinds, suitable
for different crops and uses. A configuration of sizes and
types of farm implies an allocation of labour to alternative
products: millet, and some onions, for basic subsistence,
and readily marketable crops such as tomatoes, wheat,
garlic, onions for cash needs. The balance struck between
these two categories of products depends on the person's
obligations: women, especially those with small children,
concentrate more of their effort on millet, while men,
especially those with plural wives, have greater need for
cash to meet the obligations of clothing their families, and
to save towards bridewealth for themselves or their sons.

In the course of the year, every person will need to cultivate at least one farm in each category. One may choose to
distribute the labour so that most work falls in the rainy
season on millet and tomato farms, leaving much time in
the winter for threshing, house-building, and trading, or to
allocate the labour more equally between summer and
winter crops. Individual skills and preferences, and established usufruct rights to irrigated land, will influence these
allocations.

(c) Tomatoes and wheat are produced exclusively for the
market, since they are used hardly at all as food by the
Fur; garlic, onions, etc. are partly for own consumption and
partly for sale. The weekly market-places are available to
transform these products into cash. Cash again is used to
obtain a variety of consumer goods from the market. In

(d) 1964 the annual cash needs of men in the prime of their
lives was estimated by informants, and reported for themselves, to be about £8; that of women only £1, £2, or £3. The
rate of consumption in the cash sector has, however, been
increasing rapidly over the last years.

Also purchased for cash are tools – a relatively minor
expense; donkeys, of which every man wishes to own one,

and young cattle. These last are bought from Baggara Arabs when they are about two years old, for about £6.

(e) They are then kept for some years, tended by the children of the owner, till they are ready for sale as meat on the market at the age of 5 or 6 years, when they bring about £11 or £12. No breeding or milking takes place, but the manure that accumulates where the animals are stabled at night is valued and used in the irrigated fields.

Livestock thus constitute a possible field of investment, if one has the children to tend them. Otherwise, the possibilities for investment of cash in productive enterprises are extremely restricted. Cash savings are useful as a store of wealth to secure against crop failure or sickness in the future; and amounts up to several hundred pounds are accumulated by some. But for most people who dare not use such savings for speculation and trade on the market, they remain inactive wealth, buried in a pot under the floor of the hut, and are not used as capital. A few villagers chose, usually fairly late in life, to use such savings to perform the

(ƒ) *Haj* pilgrimage to Mecca. The returned Haji tends to take little part in village affairs, and so this conversion of wealth to rank has limited consequences in the Fur system.

(g) Men may somewhat reduce their cash expenditures by weaving cloth for their families rather than buying it. Cotton for such thread may be bought, or produced by the man himself. He spins it by hand while walking or sitting idle, and weaves it on a horizontal loom which, though nominally it may be owned by someone, is in fact used communally by all.

(h) A major cash expense is that of bridewealth, involving various traditional prestations to the wife and to her bilateral kinsmen totalling about £35 in value. This expense is borne by the groom and his father. Most of it is given in purchasable objects (donkeys, cattle, swords, cloth) or their cash equivalents. Two lengths of cloth must, however, be produced by the groom himself and given to the bride's parents. For the rest of their married life, the husband is further obliged to provide his wife, and small children, with

(i) basic necessities from the market.

(*j*) In return, the wife must provide female services of sex, cooking, and brewing of beer.

(*k*) The other main kind of crop is millet. Some people find that they, in their initial allocation of labour (*b*), have struck an inadequate balance between production of cash crops and of millet. This can be corrected in the market-place: not infrequently, people run short of millet and have to buy some before the next harvest; while a few find that they have an excess which it is more convenient to store as cash than as grain. Much of the Marra mountain seems to be rather too high to offer optimal conditions for millet, and there is doubtless an overall import from lower-lying, surplus-producing areas.

(*l*) Millet is used for porridge and beer. Independent estimates in connection with sample budgets indicate that on an average about one-fifth of the total grain production goes into beer – more in the case of men, somewhat less in the case of women.

(*m*) Most of the porridge is consumed directly. On special occasions, however, connected with funerals and memorials for senior deceased relatives, or the life-crises of junior relatives, feasts are given at which porridge is also served to invited and uninvited visitors. At most feasts, beer is also given, and occasionally cattle are slaughtered. Such feasts bring honour to the person who gives them; but as they are given in the name of another person and are not formalized in grades or titles, it would be inappropriate to regard them as 'feasts of merit' in any real sense; and their effects on the political influence of the feast-giver seem to be minimal.

Beer-making is a rather complicated procedure which stretches over several days, and the product does not keep for long; so most households are unable regularly to have beer available for home consumption. Most of the beer produced thus enters the circuit of feasts and work parties,

(*n*) especially as a reciprocal in exchange for labour, as discussed above. Besides being used to mobilize labour in millet cultivation, where the large, uniform fields invite the use of communal labour, such beer-for-labour exchanges

161

Fredrik Barth

(*o*) are used in house-building. Indeed, a final marriage obligation, after a period of successful marriage, is the building of a hut by each spouse for his or her parallel-sex parent-in-law, using only labour mobilized by beer in a kinship/friendship network, and associated with special festive customs, dances, and songs.

POSSIBILITIES FOR GROWTH

The diagram thus depicts all the main forms of goods and services in the Mountain Fur economy, how they are produced and how they can be exchanged for each other – i.e. it depicts the flow of value through the system. The whole system is seen from the point of view of an ordinary villager, not a craftsman or a market-place speculator; and it presupposes the ecological and institutional facts outlined in the first part of the paper.

From the point of view of each individual unit of management, the central purpose of economic activities must be to direct the flow of his own assets in these various channels in such a way as (i) to achieve maximal increase in them while (ii) obtaining a balanced distribution of value on the various consumption items of market goods, porridge, beer, housing, *Haj*, and feasts. The balance in question is determined by each person's consumption profile.

Some general characteristics of the economy stand out very clearly in this diagram; most clearly, the limited possibilities for cumulative growth. Such growth possibilities depend on a recognized channel for reinvestment and will show up in the diagram as possible *circles* of flow, permitting what might most vividly be described as *spirals* of growth (Barth, 1963, p. 11). Only three such circles are present: (1) labour-cash-crops-cash-wife-labour, (2) cash-cattle-cash, and (3) labour-millet-beer-labour. The first of these circles is apparent rather than real; and all have built-in brakes which prevent them from serving as true spirals of growth.

As for the labour-cash-wife-labour circle, this is controlled by a number of factors such as the availability of marriageable women, the acceptance of the marriage offer by the woman and her kinspeople, and the ultimate limit of four legal wives. Of

162

more immediate relevance, however, is the fact that the labour obtained from a wife is not of the same kind as that invested in work on the cash crops. A woman's labour obligations to her husband concern the special female services only; as a cultivator she is independent, and the cash crops which she cultivates are her own, not her husband's. Though spouses often work together in the field, this is on a reciprocal basis. Thus, plural marriages will not only deplete a man's savings, but also increase his cash expenses without providing him with any source of labour, from wives or from children, which he can use in the production of cash crops. There is thus no opportunity for cumulative increase of assets in this circle.

The cash-cattle-cash circle, on the other hand, offers a genuine circle for investment and increase provided that (otherwise essentially unusable) juvenile labour is available in the domestic unit. However, the erratic supply of young cattle constitutes a brake on systematic investment: there are no markets to facilitate trade in such animals, and the supply depends entirely on the whim of the Arab nomads, who offer the beasts for sale individually through random contacts and only in response to unforeseen and urgent cash needs. In a complete census of one mountain Fur community of 212 adult householders, one person owned 5 cattle, the rest fewer, and most of them none. Though restricted in this way, profits in this particular spiral are none the less frequently cited by villagers as the source of accumulated savings.

The labour-millet-beer-labour circle is the most clearly marked one in the economy. But it also has characteristic built-in brakes. General notions of reciprocity are not effective, as noted previously; but there is a tendency for labour efficiency to correlate negatively with the size of the task: the larger the field, the more beer and the more people are present, and the more quickly does the whole occasion degenerate into a pure drinking party. The host tries to control this tendency by bringing out his beer a little at a time; but if he is too careful people will leave the site in protest.

Furthermore, the circle is essentially a closed one: millet is not treated by the Mountain Fur as a cash crop, and so wealth once in this circle remains within it, and a person's incentive to try systematically to accumulate in a spiral is limited by his view of his possible consumption needs or appetites for porridge, beer, and thatched huts.

SPHERES AND BARRIERS

The items labour, millet, porridge, beer, and houses are thus closely interconnected, and most nearly constitute a sphere in terms of exchangeability. By also considering other regular modes of circulation, especially that of a production in which the factor of land is freely available, the interconnectedness of these items is more adequately depicted. It should be noted that all items are *not* freely exchangeable for each other, e.g. labour cannot be obtained in exchange for millet. But through the brewing of beer, labour is mobilized in direct proportion to the millet invested and there are no significant restrictions on the volume or timing of this transformation – i.e. it is present in the system as a constantly available possible allocation of the re- sources in question. It thus seems most meaningful to classify these items together as constituting a single economic sphere, and to demarcate such spheres by criteria of freedom of alloca- tion and the facility with which each item or form can be transformed into any other.

The concept of spheres, then, serves to summarize the major structural features of a flow pattern. In this case, most items fall by such criteria clearly in either of two main spheres, that of labour, beer, etc. and that associated with cash. In addition, the diagram depicts conversions to *Haj* and feasts, in a sphere related to rank and influence that has no clear feedback into the economic system, and also some conversions into a sphere of kinship and affinal ties, represented here by wives as the only item with a significant, though limited, feedback on the labour side of the economic system.

The barriers between spheres, in this view, are barriers to ready transformation, i.e. all the factors that impede the flow of value and restrict people's freedom to allocate their resources, and reverse these allocations. Thus the allocation of cash to the purchase of a ticket to Mecca is a conversion to another sphere, since this amount of value can never be transformed back into cash. An allocation of labour to millet cultivation is likewise an allocation of resources to a non-cash sphere; because of the items in this sphere millet is for reasons of price and competition not a marketable cash crop, porridge has no buyers, the sale of beer is regarded as immoral, and the labour obtained for beer cannot be sold and has traditionally been used only in millet cultivation and house-building. Houses, finally, are not sold, because of the difficulty of finding buyers.[3] The barriers that prevent or restrict flow between spheres are thus compounded of a variety of factors, only some of them of a moral or socially sanctioned nature.

MANAGEMENT AND STRATIFICATION

Successful management consists in allocating labour wisely to the two main spheres, and steering one's assets through the channels of each sphere in such a way as to maximize increase. In the cash sphere, this involves agricultural skills and an adequate programming of labour input in terms of the changing requirements of hoeing, watering, guarding, and harvesting – and, in the case of tomatoes, also of drying the crop. Besides, relative gains or losses result from the choice of different alternative crops in different years, as a result of fluctuations in weather conditions and market prices. In general, cultivators seemed to feel that weather fluctuations were unpredictable; and many also seemed to choose their crops on a conventional or habitual basis, without reference to prognoses of changing prices. A steady rise in the price obtained for tomatoes over the last years none the less has resulted in a very considerable increase in the quantity of tomatoes cultivated.

Finally, the time of marketing affects the price obtained. Thus the price of onions sinks, when the new crop comes in, to less than half of the peak price that obtains in early winter. Persons with cash resources to cover current expenditure are thus able to postpone their crop sales and reap the greater profits.

The linear character of the flow channel in the cash sphere does not give much scope for management finesse, and only in the small cash-cattle-cash circle can careful saving and investment produce bonuses of any importance. Not so in the millet-beer-labour sphere, however: systematic management of millet cultivation and beer-labour mobilization is the corner-stone on which the prosperity of most villagers is based.

Let us first look at the direct relation between labour input and production. The millet-growing season extends over approximately 70 days; including the preparatory period of terrace-mending and hoeing, and the considerable concluding labour of threshing and winnowing, nearly six months are probably needed to produce a final harvest of reasonable size.

Villagers estimated that a woman with no cash-cropping commitment in the summer season should be able to produce at least 100 *mīd* (1,000 lb), by her own labour. As a daily rate this would correspond to more than 1/2 *mīd* (5 lb), per working-day.

Alternatively, much of the labour may be done with the aid of work parties. At such parties, the hosts generally estimate that a large – about 30 litre – pot of beer provides enough beer for six men for one day. By the brewing techniques generally used in the Marra mountain, millet produces about six times its own volume in finished beer. One *mīd* (corresponding to about 5 litres) of grain thus makes about 30 litres of beer. The daily consumption of beer per man in a work party is thus approximately 5 litres, corresponding to 1·7 lb millet.

Given an adequate store of millet, a person can thus mobilize labour at a cost of some 1·7 lb millet/day/man and apply it to a task that produces an average of some 5 lb millet, or three times the cost, per work-day. A reasonably skilful management in this flow circle thus secures a person an adequate supply of millet from a relatively small labour input. The person who cannot husband his resources, and whose thirst or hunger tempts him to join work parties so as quickly and directly to transform his labour into beer, will constantly be on the losing end of the deal. In Mountain Fur villages, the population thus has a tendency to fall into two strata: a majority of moderately prosperous persons, and a fraction who, because of disease, age, or bad management, have inadequate grain stores, and who supplement their food resources by frequent participation in work parties, thus serving as a labour reserve for the more prosperous villagers.

DISCREPANCIES OF EVALUATION

I have argued elsewhere (Barth, 1966) that the barriers which separate spheres and limit the amount and occasions of flow between them will allow considerable discrepancies of evaluation to persist as between items located in different spheres. Such discrepancies may be discovered when barriers break down and new patterns of circulation are made possible, in which cases an increased flow may force people radically to revise their evaluations (see p. 170 below, on the value of land). Alternatively, these discrepancies may be demonstrated where it is possible to construct some common denominator, or coefficient, for comparing evaluations in one sphere with those of another. In the present case, such a common denominator may be constructed on the basis of the market price of millet – an 'imperfection' in the separation of the two major spheres, brought about mainly by the activities of travelling merchants who bring millet in from the adjoining ecological zone, but also occasionally by the sale of millet raised by the Mountain Fur themselves.

The price of millet in 1964 ranged from 4 to 6 piastres, i.e. around an average of 1 shilling per *mīd* (10 lb) of grain. We thus get the equations:

10 lb millet=1 shilling=30 litres of beer=6 man days,
or 1 man day=5 litres of beer=2d. worth of millet.

This evaluation of what a man-day of labour is worth in beer may be compared to that obtaining in the cash sphere. The Sudan Forestry Department, and some other public bodies, make relatively unsuccessful attempts to recruit local labour in Jebel Marra. Their basic wage offer has been about 10 piastres = 2 shillings a day, or 12 times the value of the millet which a man demands for participation in a work party. Yet it has proved very difficult, especially in the initial years of recruiting in any one village or locality, to entice people to take work. Privately, I found that an arrangement for having fresh water brought to my hut, at the rate of about 1d. per 12 litre pot, was impossible to maintain because the women in the neighbourhood were dissatisfied with the rate of pay – the equivalent of half a day's 'millet pay' for 20 minutes' work. Admittedly, in these equations

I have ignored the value of the labour of brewing – as indeed I suspect that the Fur themselves, particularly the men, would do if they were to attempt the comparison. But this additional factor is far from sufficient to make good the discrepancies. Likewise, one might argue that the Fur idea that it is shameful to work for a wage should be represented as an additional cost for a man entering a wage contract, and that this constitutes the balancing factor. The empirical facts would, however, rather suggest that these costs are not so very great, since once the Fur are given enough opportunities to work for wages so that they discover the advantages of these wage rates, they eagerly accept the contracts, as in some of the Jebel Marra foothills areas. No matter how one chooses to represent it, there does seem to be a very great discrepancy between the values placed on beer and labour, and those placed on money.

INNOVATING ACTIVITY

So far I have discussed the economic activity of persons within the traditional framework of alternative allocations. But to the extent that the individual units of management really attempt to maximize their assets, they will assert a constant pressure on this framework, and will seek ways of utilizing new opportunities where they are apparent and not blocked by unreasonable risk factors or supervening social sanctions.

The most general change that is taking place along these lines in the Jebel Marra is a progressive increase in the range of crops cultivated, and a certain change in the whole agricultural regime because of the increasing importance of tree crops. This development has been initiated by some modest agricultural experimental stations, but is sustained without any supporting agricultural extension work. The development of orchards is leading to derivative changes in the views on land-ownership and tenure rights. Finally, in a few localities one can also find some truly entrepreneurial undertakings where new strategies of management and channels of conversion are being exploited. The forms which these changes take are to a marked degree determined by the economic system outlined above, and give further perspective on its structure.

Orchard development

The development of orchards requires irrigated land – i.e. the tree crop is an alternative to the irrigated winter cash crops. Such a tree crop takes four years before it gives a significant product; however, in the intervening period the fields may also be used to raise an irrigated onion crop, so no significant loss of current production is suffered during the transition. The fruits are marketable for cash – limes, lemons, oranges, and mangoes particularly for export; papaya, guava, and bananas mainly for local consumption. The ease of production, and the relatively low value of the fruit in the case of limes and lemons, make them less attractive under present circumstances, whereas some varieties of oranges have been spectacularly profitable.

The labour to establish an orchard comes in addition to that normally required, since other cash crops must be cultivated to cover current expenses until the trees start producing. The development of an orchard thus requires an extra input of labour; and this has generally been done by the innovators with the aid of work parties, utilizing surplus millet for beer. A precedent is thus established for the use of beer-mobilized labour in the cash-crop sphere. So long as a person's millet resources are large enough to provide simultaneously for the other current uses, there are no sanctions against such an allocation; but it requires careful management, i.e. a successful large production of millet by beer work parties in the year preceding the orchard development. Perhaps for this reason, only the quite successful and prosperous have embarked on this production beyond the occasional planting of single trees. In the localities of fieldwork, the first orchards were planted in a village adjoining the foothills zone in 1956, in a high mountain village not till 1962. The mature orchards give large incomes with little input of labour, individual properties producing £20 to £30 worth of fruit annually.

Land rights

This change in agricultural regime has created some uneasiness with regard to land-ownership and usufruct rights. The principle of individual ownership to (wild) trees is established and recognized. The trees which a person plants will according to this

169

principle be his, no matter who owns the land on which they grow. However, an orchard on irrigated land becomes so dense that it shades other crops and monopolizes that land. A person who obtains usufruct rights to irrigated land to which he has no title can thus, by planting an orchard, render it useless to all others for an indefinite period. Some men who held titles to land on behalf of their descent group were, in 1964, quite concerned over this, and pressed for the general acceptance of a rule forbidding the planting of orchards on borrowed land. Some few of them, on the other hand, had been quick enough to evict other users in time to secure ample areas for their private orchard developments.

Others, who had no such titular rights, wished to obtain the exclusive access to irrigated land that would make the long-term investment of orchard development a safe proposition. In the most sophisticated areas, a few sales and purchases of land had taken place by 1964, tentatively establishing truly private ownership to land. Both parties to such transactions were quite uneasy about the deal, the sellers because they were alienating rights which they held in trust for larger kin groups (and only those who belonged to nearly extinct, or emigrated, kin groups were willing to consider sale at all), the buyers because they felt that the price was excessive.

Indeed, the prices demanded are an extreme illustration of the discrepancies of evaluation that can obtain where the items, in this case land and cash, have not been in circulation in the same economic sphere. I recorded those few transactions of this kind that had taken place in one community. The first sale took place in 1961, when a field was sold for £17. The buyer planted orange trees, and proceeded to cultivate onions in the three transitional years. For these onion crops he obtained £27, £22, and £25, respectively. He expected his first proper yield of oranges to bring a larger income. He was personally no longer in doubt that the transaction had been to his advantage; but he failed by this argument to convince his friend to purchase a field for £30 which had regularly been giving an onion crop worth more than £15 annually. The man in question was willing to offer £25, but would not go higher – not because he did not have the money, but because he felt that, surely, no piece of land could be worth that much. One must assume that an increasing number of such transactions will progressively lead to a general revision of relative evaluations.

Entrepreneurial activity

On purely logical grounds I have argued elsewhere (Barth, 1966) that entrepreneurs will direct their activity pre-eminently towards those points in an economic system where the discrepancies of evaluation are greatest, and will attempt to construct bridging transactions which can exploit these discrepancies. The social factors which produce a reluctance to sell land serve as a general impediment on entrepreneurial activity in this field; besides, the profits connected with such transactions are long-term. But the disparities of evaluation between the cash and the millet-labour-beer spheres offer opportunities which have recently been discovered and exploited by a few entrepreneurs. The problem, when an entrepreneurial adventure consists in breaking through the barrier between spheres, is that of re-conversion of assets without loss – i.e. that of locating channels that allow a circle of reinvestment and growth (see above, p. 162, and Barth, 1963, p. 11).

Returning to the diagram the possibility of such a circle is apparent in the combination of channels $(k) - (l) - (n) - (b_1) - (c)$. Concretely, what happened, apparently for the first time in 1961, was that an Arab merchant who regularly visited the market-places on the northern fringe of the Marra mountain, asked for permission to spend the rainy season in a village, and asked for an area of land on which to cultivate a tomato crop. He brought in his wife and settled her in a hut, and he bought a large amount of millet in the lowlands to the north-east, where the price is very low, which he transported in on his donkeys and camels. From the millet, his wife made beer; this beer he used to call work parties, applying the labour to the tomato cultivation. Without any significant labour input of his own, he thus produced a large tomato crop, which he dried and transported to el Fasher for sale after the end of the rainy season. On an investment of £5 worth of millet, he obtained a return of more than £100 for his tomatoes.

In 1962 and 1963, more merchants, and some local people,

171

adopted the same strategy with results nearly as spectacular. The precedent of orchard labour showed the way in which assets in the beer-labour circle could be converted to the cash sphere by being used in the production of cash crops – a conversion that takes advantage of the disparity in the beer versus cash evaluations of labour. The re-conversion of assets from the cash to the non-cash sphere through the purchase of millet again takes advantage of a favourable disparity of evaluations, and is particularly simple for a trader with access to lowland markets.

The profits on trade and transport of the products also enters into the enterprise of the merchant given above. The case of one of the first local men to attempt the scheme is therefore of special interest. On the local market, he purchased:

50 *mĭd* of millet at 6 piastres per *mĭd* – 500 lb millet:	£3	0	0
Also, for the main work party feast, 1 goat for 40 piastres:	0	8	0
Total labour costs:	£3	8	0

He had all the labour in the tomato field performed by work parties. The value of the tomato crop, ready for sale within about 5 months, was £38 – profits based entirely on production and conversions within the local economic system.

Again, one must assume that this situation is unstable: a re-evaluation as between spheres may be precipitated by this flow of value across the boundary, whereby evaluations in the two spheres are brought more closely in line. Alternatively, the critical conversions may be blocked: by a refusal to give land for cultivation to the entrepreneurs, or by the discontinuation of the beer-for-labour exchanges on anything but a reciprocal basis. There is some evidence for a trend in each of these directions, but as of 1964 no effective reaction blocked these enterprises. However, the increase in wage-labour opportunities which will probably take place will no doubt also affect this situation by making it more difficult to mobilize labour for beer on a non-reciprocal basis.

CONCLUDING REMARK

In each major section of this description of the Mountain Fur economic system I have sought to make explicit the analytical steps that I have taken, and to give the argument a general form. It should therefore be unnecessary to formulate any extensive conclusion. One general feature of this analysis might however be noted. By discussing alternative allocations in terms of 'flow', and describing the concrete factors and barriers that channel this flow, one performs an analysis that is particularly useful for the study of change, and for short-range prediction. The model is, in this respect, amenable to developments and manipulations which a more strict structural representation would not allow. This increases its adequacy for the description of what is in fact taking place in the Jebel Marra area, and should also enhance its interest to economists.

NOTES

1. Based on a field visit of slightly over three months in 1964, during a year's contract with Unesco as visiting professor at the University of Khartoum. Incidental field expenses were covered by a University of Khartoum Ford Foundation research grant; an interpreter and various other help in the field were supplied by the Jebel Marra Project of the U.N. Special Fund. I wish to thank these institutions, and the authorities and persons with which I was in contact in the Sudan, for their cooperation and help.
2. In this, I disregard the members of the craftsman caste, whose numbers are very small and whose style of life differs considerably from that of Village Fur.
3. In some cases of inheritance, when none of the heirs wishes to use the house, empty houses are indeed offered on the market and bring anywhere from 6 shillings to £2. The difficulty then is to find a buyer, since those in need of a house can call on friends and relatives to contribute towards the construction of an entirely new house, at a chosen site, through expending less than about 5 shillings-worth of their own millet on beer.

REFERENCES

BARTH, F. 1963. The Role of the Entrepreneur in Social Change in Northern Norway. *Acta Universitas Bergensis. Series Humaniorum Litterarum* No. 3. Bergen; Oslo: Norwegian Universities Press.
—— 1966. Models of Social Organization. *Royal Anthropological Institute*, Occasional Papers, No. 23.

BOHANNAN, P. & DALTON, A. G. 1965. *Markets in Africa*. New York: Doubleday.

LAMPEN, G. D. 1950. History of Darfur. *Sudan Notes and Records* **31** (2).

LEBON, J. H. G. & ROBERTSON, V. C. 1961. The Jebel Marra, Darfur, and its Region. *Geographical Journal* **127** (1).

Leonard Joy

An Economic Homologue of Barth's Presentation of Economic Spheres in Darfur[1]

A flow system such as that depicted in Barth's paper can be represented in matrix form. If the matrix can be quantified, the significance of changes in particular coefficients on the total pattern of 'flows' can be measured. Such matrices are used in economics, e.g. for the analysis of transactions within an economy; for the analysis of a firm's production possibilities; or for the analysis of general equilibrium models of production and exchange. We propose here to present what might be called the economic homologue of the Barth model. In doing so we are not changing Barth's model in any way that adds to, subtracts from, or modifies the information that he gives us in the original paper. In that sense we are not making it more 'economic' than it is in his own presentation. We are, however, using a more rigorous framework of analysis. As a result, we need to be more precise in the formulation of relations, and we see that the model forces us to ask questions which we might not otherwise have asked. In relation to the original discussion it throws light on the extent to which it is meaningful to designate 'spheres'. Unfortunately, it has not yet been possible to obtain data from Darfur for the completion of the matrix and no quantitative analysis has been carried out. We do discuss, however, problems of quantification and the possibilities of quantitative analysis both with regard to the implications of changes in the situation confronting individuals and with regard to the general equilibrium analysis of the combined effects of individuals' behaviour.

ANALYTICAL PRELIMINARIES

Barth's model shows the alternatives open to an individual (male or female) for the translation of his own time and effort through production and exchange into a variety of satisfactions.

His paper discusses relationships between such entities as

175

male labour, land, millet, female labour, beer, 'beer party' labour, and so on. The output of millet is governed by the amounts of land and effort available and applied to its production. The output of beer is governed by, among other things, the millet-beer conversion ratio and the amount of millet allocated to beer production. We can present these relationships in many different ways. Here we shall first indicate a simple graphical and tabular presentation in order to explain the logic of the matrix formulation (Glicksman, 1963; Heady & Candler, 1958).

It is supposed that there are two *activities* which can be undertaken – growing millet or growing wheat. Millet will produce 400 lb grain per acre and wheat 800 lb per acre. (We assume certain yields but we could take ranges or frequency distributions.) They are, we assume, both harvested at the same time and millet requires 36 days per acre for harvest while wheat takes only 8 days per acre. There are available 2 acres of land and 48 days of harvest labour. We can represent this information in both tabular and graphical form: viz.

	Output	400	800
	Available	*Millet*	*Wheat*
Land	2 acres	1	1
Harvest labour	48 days	36	8

If land is devoted solely to one crop it will produce either 800 lb millet or 1,600 lb wheat. Assuming that, by devoting any fraction of the land to either crop, the same fraction of total possible production will be yielded, we can, on the graph, join the points 800 millet and 1,600 wheat and the line drawn will trace out the limit of all possible combinations of millet and wheat that could be grown on 2 acres of land. Similarly for harvest labour. Forty-eight days is enough for the harvest of 1·3 acres of millet (=533 lb millet) or 6 acres wheat (4,800 lb wheat) and the line joining these points on the graph traces out the combinations of millet and wheat that could be managed by the available harvest labour. It will be seen, however, that while there is enough land to grow 800 lb of millet there is only enough harvest labour to grow 533 lb. Again, while there is enough harvest labour to cope with 4,800 lb wheat there is only enough land to grow 1,600 lb. The outputs of wheat and millet for which there are enough of both land and harvest labour are confined to points on or within the shaded boundary.

PRODUCTION POSSIBILITIES

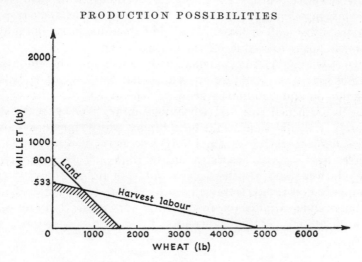

These points satisfy the following inequations:

2 acres $\geqslant$ (1 × millet acres) + (1 × wheat acres)
48 days harvest labour $\geqslant$ (36 × millet acres) + (8 × wheat acres)

which can be identified as the rows of the table already set out. These inequations can be rendered as equations as follows:

2 = (1 × millet acres) + (1 × wheat acres) + acres uncultivated
48 = (36 × millet acres) + (8 × wheat acres) + harvest labour days unemployed.

All points on the shaded boundary on the graph give values for millet and wheat acreages which would satisfy these equations.

Thus the feasible values of the boundary of production possibilities are defined by a matrix of algebraic equations. This is presented here in terms of two *activities* (millet and wheat) and two *constraints* (land and harvest labour) but it is generalizable in *n* activities and *m* constraints. Moreover, activities can include – besides production activities – purchase, sale, or

177

exchange. Production activities may be of final products or intermediate products; one crop may be represented by more than one column if it can be grown by different methods (including planting at different times). Constraints may include not only resource constraints but also social, legal, or taste constraints imposing maximal, minimal, or proportional constraints on activities (e.g. at least one plot of a famine crop; the maize acreage not to exceed twice the acreage of beans).

In this way, the information given to us about the Mountain Fur economy can be represented in matrix form. Set down below are the row and column vectors (activities and constraints) which can be identified from Barth's commentary. In one sense this matrix may be unnecessarily complex for it includes many miscellaneous activities which might normally be fitted in without competing with others for scarce time and other resources, e.g. cloth-making. On the other hand, it is almost certainly too simple in that it fails to take account of, for example, the effects of crop sequence on yields, food storage activities, etc. Many such complications could be allowed for.

Column Vectors (Activities)

Summer Raingrown Crops

P_1 Bulrush millet
P_2 Tomatoes
P_3 Wheat

Irrigated – Winter

P_4 Wheat
P_5 Onion
P_6 Garlic

Irrigated – Summer

P_7 Chillies
P_8 Herbs
P_9 Potatoes

Irrigated Orchard

P_{10} Orchard – bearing
P_{11} Orchard – establishment

Livestock

P_{12} Cattle
P_{13} Goats
P_{14} Collecting and gathering
P_{15} Hut-building

Labour and Marketing

P_{16}series Reciprocal labour given (by periods)
P_{17}series Reciprocal labour received (by periods)
P_{18} Brew beer (by periods)
P_{19} Sell labour (by periods)
P_{20} Cloth-making
P_{21} Buy cattle
P_{22} Buy goats
P_{23} Buy wives
P_{24} Buy tools
P_{25} Buy millet
P_{26} Sell millet
P_{27} Sell tomatoes
P_{28} Sell wheat
P_{29} Sell onions
P_{30} Sell garlic
P_{31} Sell chillies
P_{32} Sell herbs
P_{33} Sell potatoes
P_{34} Sell fruit
P_{35} Sell cattle
P_{36} Sell goats

Row Vectors (Constraints)

P_{101} Land – unirrigated
P_{102} Land – irrigated – summer
– irrigated – winter
P_{103} Manure
P_{104} series Labour by periods – non-brewing
P_{105} series Beer (at different times)
P_{106} Millet
P_{107} series Brewing labour
P_{108} series Reciprocal labour commitments
P_{109} series Livestock feed
P_{110} series Subsistence and feast requirements, millet for porridge, and own beer (n.b. possibly in storage form)

P_{111} Cash requirement – tools, consumer goods, etc.
P_{112} Cattle requirements, feasts, dowry, status, etc.
P_{113} Tomatoes
P_{114} Wheat
P_{115} Onions
P_{116} Garlic
P_{117} Chillies
P_{118} Herbs
P_{119} Potatoes
P_{120} Fruit
P_{121} Cattle
P_{122} Goats

EXPLANATION OF THE MATRIX

This is a generalized matrix for Fur males (excluding craftsmen, as does Barth). It shows a range of possible cultivating activities (P_{1-10}) with the direct input requirements for these activities – land, labour, and manure ($P_{101-104}$).[2] Labour resources are shown to be augmentable by 'hiring' labour (P_{17} series)[3] at the cost of beer (P_{105} series). Beer in its turn requires millet (P_{106}) and brewing services (P_{107} series). Millet can be obtained by growing it (P_1) or by purchase (P_{25}). It should be noted that if the possibility of direct purchase of beer or hire of labour by cash payment were foreseen these could be included in the matrix *as well as* the more customary form of these transactions. If payments in kind were made with goods purchased by the employer then a cash equivalent wage could be shown in the matrix. If the goods used in payment were produced by the employer then the millet-beer-labour type of relationship now shown in the matrix could be extended. Thus many ways of labour-hiring could be represented in the matrix.

The matrix formulation also allows for the recognition of custom, e.g. the role of the woman in brewing (P_{107} series), dowry commitments (P_{112}), hut-building obligations (P_{16}), etc. Other customs governing, for example, the sexual division of labour in cultivation, tribute payments, and so on could also be included were they to be relevant here. As it is, the matrix allows

179

Leonard Joy

for the provision of subsistence (P_{110} series), labour commitments (P_{108} series), cash commitments (for wives and sons and, for example, the purchase of tools – P_{111}), and a target requirement of cattle (P_{112} which could be related to dowries, status, or the desirability of a realizable capital asset). The economics of keeping cattle to improve crop yields by manure could be accounted for by including crops (singly or as crop sequences) grown with and without manure.

VALUE OF MATRIX FORMULATION

Even without quantification and computation, the representation of the described relationships in matrix form appears to have value as a powerful tool of conceptualization which takes us further than the diagrammatic representation of flows. Conceptually, the chief advantage is probably that with this method one can more readily trace potential implications of postulated relationships. One is required to undertake an explicit formulation of activities and constraints and to ask whether a coefficient is zero, positive, or negative. Therefore, one is required to make explicit the nature of the interrelationships within the system.

The mere attempt to set out the form of the matrix requires one to pose relevant questions. With this presentation one is immediately aware of the fallacy of regarding, for example, labour and land as single resources and one is forced to distinguish analytically significant differences in the timing and other characteristics of inputs, including those of a social nature. We have distinguished labour inputs not only by time periods but also by sex, and according to whether 'self-employed', hired in one of a variety of ways, or provided by reciprocal arrangements. There is practically no limit to the forms by which the terms governing the command of inputs or their specificity could be represented. But one is required to ask whether or not it makes sense to lump inputs or activities together or whether separation is called for analytically. The criteria for answering this question can readily be illustrated by considering the nature of misspecification. For example, if we treat as a single row vector both male and female labour taken together, then we are assuming that all activities requiring this input could be performed equally

180

well by male or female labour. If males are only half as efficient as females we can continue with this assumption provided we weight available male labour by 0·5. But if there are jobs which are never performed by males (or females) then our assumption might lead us to invalid conclusions and a reformulation of the matrix might be called for which recognized the division of labour. Again, if we specify a time period for a labour input it means that the operation performed in this time period (e.g. weeding, sowing, etc.) might be performed at any time within the period defined without significant effect upon output or the timing of subsequent operations. Thus, a major benefit of setting out a 'choice situation' in matrix terms is that it prompts one to ask analytically significant questions.

Quite apart from quantification, the form of the matrix enables us to trace the ramifications of change. The effects of changes in resource availabilities or in their productivity, the introduction of new crops or technologies, or changes in custom, can be traced through the system to identify the extent of their likely impact. In practice, such an exercise is likely to reveal simply the total interdependence of the whole system. This in itself would appear to be a step forward but not perhaps so large a step when one is seeking to assess where the greatest impact will be. For this one requires quantification.

Let us assume for the moment that there is no problem in obtaining data and consider the sorts of calculations possible with a quantified system. The standard economics application of such a model is to solve the matrix to give that pattern of activities (acres of millet and other crops, amounts of labour hired, etc.) which will maximize profit, or national income, or other relevant objective function – that which is to be optimized. (It is also applied to minimizing problems, but these seem less relevant to us here.) Such optimizing procedures require values to be imputed to the various activities which may be pursued, i.e. we need to assign 'prices' – positive or negative values – to wheat, onions, cattle, cloth, engaging in reciprocal labour arrangements, and so on. The solution obtained is that pattern of feasible activities which produces the greatest total return – given the values assigned to different activities. Different patterns of 'prices' (i.e. assigned values) will indicate different patterns of activities as optimal. Now, although we must assign prices in order to 'solve' our matrix, we may assign hypothetical prices and permute them simply for the purpose of tracing the bounds of possible choice.[4] (In fact, we need only permute price *ratios*, which is simpler.) With a large matrix this might still be expensive in computer time, but in primitive situations subsistence constraints may reduce the practical choice range to manageable proportions.

In the context of a market economy, price parametrization (or the process of determining cornerpoint solutions over a range of relative prices)[5] is significant for assessing the effect of changing price relatives on optimum output patterns. Indeed, it is one approach to supply prediction. In a primitive economy one might work in the reverse direction and ask what 'prices' are consistent with observed behaviour. It is true, of course, that such a procedure for imputing values assumes, at least, maximizing behaviour and the observation of equilibrium states. But an attempt to carry out such an analysis might throw light on the question of the extent to which behaviour is maximizing and in equilibrium.

Imputation of values may be attempted also by comparing the consequences of relaxing social and other constraints. Custom which constrains men from getting on to their knees and weeding may have a changing significance with growing land pressure, new markets for cash crops, and so on. One might compare production possibilities with and without the recognition of this custom to assess its significance and the extent that it might come under pressure with the availability of land and markets.

In general, one might use matrix analysis (more generally referred to as mathematical or linear programming) to explore the consequences of change in respect of changes of resource availabilities, technologies, markets, customs, and values. The non-decomposability of the matrix emphasizes the complexity of tracing the ramifications of change. (By non-decomposability is meant the inability to abstract any part of the matrix from the whole without affecting its properties; alternatively, the inability to solve part of the matrix independently of the rest of it.) Changes in the availability of land, market prices, and attitudes to cash hiring of labour or wage employment would affect not only the relative attractiveness of various activities but also the relative valuation of various resources and the economic significance of various customs. Any attempt to trace these ramifications needs to be systematic and based on some such analysis as is presented here. The demonstration of non-decomposability is important because it qualifies Barth's use of the concept of spheres.

It is of interest to trace in the matrix the spheres depicted by Barth. The labour-millet-beer-labour sphere is covered by the coefficients shown as * in the abbreviated matrix below.

		P_0 Resource available	P_1 Millet	P_{17} series Hired labour	P_{18} series Brew beer
P_{101}	Land	*	*		
P_{104} series					
	Labour ⌠1	*	*	* _ _ _ _ _ _ *	
	by ⎱2	.	.	/ / / / / / /	
	periods ⎰.	.	.	/ / / / / / /	
	⎱.	.	.	/ / / / / / /	
	⌡.	*	*	/ / / / / / /	
				* _ _ _ _ _ _ *	
P_{105}	Beer	*		* _ _ _ _ *	* _ _ _ _ *
P_{106}	Millet				
	retained	*	*		* _ _ _ _ *
P_{107} series					
	Brewing				* _ _ _ _ *
	Labour ⌠1				/ / / / / / /
	by ⎱2				/ / / / / / /
	periods ⎰.				/ / / / / / /
	⌡.				/ / / / / / /
					* _ _ _ _ *

* Shows non-zero coefficients

This abbreviated matrix shows the interdependence of millet production on land and male labour and the possibilities of augmenting male cultivating labour by hiring through beer payments which are in turn dependent on the availability of millet (after retentions for consumption) and brewing labour. What it does not show is that there are alternative uses for land and labour (own and hired) and that millet may be bought as well as grown. These aspects are revealed in the Barth flow diagram, but what we notice here is that in representing them we introduce ultimately the whole of the matrix. For we have to include all other activities that use land, labour, millet, and cash. Similarly, it follows, the cash crops-cash-cash purchases sphere when represented in an abbreviated matrix fails to show alternative uses of land and labour, or of crops sold, unless it includes what we have confined to the labour-millet-beer-labour sphere. In Barth's diagram the wife appears as a sphere on her own, but we have already included her here in the labour-millet-beer-labour sphere, and she similarly must be related to the cash sphere. The Haj-Feasts sphere is again clearly interdependent with all other spheres.

Thus, while it is of interest to show the links of interdependence between various activities, it is clear that there is in fact a totally interdependent network.

So far we have discussed the possibilities of learning more about the situation of the individual (or family). Theoretically, it is possible to go beyond this to examine the implications of values, customs, social institutions, resource availabilities, and so forth for the economy as a whole. Given that we can define individual situations in the economy we can theoretically take the matrix for each individual – or groups of similar individuals – and link them into a general equilibrium system. Individuals are linked through exchange in its various forms, including, for example, reciprocal labour. To make the system work we need to impute values placed by individuals upon various forms of consumption (including 'non-material' consumption). Conceptually, such a model might be used to determine the existence of disequilibrium – actual or implied prices or valuations out of line with those necessary for general equilibrium. The implications of equilibrium prices for exchange patterns might be traced in relation to, for instance, bride-price, communal labour obligations, and so on.

However, such calculations depend on the existence of quantified individual basic matrices. If we have these we can impute individual values from observed behaviour provided we can also assume that individuals' expectations, on which their behaviour was based, were substantially correct. Whether in practice the attempt at a general equilibrium analysis would be

Barth's Presentation of Economic Spheres in Darfur

more rewarding than the straight observation of disequilibrium situations, as in Barth's paper, will remain unsettled until some attempts have been made at this. Even where such analysis is shown to be feasible it will only be superior where complexities are such as to be not readily traced by direct methods.

QUANTIFICATION

A number of studies of semi-subsistence farming situations have now been made using linear programming (McFarquhar and Evans, Clayton, Desai, Heyer). Of these, Heyer's study of Wakamba is remarkable for its meticulous – indeed anthropological – approach to data collection and analysis. In general, while data collection has many problems, it is not infeasible, and the problems of data collection are less than those of analysis. Judith Heyer's data revealed a very considerable range of farmer experience in relation to labour inputs and their timing for various cropping operations. She found also a considerable range of practices with regard, especially, to crop mixtures. In linear-programming terms, this meant that almost each crop-growing activity which was observed amounted to a unique activity vector. Thus any attempt to produce a generalized basic matrix would include one column per farmer per production activity. This might make sense if each column vector process[6] per crop activity represented one point on the production function for that crop chosen as optimal by individual farmers in different situations. Analytically, the problem is to determine how far this is the case and how far differences are random or accountable as differences in, for instance, labour efficiencies of different farmers.

The question is very much whether the recording and analysis are worth the effort. There seems to be no doubt that Heyer throws light on such factors as the influence of family and holding size on the choice of cropping system. Studies that she is pursuing of such issues as the effects of population pressure, labour emigration for wage employment, opportunities to purchase staple foodstuffs, etc. seem to be directly feasible from this basic work.

Unfortunately, we do not have data – even for a single

185

Leonard Joy

individual – which would allow us to quantify the Fur matrix. This is hardly surprising since Barth did not contemplate initially the quantification of our matrix. Personally, I would imagine it to be not too difficult to ascribe typical values – or ranges of values – for the relevant coefficients by asking individuals for their own estimates. This may seem a very dubious procedure but it may not be so questionable as it looks. In the first place, such coefficients as are critical are likely to be known to cultivators. They may not know how many standardized man-days per acre would be required for digging, but they may well know how much time they would allow for the preparation of a specifically identified plot (whose area might subsequently be determined). Those data which are less confidently known are likely to be less critical in affecting the conclusions drawn. Secondly, whereas an actual observation may record only one year's objective experience, it may be more important to recognize year-to-year variance which cannot be readily obtained by direct observation. In this event, reported ranges may form a useful basis for simulation (see below).

It may be argued too that one is interested in subjective as well as objective assessments. In this respect it is important to be sensitive to the possibility that one is asking farmers to provide assessments in terms which are not their own or about things which they do not normally consider – a problem of which anthropologists are fully aware.

The effects of variations in input-output coefficients have been studied by simulating likely values of variable coefficients. Similar procedures might be adopted in situations where coefficients are not known with precision to assess how critical is the accuracy of a coefficient. In one simulation study of presumed profit-maximizing small farms in Sweden (Renborg, 1962), the conclusion was reached that, in spite of coefficient variations, there were considerable stable elements which should appear in any profit-maximizing farm plan in the environment under investigation, i.e. regardless of the effect of weather and other causes of coefficient variation.

While the implications of coefficient variation for production possibilities can be explored by simulation, the representation of actual behaviour in the face of uncertainty is a somewhat

186

different matter. However, we can investigate the consequences of observed behaviour in the face of simulated vagaries of nature, and compare the results with those relating to simulated alternative behaviour patterns. Attempts have been made to test the consistency of postulated decision-making analogues of behaviour in the face of uncertainty (Das Gupta, 1964). These at least provide us with working hypotheses to account for farmers' behaviour.

It should be noted that no claim is being made to represent actual behaviour. What we are interested in here is the analysis of alternatives implicit in the ecological, technological, economic, and social environment, and the way choices bear on one another. It may be interesting to attempt to represent this both object-ively and subjectively – though, as people learn, the latter may approximate to the former.

Barth briefly discussed questions of accumulation, and here the flow diagram is considered for possible 'growth spirals'. The programming formulation may also be considered over time. A recursive system may be built, in which the results of one period feed into the next – a technique known as dynamic linear programming. This is distinct from dynamic programming (Throsby, 1962), which gives criteria for decision-making through time when decisions are made in sequence on the basis of outcomes of previous decisions not previously predictable.

CONCLUSION

A matrix presentation can be made to represent exactly the properties of the flow system outlined by Barth. When this is done so as to incorporate the full information included in the paper it includes much that does not appear in Barth's diagram (e.g. the distinction of sub-periods for labour supply and crop-input requirements). While this makes the matrix formulation less readily assimilated than the simple flow chart, a complete flow chart would also become difficult to comprehend.

It is shown that the matrix is not decomposable, which implies interdependence between activities and between alternative resource allocations – the spheres are not separate.

Conceptually, it is argued that the attempt to formulate a

187

matrix requires one to ask analytically significant questions. While it is not suggested that a matrix must therefore be necessarily 'right', it is argued that the process of drawing up a matrix generates significant hypotheses about relationships, and that the matrix formulation offers criteria for significance for the 'rightness' of vector specification.

Quantification is both theoretically and practically feasible in some situations. It appears likely to throw light on a range of issues concerning the significance of existing or possible new situations in relation to resource availabilities, techniques, market opportunities, social institutions, customs, and values.

It is suggested that mathematical programming and allied procedures could provide a powerful analytical tool for social anthropology.

NOTES

1. This paper is a contribution made subsequent to the conference. The author acknowledges his debt to Fredrik Barth not only in respect of the initial article on which this note is based but also for the very ready and stimulating personal exchange which we have enjoyed. We had hoped for the presentation of a joint article based on a quantitative analysis but it proved impossible to complete the matrix simply from data collected in previous fieldwork. The present discussion is therefore more exploratory of economic theory than of anthropological analysis. But it is hoped that the nature of the potential joint participation between the economists and anthropologists in quantitative analysis has been sufficiently indicated.
2. Rows are numbered sequentially from 101 as a computing convenience. This also makes it easy for readers to distinguish row vectors as those Ps with numbers higher than 100.
3. The addition of 'series' to a row or column number means that there may be more than one row or column, for instance, as in this case, to show labour hiring at different periods.
4. Referring back to our graphical illustration, maximization would mean identifying the most valuable point on the production possibility boundary. This depends on the values ascribed to millet and wheat. If millet is infinitely more valuable than wheat then only millet will be produced and vice versa. There will be some relative valuation which will indicate the point of inflexion of the production boundary to be the point of optimization. Thus, by tracing the range of relative prices and identifying for each the optimum pattern of activities we define a sequence of optimal points which is the production possibility boundary.
5. Exploration of production and exchange possibility boundaries might also be undertaken by parametrization with a variable resource.
6. Each different way of growing a crop has to be represented by a separate column. For convenience, a distinction is made between an activity (growing wheat) and 'processes' of that activity (different ways of growing wheat).

REFERENCES

CLAYTON, E. S. 1961. Technical and Economic Optima in Peasant Agriculture. *Journal of Agricultural Economics* **14**(3).

DAS GUPTA, S. 1964. Producers' Rationality and Technical Change in Agriculture with special reference to India. London. (Unpublished Ph.D. thesis.)

DESAI, D. K. 1963. *Increasing Income and Production in Indian Farming.* Bombay: Indian Society of Agricultural Economics.

GLICKSMAN, A. M. 1963. *Linear Programming and the Theory of Games.* New York: Wiley.

HEYER, J. 1966. *Preliminary Results of a Linear Programming Analysis of Peasant Farms in Machakos District, Kenya.* Mimeo. E.A.I.S.R. Conference, Kampala.

HEADY, E. O. & CANDLER, W. 1958. *Linear Programming Methods.* Ames, Iowa: Iowa State College Press.

JOHNSON, G. L. *et al.* (eds.). 1961. *Managerial Processes of Mid-Western Farmers.* Ames, Iowa: Iowa State University Press.

MCFARQUHAR, A. M. M. & EVANS, A. 1957. Linear Programming and the Combination of Enterprises in Tropical Agriculture. *Journal of Agricultural Economics* **12**(4).

RENBORG, U. 1962. *Studies on the Planning Environment of the Agricultural Firm.* Upsala: Almqvist & Wiksell.

THROSBY, C. D. 1962. Some Notes on Dynamic Linear Programming. *Review of Marketing and Agricultural Economics* **30**(2).

—— 1964. Some Dynamic Programming Models for Farm Management Research. *Journal of Agricultural Economics* **16**(1).

Sutti Ortiz

The Structure of Decision-making among Indians of Colombia[1]

INTRODUCTION

Much has been said about the backwardness of part-subsistence farmers and how they affect the economic growth of under-developed countries. They contribute little to the gross national income (Agarwala & Singh, 1963, p. 384) and fail to release labour for activities that will bring a higher marginal return and a greater margin of saving. No social scientist will argue with this point. But the low gross agricultural output of peasant economies cannot be attributed simply to lack of ability or of thrift, or to the higher value assigned to leisure than to labour. A considerable number of studies carried out by social scientists will discredit such simple explanations.[2] My own fieldwork amongst Páez-speaking peasants in Colombia has convinced me that careful and rational allocation of resources has given a great deal of adaptability to an economy which has to compete with a better-informed and more highly capitalized peasant economy.

In terms of technology, there is no question that part-subsistence peasant farming leaves much to be desired and that yields could easily be increased by improving agricultural practices. D. Edwards, in a study of small farming in Jamaica, remarks: 'The small farming studied was technically bad, but economically it appears to represent a reasonable response to the conditions under which farming is practised' (Edwards, 1961, p. 282). Schultz suggests that new technical factors of production made available to farmers and backed by proper incentives and rewards will make the transformation of traditional agriculture possible (Schultz, 1964, pp. 205-206). Technological innovation, even with the qualifications made by Schultz, has to be treated with a certain amount of caution. Anthropologists have pointed out that some of these improved techniques may

191

affect social relations upon which rational farming depends and that, therefore, economic action cannot be treated separately from the social context in which it operates.[3]

As anthropologists, our contribution lies not only in listing social factors of production that might be overlooked by economists, but also in trying to outline the structure of the situation within which the farmer has to make his own productive decisions as well as the process of decision-making itself. Social factors may affect factors of production differently in accordance with the total social and economic context within which they operate. I fully sympathize, though I cannot agree, with Meier's despair, that socio-political factors are relevant but that in many respects it is 'too easy a way out' (Agarwala & Singh, 1963, pp. 55-56). To determine when and how these factors are relevant it is best to analyse them in the context of decision-making.

Economists have based their models on the assumption that individuals act rationally. The use of this term to describe the nature of the outcome of a decision does not imply a value judgement on the part of the observer-analyst. Rationality implies that when the actor is faced with a set of alternative actions he will evaluate and rank them according to his own particular preferences. He will choose that course of action which he ranks highest, in other words he will try not to forgo a high-preference action. It is just as important to consider what he would have to forgo as to consider what he will receive, since preferences may be closely ranked or linked into pairs or sets.

Preferences are measured in terms of outcomes. In other words, it is assumed that a particular course of action is selected because of what the individual will receive. This may not be strictly true in certain cases. For example, when labour exchange is decided upon, one type is preferred not because of efficiency but because it is a more bearable means of accomplishing a task; however, one could include this benefit as part of the total benefit received.

The outcome need not be sure prospects but expectations of prospects. In fact, a farmer expects a number of possible outcomes and tries to evaluate which ones are more likely to occur.

In this particular Colombian case study the evaluations are subjectively estimated by evaluating past experiences without calculating probabilities. In this case I make the assumption, validated by observed behaviour, that farmers adjust their decision to the range of expectations and not to any one of the more possible outcomes.[4]

For a farmer, an expectation of a return depends on climatic conditions, technical problems, price fluctuations, etc. A peasant farmer does not possess either the information or the technical knowledge to make accurate forecasts of yields or pay-offs. He has to evaluate subjectively the range of possible outcomes and is unable to estimate with certainty which one is more likely to occur. Hence farming decisions are made under uncertainty. It has been said that under such conditions decisions cannot be rational, but Das Gupta (1964) has ably countered this objection and Arrow (1951) has pointed out that in fact most decisions are made under uncertainty. However, the level of uncertainty is of importance in determining the choice a farmer is likely to make, a point to which I shall return later.

I have said that preference ratings are based on expected outcomes. The significance of the outcome for the farmer does not depend on the product itself but on the number of wants it may satisfy. Therefore, when discussing rationality, it is more significant to consider outcomes in terms of utility than in terms of quantity. The word 'utility' has often been used to express the degree of satisfaction achieved by a particular outcome. It has also been used by von Neumann and Morgenstern (1964, pp. 15-31) as a statement of relationship of one outcome over another, in other words as a numerical expression of preferences; and used in this sense it does not explain choice. There is, of course, a motive implied in each preference and this motive has been assumed to be income. In classical economics income can easily be measured in terms of money. This is not the case with peasant farmers, and we are thus left with the problem of assuming that preferences are guided by the desirability of satisfying given wants. As in our case, wants or means of achieving certain wants are not easily transferable. Preference must involve a consideration of the relation of wants to means. Numerically speaking, the relationship could be expressed as constraint over certain preferences, because the choice of these would mean that other subsequent preferences would have to be forgone.

Social scientists have pointed out that wants are socially defined and that they vary from culture to culture. It is not a simple matter of magnifying quantities of products. Rather, it is a matter of achieving an end which has utility because its consumption is socially or physically required by the producer, or because it may be translated into any given want (i.e. money in our society), or because it is a means of continuing a certain course of action. Thus the concept of rationality has to be considered not as a simple means and ends relation but as a sequence of social actions (Smelser, 1963, pp. 20-34). In other words, when an Indian decides to plant more coffee he has to take into account that he may be able to do so only by asking for exchange labour and that in order to attract his neighbours and kinsmen he must remain in touch with them. If he had a greater amount of capital available he might have been able to hire labourers and to buy goods he needed. But if he must depend on exchange labour and on credit, which is to be repaid in labour, a commitment to expand coffee plantations may lead to conflicting demands. If an Indian maintains close interaction with his neighbours and kinsmen he expects them to reciprocate in kind; if he enters into a close relationship with a White trader the reciprocal action expected is different. I am not referring simply to expectations of a return of goods and services, but of sanctions of approval, moral support, prestige, etc. It is in this wider sense, where social and so-called economic returns are interlinked with each other, that I am using the concept of utility. Preference may be to increase productive assets or to increase social assets. By using the term 'utility' in this way, rationality of consumer behaviour in a highly industrialized, individualistic society can also be understood. Peasant societies give us more dramatic examples, perhaps, but they are not totally different from market economies.

It is true that rational behaviour cannot be analysed except in terms of a preconceived principle which assumes that human wants are unlimited. Individuals act rationally in an attempt to maximize social and material assets; when they do not, it is because the rewards are less than the effort required. In a society structured into classes, where social mobility is possible, an individual is expected to achieve higher social status; in an egalitarian society he is expected to achieve greater respect and friendship. This assumption may prove false under certain circumstances, but it is basic to the concept of choice and the relations of means-ends. Certainly it applies to the case under study.[5]

Since preference-ranking can be made only in terms of expected outcomes, the differential probability of results will affect rational behaviour. For example, if the probability of a given income from coffee is greater than the probability of the same income from maize, coffee will be preferred to maize. In some cases the probabilities, or the subjective evaluation of probabilities, are so similar that preference will not be clear-cut. The situation can get more complicated if we consider that not only is it difficult to calculate what the yield of the two crops will be but also it is just as difficult to calculate whether the price of coffee or of maize is more likely to increase or remain stable. In long-range investments it is almost impossible to decide on a preference with equally uncertain outcomes. In such cases one would expect the choice to be based not on price or yield but, for example, on desirability of family consumption of one of the two crops, or the availability of cheaper labour at a time when one and not the other of the crops has to be planted or harvested. In other words, low level of expectation of any one outcome means that preference is based on other more discernible factors such as cost of production or alternative use of the products. In one case the decision is based on cost reduction; in the other, it is made in terms of possible loss. For example, if coffee is not consumed by the farmer, low price represents a greater loss than with maize, which can be used as a substitute for other purchased staples. Choice thus follows a preference not only for a maximum outcome or a sequence of linked outcomes but also for a minimum of cost or uncertainty. The weight of these factors depends on the income or subsistence level of the individual. In the case of peasant farmers the third factor is of particular importance.

Rationality of behaviour does not imply that there is a constant conscious awareness of having made a choice or even the ability to express it verbally in terms of quantities or factors. It would be unfair to expect highly analytical modes of behaviour when we ourselves barely practise it in our household budgeting. When a farmer answered me, rather impatiently, that he really could not tell me how many stems of manioc he was going to plant, because he stopped planting when he could see he had enough, he was quite clear as to the amount required. Thus our task is to be able to point out the form and the process of decision-making, and how in itself it may affect the outcome. Does the process as well as the timing affect the outcome and the discovery of new factors?

The above discussion of rationality does not imply that tradition, habit, and even impulse do not play a role. Those acquainted with the enormous amount of literature on consumers' behaviour and the behaviour of the firm[6] should not find this surprising. Indeed, following 'traditional' means of cultivating the soil can be taken as part of rational behaviour. A constant re-evaluation of means in terms of preference can be extremely wasteful. It requires time and increases uncertainty. Is it not, after all, one of the purposes of rational action to minimize consumption caused by unnecessary risk?

The question is not whether tradition does or does not play a role, but whether Páez farmers ever alter their course of action when alternatives backed by positive sanctions and higher returns are open to them. In other words, do they define problems and try to resolve them rationally or not?

In the preceding paragraphs I have discussed briefly the concept of rationality and how it can be used, not as an explanation of behaviour but as a means of predicting outcomes with greater precision. It has been suggested that uncertainty and expectation should be considered as part of the model and that outcome should not be restricted to monetary returns if the model of decision-making is to be used to predict accurately decisions taken by peasant farmers.

In this study it is suggested that if decision-making models have not always accurately served to predict behaviour, it is because they have assumed that the decision depends on the set of choices, the expectations, the level of uncertainty, etc. Studies of the behaviour of the firm or consumers' behaviour have also included psychological and organizational factors which may affect the weighing of preferences, the availability of information, and the implementation of decisions. In other words, models have only taken into account the factors impinging at the moment when the choice is made or when preferences are ranked. I suggest that the set of factors taken into account are determined not solely by the information available, the personnel making the decision, aspiration levels, the expectation of outcomes, the outcome itself, and the level of uncertainty, but by the structure of the situation which will define when and how these decisions are taken. Here I shall try to consider on the basis of the analysis of the behaviour of Páez farmers:

1. What factors determine whether or not a managerial act is posed as a problem which requires a decision;
2. How the decision is arrived at, and how the process affects the outcome of the decision.

These factors could be expressed in numerical relations, and I have attempted to integrate social factors as part of economic relations so as to make this possible. However, no numerical evaluation is attempted here, because further refinement of the relevant factors and interrelations between them will have to be made.

A producer is here believed to continue acting as he did previously, that is to choose 'traditional' means, until the structure of the situation changes so as to motivate a reconsideration of the original decision. The question which still remains unanswered in this study is how much, or how little, the structure of the situation has to change to define a decision-making point. I suggest here that not all decision-making points are similar in character and that the change in the structure of the situation affects the process of decision-making as well.

I am here considering only peasant economies and, in particular, peasants who not only produce for their subsistence but also produce a cash crop which is, practically speaking, purely for export. In reference to decision-making, I think it matters whether the cash crop produced is also a subsistence staple or not. Therefore I would like to make a plea for a careful typology of peasant economies.[7]

THE PÁEZ INDIANS

The particular case I have studied is that of the Páez Indians in Colombia. In the western part of the Department of Cauca, the Southern Andes form a dense knot of criss-crossing mountains ranging from about 6,000 to 12,000 feet. This region has been called Tierradentro and for topographical reasons it has remained in marginal contact with the adjacent wealthier lowland valleys. Only recently, from about 1958 to 1960, have dirt roads penetrated this dense and steep mountain region. Indian and Colombian peasants who farm on these slopes have remained equally isolated from the bigger towns and Departmental capitals where commercial activities and urban settlements open new market opportunities to peasant farmers. This area therefore represents a pocket of economic hardship within a Department of Colombia known both for its high Indian population (20 per cent according to 1954 census) and its lack of industrial development. The population of Cauca depends mostly on mixed-farming activities. Even in Popayán, the capital of the Department of Cauca, 22 per cent of the population are either absentee landowners or farm workers. In the region of Tierradentro this percentage is as high as 99 per cent. Coffee, corn, and potatoes are the main crops and are often combined with cattle-raising enterprises. In the particular settlement studied coffee is the only cash crop, and maize, plantains, manioc, and beans are planted for local consumption.

The population of Tierradentro (about 27,000) is scattered over a wide territory. There are two settlements, Inzá and Belalcazar, with a population of between 500 and 600 each; other settlements have a population of 100 or less. Larger settlements to the west are separated from Tierradentro by high-altitude plains and mountains. A five-hour bus trip connects Inzá and Belalcazar with the town of La Plata, the closest bigger market centre, with a population of about 2,500 inhabitants. But La Plata is not commercially active enough to make it an attractive stop for Tierradentro traders, who will instead travel another 5 or 6 hours to get to Popayán or Neiva (population of about 30,000 to 50,000).

The Structure of Decision-making

The rest of Colombia is not so very different from Tierra-dentro. Most of the country's population is concentrated in the Andean region. Each region is separated from the others by difficult terrain and connected only by one main road, which travels from north to south, and branches into a few secondary roads (a total of 36,890 km, of which 1,459 km are for Cauca). Settlements are small and quite distant from each other; Colombian farming population is sparsely scattered. This demographic picture does not encourage commercial activities, which are made even more difficult by the incidence of violence – banditry and political upheaval have claimed a toll of approximately 200,000 deaths since 1948 (Guzmán Campos et al., 1964).

Though this southwestern area of the Colombian Andes presents unique problems of isolation for small peasant and Indian farmers, much of what is said here applies to other areas of Colombia as well. Coffee production for most of Colombia comes from small peasant holdings where subsistence crops are also grown. In fact, 36 per cent of coffee plantations are of one hectare or less, 58 per cent are of 1-10 hectares and only 6 per cent are of more than 10 hectares (Food and Agriculture Organization, 1958, pp. 1-104).

The Department of Cauca is divided into a number of municipalities, which are entirely dependent on directives initiated in Popayán, the capital, a very famous colonial city. The municipal mayors are appointed by the governors, who may also veto any administrative act. Local municipal government has very little authority and autonomy.[8]

In the area of Tierradentro there are 19 Páez Indian reservations distributed within two municipalities. They are constituted as political and land-holding corporate groups directly dependent on municipal authority. Every reservation has a council formed by the male heads of all households. They are expected to meet regularly and discuss and initiate administrative actions pertaining solely to the reservation community. It is this council which annually elects a number of officers. The functions of these numerous officers are rather vague. Recent government laws and regulations have restricted their authority to such an extent that they now are allowed only to mediate in minor disputes and implement orders dictated by municipal mayors.

The reservations came into existence by acts of the Spanish Crown. Land grants were made to small settlements of Indians from 1593 onwards. The territory assigned to each so-called settlement – Páez Indians it seems were never concentrated in settlements – was large enough to provide subsistence for existing families, but did not take into consideration a rapid increase in population. Indians are not, in fact, restricted to live within these territories, and many have migrated to larger towns or acquired land as tenants.

Reservation land is not taxable and as long as there is unused land any descendant of the original settlers has a right to a free lot. Therefore, as long as there is land available, it is to the advantage of an Indian to establish residence therein. Outsiders, whether of White, Mestizo, or Indian stock are not allowed to settle within the reservation. They usually settle in surrounding territory and become close neighbours to Indian farmers. In the settlement studied, these so-called White peasants also plant coffee and subsistence crops in exactly the same manner as the Indians. Others have large areas of pasture land as well, and a considerable number of cattle. Most of the non-Indian settlers specialize in some trading activity, however small.

Scattered over the slopes and crevices of the mountains which surround the minute settlement where I resided – San Andrés – are approximately 300 Indian households, the total population of this particular Páez reservation. Sometimes, if the terrain allows it, houses cluster into small neighbourhoods. Each of them is given a name indicative of its geographical location. Resident families of each of these neighbourhoods are believed to be distinctive in that they share similar economic aspirations. Some are thought to be very traditional in their economic endeavours, others to be lazy, because of their preference for wage-labour activities. Because of inheritance of land by male descendants and limitations set upon any other form of land transfer, these neighbourhoods consist mostly of descendants of one or two original settlers. Their imputed ideology and their aspirations are, in fact, the result of shortage of land resources and climatic differences that affect their economic activities, rather than basic differences in value orientation. I think this is a good illustration for the following general discussion on the relevance of using value systems to explain differences in economic behaviour.

Not all members of a neighbourhood are closely related. Land fragmentation, epidemics, and migrations have, through the generations, scattered the descendants of the original settlers. Propinquity brings families together into cooperation in agricultural tasks and in upkeep of common paths and of canals that bring fresh water within easy reach of their houses. Neighbouring Indians tend to visit each other more often than relatives further away. Not all Indians have close neighbours; frequently one can find a lonely residence perched on a steep slope or hidden between mountain crevices.

In these simple thatched dwellings live a husband, his wife, and their children. Together they work the land that has been assigned to them and often pool the cash earned by each of them. The father controls the land and he by custom should make all final decisions. A woman has to have her husband's permission before she sets up the loom to weave a garment or accompanies him to work in the plantations of White settlers. She will, however, have a say in big transactions. The elementary family operates as a socio-economic unit. Land and tools of production as well as animals, though controlled ultimately by the husband, are thought to belong to all members of the household. Paternal control and authority are not absolute. When sons reach the age of about 18 they begin to question this authority. As they grow older, whether married or not, they do seek more independence. The final break is reached when the father gives his consent to his son's marriage and has to assign him the lot of land that will be due to him in inheritance. Even before this, young men begin to work as wage labourers and retain the money they earn. They cease to help their fathers regularly in the family fields and mark time until they will be given their share of land.

Páez kinship system can be classed as bilateral. Kinship obligations are recognized within the range of parents and siblings but not beyond it except for a minimum sign of hospitality and a minimum amount of trust. Kinship, to be operative, has to be reinforced by a friendship tie and to have an economic utility. Maternal kin are as important as paternal kin, but it is from a father that one receives the land one tills (except when in former time there was enough available land to petition for a virgin lot on the reservation of residence) and one receives one's surname. There is a vague feeling of kinship among all individuals who share the same surname. We are cousins, they will say. Each patronymic group is exogamous; it is for this reason that Bernal (1955) has suggested, I believe without foundation because the patronyms had been introduced by Spanish missionaries who also prescribed certain marriage rules, that these groups represent survivals of previously existing clans.

There are no Indians in San Andrés who have completed a primary education that would at least have taught them to read, write, add, and subtract. But there are some non-Indian peasants whose successful business ventures allowed them to send their children to technical schools farther away. Tierradentro is not a suitable place for intensive advanced farming practices. Markets are distant and cost of transport would have made intensive food production for market prohibitive. Mountainous countryside is not suitable for any of the more popular methods of mechanized agriculture.

THE ORGANIZATIONAL CONTEXT OF ECONOMIC RELATIONS

Each farmer makes his own productive decisions according to his own particular preferences and a particular set of variables that affect his situation. The sum total of the decisions of our 300 Páez farmers and the consequences of the same, that is the quantity and types of goods produced and the economic relations entered upon, give us a full description of Páez economy. These decisions and these variables are, of course, not random. They are the consequence of a long sequence of previously realized social and economic exchanges. This set of pre-existing relations can be described summarily as the organization of social and economic relations. Static macro-descriptions of outcomes of social and physical acts often leave much to be desired, but have the advantage of allowing us to describe briefly an immense amount of relevant material and to order it into categories that are meaningful for our own problem – the study of individual decision-making. The intention here is to attempt to reduce the number of categories to the minimum of those which will, in fact, determine the modal outcome of productive decision-making in part-subsistence economies. These factors represent the inescapable situation. Each farmer acts within a given socio-economic situation and makes his own decisions according to his own personal aspirations and his own variables.

It will be noted that cultural values and ideologies are not given as fixed organizational features. I have not done so for several reasons. First, ideological differences between the Páez Indian community and the peasant Colombian community do not explain existing differences in economic behaviour; the same point holds then for differences within the Indian community, as has already been pointed out. Secondly, I am not convinced that ideological systems are determinants of economic behaviour. Ideologies may be symbolic statements about pre-existing arrangements or alternative ones and, as such, serve as guides to individual behaviour. Therefore, in our analysis, ideologies are considered as information available to each one of the producers. For example, the insistence of subsistence farmers on retaining their small properties, even though marginal returns may be lower than if they worked as wage labourers in the city, has often been described as the emotional attachment of Latin-American peasants to their farms; it may also be discussed as a reaction to known returns and uncertain futures. Ideologies may also act as devices to ease situations of strain,[9] or to justify existing arrangements. Indians are said to be lazy, not to pay debts, and to be irrational. Hence it is considered morally justified to force them to work as wage labourers and to cheat them in transactions to make up for the debts owed. But this statement has no factual validity, and traders and landowners are well aware of the fact. Thus, in so far as ideology is information, it will be considered with opportunities and, in so far as it may state social goals and relations, it will be dealt with in the concept of utility.

In part-subsistence economies the producing and consuming sectors
    overlap

Farmers do not attempt to maximize indefinitely their marginal revenue by increasing production. Quantity produced, therefore, should be restricted to the needs of the producing unit. Páez economy is an interesting case because, on the one hand, farmers produce a cash crop for export and, on the other, they produce food crops for their own subsistence. When discussing the size of the coffee plantations, a Páez farmer justified his inability to expand his original acreage in terms of the resources available. When I asked him about the acreage of his subsistence crops, he felt it was sufficient to explain that he planted what he thought was necessary. Thus the presence or absence of an unlimited sector of consumers will determine the attitude of a producer. The obvious question of why subsistence crops are not produced for a market, or why producers do not become specialists and develop within the Páez economy a sector of producers and a sector of consumers, will be answered in the course of the next section and the concluding statement.

If there are not two separate sectors, one of producers and another of consumers, exchange is not basic to the process of production and, therefore, does not affect deeply the structure of decision-making. An extreme interdependence between different types of producing units is of more relevance to the study of the behaviour of the firm. Páez farmers act, in this sense, quite independently of each other. They do not have to sell their coffee to feed their families, to hire labourers, and to keep investing at a high enough rate to continue production at the same level. Subsistence decisions are oriented to satisfy the needs of the family rather than to maintain a certain level of production. Dalton's statement that 'without purchased ingredients of production, and without reliance upon market disposition of output, the input and output decisions of producers cannot be based on factor and output prices as guiding parameters' is true (Dalton, 1962, pp. 361-363). But his assertion that in the absence of market dependence, as dominant economic organization, production is invariably socially controlled by kinship, religion, and political organization, would have to be modified.

Because the production of Páez farmers is not entirely geared to the purchasing of productive assets or even consumer goods (I am referring here to the subsistence sector of production), quantities produced are relatively independent of the economic behaviour of similar units. If the goal of subsistence production is to satisfy socio-economic needs internal to the producing unit, then output is not strongly affected by the amounts produced by other similar units. The size of a field of manioc depends on time, seeds, labour, and land available to the farmer and not on the size of manioc fields of other farmers. Competition is in the field of control over resources rather than in outcome and orientation of production.

It may be argued that this statement would not hold true for coffee production, where prices and therefore marginal returns might be affected by the behaviour of other producing units. San Andrés Indians (only 113 had land suitable for coffee production) produced an approximate yield of 200 loads of coffee during the main harvest of 1960-1961, and the Colombian peasants around the reservation produced, for the same period, 230 loads. Thus the amount produced locally was too small to affect buying prices in the important coffee-buying centre of Neiva, which I would estimate handled more than 100,000 loads in the course of a season. It should be noted that it was very high-quality coffee, and beans were carefully selected, so that local buyers had no fear of getting lower re-sale prices. The Federation of Coffee Growers in Colombia have agreed to a national price system in which regional variations are in direct proportion to transport cost and distance to export areas.

From the point of view of the Indian and White peasant producer, price fluctuations are relevant and taken into account, but they are felt as accidents far removed from their environment, over which they have little or no control. It never occurs to them that if production is lowered prices might be higher. In fact, given the limited quantity of coffee produced locally, their behaviour would not at all affect the demand and supply equilibrium. It is more useful for them to act in coordination and base their decisions on consensus than to venture into new cash-crop enterprises that might be risky and where they would lack the advice and experience gained from others. It was interesting to be present at a time when, owing to a growing dissatisfaction and uncertainty over coffee prices, Indians were discussing the substitution of wheat for coffee as a cash crop. On the higher slopes Indians still continued to plant some wheat because coffee yields were too low. Long discussion ensued as to the difficulties of each enterprise, and the advisability of reintroducing it in lower areas (coffee was introduced to San Andrés about 1930, and before that all Indians were wheatgrowers). The difficulties were not only technical knowledge, and uncertainty of prices and of response of buyers, but also the availability of mills and the cost of running a local primitive stone mill. Organized collective action, given that their joint production could not affect market prices, would be much more rational than individual farmers' venturing on their own. Thus marginal participation in market economy strengthens joint action rather than encouraging innovation.

The independence of producing units (in reference to plans regarding output) will vary with the type of peasant economy. The Páez are an extreme case because they produce a cash crop which is not consumed. In other part-subsistence economies, the cash crop is also an important item of consumption, for example, maize in Guatemala. The question to be asked is whether in this latter case a producer will take into account the behaviour of another producer or whether the required adjustment to maintain the same marginal return is made by increasing productivity. It might also be that middlemen reorganize their buying and selling activities and expand the demand sector.

In a non-market economy, where competition is restricted to control over resources and interdependence is minimized, a producing unit will seldom be excluded from independent farming activities. One would expect, and in fact does find, a very heterogeneous population of producing units – heterogeneous, not just with regard to socio-economic aspirations, but also with regard to managerial ability and productive outcome. Thus it will be harder to test predictions by statistical methods. A 'bad farmer' may continue to farm because he manages to survive. He is unlikely to become a full-time wage labourer and thus release his work potential to those farmers with greater managerial ability, for the simple reason that subsistence farming, as carried out by other producers, could not absorb a large number of permanent labourers. Only in this sense is subsistence farming a wasteful system. On the other hand, it makes it possible for producers to take greater risks than are prudent considering their incomes.

In summary, the relevance of non-divisibility of the economic population into consumer and producer sectors in the peasant society under consideration is this: it orients decision-making to demands internal to the producing units; it restricts competition to availability of resources; it encourages joint action rather than individual innovation; it allows the incompetent manager to continue farming and impedes specialization.

Levels of capital assets and savings are generally low in peasant economies. The Páez peasants are no exception to this rule. This is not for lack of interest or effort in investment and saving. Farmers spend more of their cash income on productive assets than on social expenditures. Saving is a purposeful action and therefore has to be discussed in the context of production and factors that affect it. What is relevant to point out here is that the low level of savings and capital assets does not allow the peasant farmer to plan production on the basis of long-term expectations. This is further restricted by the limited liquidity of some of their assets. However, because of the subsistence character of the economy, farmers need not be in a hurry to sell their crop.

Practically speaking, credit is unavailable to Páez farmers. Stores sell only expensive tools on credit and usually do not stock these items except shortly before or during harvest-time when Indians are likely to have money. The 'Caja Agraria', a governmental credit institution, has no agents in the area, and Indians are not well informed as to the facilities available to them. Requirements set for extension of loans make the services of the 'Caja Agraria' more useful to middle-income farmers than to very poor ones.

Institutional arrangements for the distribution of agricultural products

In peasant economy, the institutional arrangements for the distribution of products and resources may take place either through a network of market-places linked by the activities of middlemen, through traders, or directly between individual producer and consumer.

207

In the area studied, coffee is sold directly to traders who export it to larger commercial centres. From the same middlemen an Indian farmer buys his supply of potatoes, salt, unrefined sugar, etc. Traders concentrate in the relatively more densely populated areas or at key points along the few roads that cross the territory. Farmers living farther away, of either Indian or White extraction, have to bear the cost of transport to the closest buyer. Transport difficulties, as well as danger from bandits, have discouraged ambulant traders from venturing inland. As a result, there is no extensive chain of intermediaries, as one finds in other peasant societies. The buyers may be individuals residing locally or in larger commercial centres. No subsistence crop is exported from Tierradentro, and some staples are imported.

Owing to transportation difficulties and low population density, there is no close-knit network of market-places throughout rural areas. Nor are these areas interconnected by a large number of ambulant traders who may one day visit a market, and then move to another. Ambulant traders attend one or two local markets and, if they move farther away, it is only to remain there for the whole of a harvesting season. Markets are served from larger commercial centres.

Regional price fluctuations are quite marked. The purchase of potatoes, for example, in one area for resale in the next market could bring high revenues. But cost of transport discourages such ventures. A middleman would have to find a seller – which might not be an easy thing to do unless he travelled far and wide – and then bear the cost of difficult transport to the market centre, and storage of products until the sale was made.

A similar problem is encountered by Indians who may want to consider production of subsistence goods for local consumption. Production for sale would have to be in large enough volume to attract outside buyers (if and when it succeeded in attracting them). If the food was intended for local sale, then the demand would have to be large enough to warrant its production. This was not the case in San Andrés; in fact, if about 15 Indians had doubled their food-crop production, they would have managed to supply all White farmers.

Food may be exchanged between producer and consumer by

special agreement. A Pácz farmer does not offer food for sale on the market-place, but to special clients who may belong to his community or to the community of White traders ánd coffee-growers. What is important to note is that, with rare exceptions, food is offered only to clients; the individuals must be bound by reciprocal obligation for a Páez to consider the transaction worth while. This is not because food is given a different value from other goods, but because limiting exchanges in this way has served to minimize the risk of famine. A farmer may purchase or borrow food from another with the understanding that he will lend or sell him food on another occasion. Thus, a shortage of cash will not lead to starvation. A Pácz will sell to a Colombian peasant if he is willing to reciprocate with small favours (e.g. credit). Even if he sells his food for a price, it will be lower than the ongoing market price. Indian wages are lower and their level of subsistence would be considerably lower if, when in need, they had to buy food at the rates established on the basis of the acquisitive power of better-remunerated White labourers. It is thus not surprising that Indians selling food consistently in the market place, or selling after refusal to exchange it with an Indian or Colombian client, are heavily criticized.

Distribution among clients serves as a means of coping with uncertainty. It is equivalent to an institutionalized insurance mechanism. The sanctions regulating the arrangements are both social and economic and the amounts demanded and the identity of the demandant are known.

Cyclical nature of farming revenue

Patterns of investment depend to a certain extent on the timing of cash revenue from farming activities, since credit facilities or loans are not made available to most farmers. Coffee-farming and labouring in coffee plantations during harvest season are the two main sources of cash earning to Páez Indians. Thus planning productive activities which required a cash investment could only be carried out after the coffee harvest.

The same pattern does not apply to household consumption patterns. It is true that beans, maize, potatoes have definite seasons, but the two main staples, manioc and plantains, are available all the year round. Certain basic commodities have to be purchased: kerosene, candles, soap, salt, sugar, and spices. Meat, clothing, and luxuries make extra demands on available cash resources. Chicken- and pig-farming supply a household with most of its meat requirements. Clothing purchases are delayed until money is readily available. I have calculated that the minimal annual cash requirements for regular purchases for an average household of two adults and three children is 243 Colombian pesos or the equivalent of 81 days of wage labouring by an adult male. This minimal budget requirement can be met by occasional work for Colombian peasants or by small sales of one or two pounds of beans in order to purchase sufficient salt or kerosene. In other words, in Páez economy, the cyclical nature of their main cash crop affects only productive investment or the fulfilment of certain social obligations (feasts, weddings, baptisms) rather than seriously interfering with daily household consumption.

Social and political organization

Each farmer, as a member of the Indian community, has moral and legal rights to receive aid from other members of his community, namely, kinsmen, friends, neighbours, or administrators. These people represent his human resources; if he so chooses, he may mobilize them as labourers or as a source of credit, cash, food at special rates, or special favours. These rights are backed by vague moral sanctions. One works for a kinsman or a friend if the kinsman and friend have been helpful. Kinship and friendship ties are a valid excuse for initiating a request, but kinsmen, other than parents or siblings, can refuse without difficulty. Furthermore, parents have, in fact, very little authority over their grown children, who in turn are divided among themselves by arguments and fights over land. Once an economic and social interchange is established its continuation is backed by the threat to withdraw reciprocal obligations. This means that a Páez Indian must cultivate his friends and kinsmen if he wants help from them. He must visit them once in a while, invite them for a drink when he grinds sugar-cane or gives a feast.

Social rewards and punishment not only sanction behaviour

but also motivate specified actions. Social stratification, the possibilities for social mobility, and the means necessary to achieve it may guide a particular line of economic action. But it must be remembered that peasant societies are not self-contained and that a peasant farmer can opt for 'traditional' social rewards or for rewards intrinsic to the market economy, in this case to non-Indian peasant society.

Given such a heterogeneous population, an individual is always faced with a number of alternatives. The choice may be motivated by one of the two 'value systems' (Indian or Colombian) or, more likely, by what he knows the outcome of his actions will be from his own experience. At the moment when the choice is made he is already interacting with some Indians and some non-Indian peasants. If he manages to accumulate enough money to buy a horse, a suit of clothes, etc., he may be treated with greater respect by the non-Indian peasants he is in contact with and perhaps he may be invited to gamble with them.

A farmer may accumulate enough money through luck, or ability to make the 'right' decisions, or ruthlessness, or any combination of these qualities. Theoretically speaking, social mobility from Indian to Colombian peasant or Colombian urban worker is possible, and in my community I could cite examples of individuals who had ceased to be Indians simply by virtue of their economic success and willingness to socialize with traders rather than just with poor Indian farmers. But these examples are rare because the resources and opportunities open to Indians are limited.

The choice to expand cash enterprises has to be made early in life, particularly in the case of coffee. But at that time an Indian may not have had enough experience with non-Indian peasants to want to intensify contact with them. Early efforts are probably, in such cases, directed to a diversification of production in order to minimize risk, to allocate scarce labour resources better, and to fulfil social obligations. Within the context of the Latin-American Indian situation, the apparent unwillingness of some Indians to give up certain 'traditional' expenditures and systems of distribution may not be because community solidarity and economic equality are highly valued. I suggest that a

211

closer scrutiny of the economics of the distributive mechanism will bring to our attention relations of consumption and production factors that will uphold a more positive economic function than is otherwise contended, in this case the minimization of uncertainty and the stimulation of food production. Within the community all members are considered equal. Differential prestige is the only distinction made between individuals and it rests purely on personal qualities such as ability, friendliness, and hospitality. A capable man is, of course, a good farmer but it is difficult for a poor Indian to offer hospitality to his friends and kinsmen. Thus wealth is just as important for success within the community as outside the community. However, if an Indian becomes very wealthy he is regarded with a mixture of admiration and suspicion. He is suspected of having withdrawn help and hospitality from friends and kin and of attempting to break away from them and to become non-Indian. An Indian who has a good number of cows or a successful coffee plantation must decide whether he wants to spend his money to get support and admiration from Colombian peasants or reinvest his capital in strengthening his ties with Indian kinsmen and friends. In this last instance he will offer a feast to dispel any doubts about his hospitality. His decision will rest on his evaluation of the situation and the chance of being admitted into non-Indian circles.

Sanctions are important to ensure that contractual agreements are carried out. In the case of Páez Indians, practically speaking, there are no legal sanctions that could be applied to Indians who did not fulfil their contractual obligations. Theoretically, Colombian authority should interfere when appeal to them is made, but in practice they do not want to be bothered with Indians. Therefore contractual arrangements are restricted to individuals with whom one has already established reciprocal exchanges. Money or resources are not otherwise loaned. Colombians also have great difficulty in collecting debts through municipal authorities, and, as a result, local traders are not willing to extend credit except to special clients.

Land is inherited. Traditionally, a family could expand farms by clearing virgin land, but nowadays all available reservation land has been allocated. Only sons can inherit land, except when

212

descendants are only females. Ideally, the land should be equally divided among sons, but since they receive the lot at time of marriage and at a period when offspring are able to challenge parental authority, the amount of land assigned to each of them depends on the ability of each son to bargain for a better or larger lot by offering or threatening to withdraw labour co-operation from the parental farm. To a certain extent this depends on the number of sons, the age-span between them, the extension of the parental farms, and the extra-familial labour resources available to the father. But it also rests on the managerial ability of Indians to bargain for a larger lot than they would otherwise receive.

It is illegal to transfer land from one family to another, either by gift or by sale. Land can be borrowed on a short-term basis, but since there is a general shortage of land, it is infrequently done. Indians can expand their fields by purchasing land outside of the reservation, but high land prices in adjacent territory make expansion difficult. An Indian can only afford land on the more distant mountain ranges but unless he has enough capital to invest in cattle-raising this will not be worth while. The only other real possibility for expansion is to become a tenant of a wealthier Colombian farmer. In exchange for a lot of land, theoretically of undefined size – practically usually restricted to 2 or 3 acres – the Indian has to give three days a month of free labour to his landlord, whenever it is requested. As these requests conflict with the labour needs of the Indian farmer, Indians become tenants only when absolutely necessary.

MANAGERIAL DECISIONS

I have already indicated that in order to understand the outcome of decisions it is not enough to consider preferences, expectations, and uncertainties within a model of rationality; the process of decision-making should also be considered. I have raised two questions in the first section of this paper which, I believe, are of the utmost importance in understanding outcomes:

1. What are the factors that determine whether or not a managerial act is posed as a problem that requires a decision?

2. How is a decision arrived at? Does the process affect the outcome of the decision or not?

Páez farmers plant subsistence crops and coffee trees. From what has been said so far, it will be useful to answer the above questions in terms of the choice involved in coffee and subsistence agriculture separately, not because they constitute entirely separate spheres of activities, but because they can be used as two examples which convey clearly the relationship between process and outcome. In the following sections I will show how the organization of economic activity defines the moment of decision and how this in turn will affect action.

Coffee plantations

Coffee is planted only after careful consideration by members of a household. Plantations are started once and sometimes twice in the lifetime of a farmer. Once the shade and coffee trees have been planted peasants do not seriously consider expansion. They will concentrate their efforts on weeding and at most replacing a few dying trees. It is not just because coffee trees produce for about 15 years, but also because Páez peasants think of cash-crop expansion as involving two sets of choices:

1. They use their limited land resources either for new coffee plantations or for subsistence crops.
2. They either retain the good will and cooperation of their children by giving them land when of age, or they expand their fields.

When a young Indian marries, or perhaps even before, he will start to plan his new fields. He must then decide how much coffee to plant and will do this by evaluating his chances of being successful as cash-crop grower and the resources available to him. The original plantation does not require a high capital investment if exchange labour is used. If he has a fair amount of land he might be able to plant enough coffee, at least during two seasons, to become independent of other Indian farmers. During the first few years he will need little in terms of cash-crop requirements, except what he may need to feed labourers. Later on in life, if he is successful enough, he will be able to add to his

214

family's diet with purchased goods. But if he thinks it is unlikely that he will ever be able to produce much coffee because of the restricted amount of land available, the poor quality of the land, or the altitude, he will make sure to reserve enough acres to plant subsistence crops for his own needs and to exchange with others.

A Páez farmer will not think of planting coffee again unless his own brothers die before his father, and he thus receives more land than expected, or if he has only daughters or perhaps just one son, who will make minimal demands on his land resources. It is unlikely that he will increase his cash assets to such an extent that later on in life he will not need to depend on subsistence farming. If he is thinking in terms of the latter, he will invest in pigs or a cow.

Thus limitation of resources and subsistence farming – as a means of resolving how to eat if the coffee-harvest does not produce enough to buy sufficient food and to pay labourers – define decision-making in coffee agriculture as a conscious act which takes place once, or at most twice, in the lifetime of a farmer.

The choices made proved to be rational in most cases. On the whole Indians did not only consider what would be a suitable combination of resources but were able to evaluate future expected returns. They were not extremely daring and there were no spectacular successes or failures. Low-cost planting techniques were preferred. This can be explained by the fact that coffee prices had fluctuated greatly in the past years, and farmers expected continued price changes. Capital investments were made to improve harvesting and processing methods (hiring efficient labourers; equipment to hull, dry, and select beans) in order to increase yield and improve the quality of the product. These expenditures were incurred shortly before harvest-time when the farmer had some information about ongoing prices and crop yields, and could therefore estimate revenue. The personality of the particular farmer, the amount of confidence he had at the age of about twenty in his ability to handle cash or bargain with traders, as well as coffee prices at the time, affected his decision. But increase in price could not encourage him to plant more trees later on in life. At most an increase in price will encourage an Indian farmer to harvest and dry the beans with more care and weed the plantation a sufficient number of times to ensure the greatest possible yields.

Decisions are carefully planned, not only because they are taken once in a lifetime, but also because starting a new plantation requires a concentrated amount of effort and the outcome of this decision affects the total organization of production. Planters have to be approached in advance to obtain the required number of saplings (which are given free of charge), and food would have to be grown or purchased for the extra labourers.

Advice of other farmers is asked and discussed for a long time. Future expectations and past experience are taken into account. Their decision is determined by resources and risks involved. Farmers are not willing to threaten their very basic subsistence, but otherwise they attempt to maximize cash resources as far as possible by planting as much coffee as they can when they are young.

The factors taken into account are those which a farmer controls, either directly or indirectly. If he controls them, he can then have a sufficient degree of certainty as to the eventual availability of factors to allow him to state a decision. Weather, price fluctuations, etc., can only be estimated subjectively on the basis of past experiences. But a farmer is not able to predict whether a good year for yield or prices will be followed by a bad year, nor does he have the technical knowledge to determine annual variations in revenue. He expects a certain range of variation and makes his original decision in terms of what he thinks vaguely is most likely to be his revenue and on what he thinks may be his lowest revenue. These were the two estimates farmers discussed among themselves. Prices are taken into account only in so far as they are expected to rise and fall within a certain range; more specific calculations are not made, and would, in fact, be an impossible task for a peasant farmer. In the case of coffee, readjustments to price changes are difficult because it takes the trees four years to produce, and they continue to bear for at least fifteen years. But, in general, I would not expect a farmer to readjust to small fluctuations, except when the new price is known, that is, at harvest-time and by improving or intensifying his harvest activities. Prices are taken into account as factors in decision-making only when they fall below the lowest expected revenue.

Subsistence crops

Planting of subsistence crops (manioc, maize, potatoes, beans, sugar-cane, etc., depending on altitude) can be done at least twice a year and, in fact, some (like manioc) can be planted at almost any time during the year. Extensive fields cannot be prepared for planting except during the short dry-season; but smaller plots, in fields already cleared of heavy vegetation, can be used at other times.

Scarcity of labour resources and flexibility of the agricultural cycle account for the fact that tasks are carried out when the farmer is able to work himself. Often a task is not completed during a continuous span of time because of multiple demands on his own labour potential. An Indian may be called to pay off his debts by working in a trader's fields, or to repay exchange labour, or to process sugar-cane to make a contribution of drink for a feast. It is easier to plant when time is available than to sort out the multiple demands made on his own labour. It is too expensive to hire or contract exchange labour and such arrangements are reserved for clearing and weeding tasks, considered to be too heavy or too boring to do by himself.

Exclusion of crops from open market exchanges means that it is not important to combine resources in order to increase productivity in unlimited fashion. A small amount of food may be sold; but the marginal return is so small that even if allowed to sell freely, food crops are not likely to be planted in order to increase cash revenue. Cash enterprises are limited to coffee production, cattle- or pig-breeding, sugar production, and wage labour. Thus need for cash increases the number of demands made on labour resources. An Indian farmer does not have full control over these demands; for example, he has to work in the landlord's field when he is called and not when he is free to do so.

It is more important to time the planting or harvesting of a crop properly according to the specific need it will satisfy, than to fix agricultural tasks according to a preconceived evaluation of optimum combination of resources. If a woman becomes

217

pregnant, or a close kinsman dies, cash and/or food will be required, and more food may have to be planted.

Thus there is no single critical moment at which decisions have to be made. Only partial decisions are normally made and a careful plan that will encompass all the various future subsistence activities is never drawn up. Decisions concerning resource allocation are made when the resource is made available, and then alternatives are evaluated against the particular resource. When a farmer has a small amount of cash (apart from the proceeds from coffee plantations or the sale of animals), he decides at once how he will employ it. When he is free to work he will decide on the spot whether to plant more, or weed the existing fields, etc. This means that tasks are not always adequately coordinated and resources may be wasted. But, on the other hand, time is not unnecessarily spent making plans which farmers will not be able to implement.

Input and output relations are not carefully evaluated; in fact, it is almost impossible to do so when tasks are never completed within a short period of time. The amount produced is more critical in subsistence agriculture than the cost of production. I do not mean to imply that Indians do not take into account that in their particular field maize does not produce a very good yield and that it is best instead to expand their plots of manioc or beans. However, finer evaluations of resource combinations are not necessary.

When decisions are made in advance, the task is simplified by considering only the obvious factors of production, the obvious resources, and the obvious ends required. In order to be able to make a decision, the model describing means-ends relations must be kept simple. An individual must also have set expectations and believe in them. Since only minimal information is available when a decision is made in advance, models are not too complicated.

When a farmer makes his decision as he is planting, the obvious is of a very different nature from that of decisions made in advance, and he focuses on the obvious. It is the size and quality of the stem of manioc which he is planting that will make him decide whether or not it will produce and how many tubers it is likely to bear. He will plant more tubers if the stems he is using are not of good quality, if rains do not hamper his work, if he is not exhausted, and so on. This is what I mean when I say that Indians plant until they can *see* they have enough[10]; there is no exact measure of how much is enough. The number of relevant factors that would have to be taken into account at the moment of planting is too great for all of them to be considered; to do so would make choice impossible. Unconsciously, an Indian minimizes the number of factors by concentrating on what is obvious at the moment: the resources available at that point and the future needs which that particular crop can satisfy.

The nature of the decision-making process in subsistence agriculture affects disadvantageously an efficient combination of resources, but it allows for the readjustment of agricultural activities as the needs of the family change from month to month. This constant readjustment is automatically made because change in needs constitutes one of the obvious elements in the mind of the Indian. Is it not the main purpose of subsistence agriculture to satisfy a set of well-defined wants by producing directly for their satisfaction? With this qualification in mind, the process of decision-making is well adapted to its task.

CONCLUSIONS

An analysis of Páez farming behaviour has elucidated one important point that ought to be considered in economic behavioural analysis. A model of decision-making based, for example, on combined coffee and subsistence crops would not have been able to forecast output in the subsistence sector, and discrepancies would have to be accounted for by difficulties in implementing the decisions previously arrived at. It would be serious if new opportunities, offered to farmers on the basis of these models, were not made use of by the intended peasants. This failure would not necessarily be due to an unwillingness to accept alternatives or innovations, but to the fact that they cannot be integrated within the decision-making process, and thus they are never evaluated against other relevant preferences. To give an example, the price of beans was considerably higher during the year I was in residence than it had ever been before. When the beans had to be harvested the farmer was then faced with the decision of selling them or consuming them. His decision was based on his preference of one over the other, the amount harvested, and the availability of the buyer. Though in this case it is fair to say that producers had knowledge and reason to believe that the price would remain high long enough for them to plant, harvest, and profit from the venture, they did not plant. One would have expected them to do so, if their behaviour was to be in accordance with decision-making in the coffee sector. The discrepancy would have to be explained as, by assuming that they act rationally at some times and not others, or that cash is ranked in preference higher than coffee but lower than food, or that there are two entirely separate economic sectors which are defined not only by the nature of the goods produced, and the utilization of the same, but also by the fact that one is associated with 'traditional' behaviour and the other with 'rational', market-oriented behaviour. I am sure that there are other possible explanations which may ring true in that particular context. But although a relatively recent crop, coffee has come to be regarded as no less 'traditional' than subsistence farming. The amount of coffee produced depends on the availability of land for subsistence crops, and the bulk of manioc produced depends on the money expectations to buy subsistence foods or meet other payments that could be made in kind. If one takes into account the process of decision-making, then it will be clear that the alternatives considered for bean-planting would be different from those operative when coffee-planting only is considered. If bean prices remain high for a number of years, farmers are likely to discuss the possibility of treating beans as a cash crop, and substitution or diversification of cash crops may occur, as has already happened in the change from wheat to coffee.

What I have pointed out in this study is that choice does not depend on preference, expectations, and uncertainty alone. The number of alternatives as well as the expectation do depend on the information available and consequently vary with the individual. There is a more fundamental point: unlike the gambler who is confronted with a set of odds and pay-offs, the farmer confronts himself with his set of choices. This confrontation is not simply regulated by some internal ideological or psychological mechanism. It is mainly determined by the organization of productive activities. Which factors are considered as alternatives, and when, is then not a matter of chance. Different choices may not imply a contradictory scale of preferences, but decision A may have involved consideration of a different set of factors from those affecting decision B.

Fieldwork amongst Páez peasant farmers has made it possible for me to follow up closely the processes of decision-making in production. It was observed how solutions depended on how the decision was arrived at, and in this study I have shown two distinct types of decision-making. I do not postulate here that there will be the same two types of processes in all societies; I suggest only that decisions may be arrived at in more than one way.

In the two types cited, we have seen how the decision process affected the output. Some decisions are made before the task is organized; other decisions are left to be made on the spot. When decisions are made before the task is organized, factors relevant to the production of that particular crop are taken into account and marginal returns are evaluated. Indians explore alternatives and even consider the re-introduction of wheat as a cash crop. Where decisions coincide with action, decisions are piecemeal, and are evaluated in terms of needs, and of resources made available at that particular moment. In this case it is unlikely that individual farmers will search for new alternatives, or for means of freeing resources. Thus production of food will not increase as much as factors would allow.

The timing and the process of decision-making determine with how much care planning will be carried out and how thoroughly alternative possibilities will be evaluated. Conscious planning of coffee-planting allows for more long-term decisions but for minimal readjustment after decisions are made, while in subsistence farming, decisions can be corrected through the course of the year.

I have indicated that the individual producers unconsciously select for consideration what to them are the obvious elements at the time a decision is taken. The level of uncertainty as conceptualized by a farmer has to be taken into account when we summarize models of decision-making. Risk over and above a minimal level of subsistence may not affect behaviour in the same way as the risk of losing the only source of subsistence, particularly if there is no operative insurance mechanism. It was my experience, when talking to Páez farmers, that if, owing to the economic position and degree of specialization, the level of uncertainty was high, farmers were very conscious of impending danger and much more likely to consider the risk inherent in any enterprise. Food-producers with no coffee plantations, or very small ones, have an assured minimum subsistence – the inter-community loans and sales already discussed – and therefore are less likely to be concerned with the risk entailed in, for example, pig- or cattle-farming. In fact, it is only this type of farmer who keeps a large number of pigs. The same holds true for the wealthier farmer who can apply for government loans. Thus the subsistence producer and the wealthy coffee-producer are more concerned with the relation between return and risk than with risk *per se*. The small producer who does not have enough land or labour to plant food crops as well, or who does not have enough kinsmen and friends to exchange with, is very concerned with ensuring his subsistence by avoiding any enterprises that may seriously affect it. In fact, discussions on farming are, in the case of these farmers, preceded by complaints about possible risks. The decisions of these farmers are bound to be more cautious and conservative. They reduce risk by diversifying productive enterprise.

There is another type of decision that I have not considered here, for lack of space, and because it falls more or less in the first type. If a new opportunity which will bring a cash reward is made available, for example, purchasing a pig or a cow for breeding, an Indian makes the decision on the spot. At that moment he carefully evaluates not only the risk entailed and the return expected, but also the chances that the same opportunity will be available in the future. For ecological reasons, none of the farmers studied could consider dedicating most of their efforts to cattle-breeding or pig-farming.

What is postulated in this study is that the particular set of factors taken into account depends on the timing of the decision, and this in turn is determined by the organization of productive activities. A farmer starts, continues, and stops planting, following production programmes arrived at in the course of previous years. Decisions are, of course, taken all the time; to initiate an action or cease the action, implies a decision. But, as we have seen, these action-oriented decisions do not call for an evaluation of all relevant factors.[11] Only when there is a basic change in the organization of economic activities will plans be considered carefully and decisions made. Thus what determines changes in output are changes in the structure of the situation. A change of a factor may not be sufficient unless that change is responsible for subsequent changes which will sufficiently alter the context of economic activities to stimulate the definition of a decision point. Price changes by themselves may not bring about the definition of a decision-making point, they may only stimulate a readjustment of an existing situation in order to take advantage – within the scope of the already established means of production – of higher revenue or of a decrease in revenue.

It is impossible at this point to suggest an hypothesis that would define the decision-making points in agricultural production at such a peasant level. I can only point out some of the factors that ought to be taken into account, and add that such a model will help to solve some of the riddles encountered in attempts to predict the behaviour of individuals and of firms. There is no constant reconsideration of alternatives to maximize profit, nor a reconsideration until a so-called satisfactory level is reached. Reconsiderations only occur when organization of production is affected; until then, adjustments are made so as either to maintain or, if possible, to increase income, e.g. in the case of sale of beans, basically a subsistence crop.

In the course of the discussion, I have considered the following relevant factors:

- social and economic rewards;
- availability of resources;
- institutional means of reducing uncertainty;
- economic organization (which in this particular case leads to what I call the ego-orientation of decisions);
- technical aspects of agriculture;
- interdependence of productive activities.

These factors fall into three categories: objectives, controlled variables, and uncontrolled variables. An individual may change his objective or objectives, and may attain them by a recombination of controlled variables. Uncontrolled variables will affect the level of uncertainty, which may be high enough to require perhaps a reconsideration of his objectives, or may be too high and equally affect alternatives to make preferential choice impossible. These categories are systematically related to each other, and a testable model of decision-timing should be based on their functional relations.[12]

Any attempts at influencing allocation of resources by providing the farmer with carefully investigated solutions, either by means of farm budgeting or linear programming, will affect the purpose of decisions. I can foresee no obvious problem when the decision refers to the cash sector of the economy. But when the solution applies to the subsistence sector it would seem to me that it would reduce the efficiency of the farmer. It will change the orientation of the decision from ego's needs to market's need, i.e. more food products. In the first place, the farmer's needs may unforeseeably change during the course of the year. Secondly, his constant re-evaluation of his decisions allows him to make the best use of his resources and balance out conflicting demands. In order not to affect the peculiarities of part-subsistence peasant farming, i.e. low-cost production and adaptability, it may be more useful to set decision problems only in the cash sector of the economy and allow the farmer to decide how and when he will plant his food crops.[13] Technical information may suffice to improve the marginal utility of his labour in the subsistence sector.

Any attempt at problem-solving should take into account not only any commitments that a farmer may have towards other members of his community and the economic value of such commitments, but also the fact that these commitments change through his lifetime. In other words, there are optimum times for expansion of certain enterprises, according to given social and economic factors. These will vary from society to society. It may be more useful to determine the optimum points than to attempt a uniform development of farms.

It is obvious from the information presented here that Páez

farmers would greatly profit from any efforts to supply them with technological information, cheap devices to increase productivity, and better credit facilities. Yet these simple and obvious solutions raise a number of problems – for example: (*a*) what are the best means of reaching such a heterogeneous and widely scattered population? (*b*) is the existing formal organization suitable for such a task, or should existing informal channels be utilized, or again should a new organization be created?

Land shortage is one of the serious local problems. Granting of individual titles would certainly allow for a redistribution of land. It will also mean that poor managers might be tempted to sell their land, thus freeing their own labour potential which could be used by other more capable farmers. But before sponsoring such a recommendation, we must ask who is likely to buy Indian land? In Tierradentro it is not going to be better managers who buy the land, but the local speculators, who will eventually resell it, either to another Indian farmer, or to a Colombian peasant (both probably incompetent), or to a wealthy landlord with Indian tenants. The result will be that land thus transferred will not yield higher productivity and that the ineffective poor farmer will become still poorer. Furthermore, land sales would have an important socio-economic result – they would affect the permanence of the reservation population, and with it assurance that individuals on whom a farmer has to depend will continue to be his neighbours.

Much has been said recently about the suitability of small-holdings for the production of certain cash crops such as coffee; peasant farmers can be low-cost producers. Some argue as well that subsistence farming allows the peasant to face a greater margin of risk than he would otherwise be able to cope with. I would add here that food production has the same inherent uncertainties as cash-crop production, and that if a peasant is going to plant food crops, so as to assure his family's subsistence, he will have to insure against failure of these crops as well. Thus, before any reorganization of peasant farming is attempted, one ought to establish first: (*a*) the institutional means of coping with risk and (*b*) how reorganization would affect risk. If so, what other insurance mechanism can be developed, so as not to affect the efficiency of small peasant holdings?

Sutti Ortiz

NOTES

1. Fieldwork among the Páez Indians was made possible by a grant from the Organization of American States.
2. There is, of course, a considerable list of publications on the subject. The most relevant studies of Latin-American peasant economies are: Tax (1953) and, with particular reference to Colombia, Fals-Borda (1955).
3. Mary Douglas (1962), in a study of Lele economy, shows how preference for certain techniques – in spite of awareness of more efficient methods – rests on Lele institutions and environment.
4. For a discussion of the importance of the inclusion of expectations in the model of decision-making, as well as for a review of relevant hypotheses, see Ozga (1965).
5. Many are the implications of the rational model of economic man. I have not attempted here a thorough discussion of all the ramifications of the concepts used. For more detailed discussion see Das Gupta (1964) and Arrow (1951, 1963).
6. For a discussion of problems relating to decision-making and the use of decision-making models, see Oxenfeldt (1963), Simon (1959), and Katona (1953).
7. For a discussion of 'peasant' as an analytical type, see Firth (1964), Fallers (1961), and Wolf (1955).
8. Lack of autonomy and authority of local government is not unique to hinterland areas. Fals Borda (1955, 1957) cites a similar case for the Departments of Cundinamarca and Boyacá.
9. For a discussion of the relevance of ideologies to economic behaviour, see Smelser (1963) and Samuelson (1957).
10. In discussion of my conference paper, Audrey Richards pointed out that careful measurement of crops as well as means used to compare yields quantitatively reflect attitudes about production. One should consider the wants a particular crop satisfies, in order to understand how its yield is evaluated.
11. Raymond Firth has suggested that a typology of decision should be taken into account when discussing factors affecting the process of decision-making. He has proposed a threefold classification:

(a) policy decisions; (b) management decisions; and (c) operational decisions. These classifications will certainly help comparative studies of decision-making process. See Firth (1965, pp. 28-31) for further discussion of this point.
12. Halter and Dean (1965), in an article on the use of simulation models, describe the outcome of farm-management decisions and point out, just as I have attempted to do for peasant farming here, that the technique of production as well as the exogenous character of price fluctuations determines the elements which are considered in the decision-making process. In the cattle-ranch case discussed, decisions about cattle purchases depend on cattle and feed prices, capacity of feedlot and price of slaughtering. The authors make use of models which simulate actual decisions and evaluate desirability of policy. It is assumed that certain decision points are more critical in the production process. However, it is not taken into account that, if there is a change in the definition of the decision point, it will affect factors taken into account. In the case analysed, decision points are discussed as if they depended solely on techniques of production.
13. Another relevant problem is how Páez Indians react when faced with uncertainty or new opportunities; this would require the analysis of further detailed case material and is beyond the scope of this paper.

REFERENCES

AGARWALA, A. N. & SINGH, S. P. (eds.). 1963. *The Economics of Underdevelopment*. New York: Galaxy.

ARROW, KENNETH J. 1951. Alternative Approaches to the Theory of Choice in Risk-Taking Situations. *Econometrica* 19: 404-437.

—— 1963. *Social Choice and Individual Values*. New York: Wiley.

BERNAL, VILLA, SEGUNDO. 1955. Bases para el Estudio de la Organización Social de los Páez. *Revista Colombiana de Antropologia* 61. 165-188.

DALTON, G. 1962. Traditional Production in Primitive African Economies. *Quarterly Journal of Economics* 76: 360-378.

DAS GUPTA. SIPRA, 1964. Producers' Rationality and Technical Change in Agriculture with Special Reference to India. Unpublished Ph.D. Dissertation. University of London.

DOUGLAS, M. 1962. The Lele Economy Compared with Bushongo: A Study of Economic Backwardness. In P. Bohannan & G. Dalton, 1963, *Markets in Africa*, pp. 211-233. Evanston: Northwestern University Press.

EDWARDS, D. 1961. *An Economic Study of Small Farming in Jamaica*. Glasgow: Maclehose.

FALLERS, A. L. 1961. Are African Cultivators to be Called Peasants? *Current Anthropology* 2 (2): 108-110.

FALS BORDA, O. 1955. *Peasant Society in Colombian Andes: A Sociological Study of Saucio*. Gainsville: University of Florida Press.

—— 1957. *El Hombre y la Tierra en Boyacá: Bases Sociológicas e Históricas para una Reforma Agraria*. Bogotá: Antares.

FIRTH, RAYMOND. 1964. Capital, Saving and Credit in Peasant Societies: A Viewpoint from Economic Anthropology. In R. Firth & B. S. Yamey, *Capital, Saving and Credit in Peasant Societies*, pp. 15-34. London: Allen and Unwin.

—— 1965. *Primitive Polynesian Economy*. London: Routledge & Kegan Paul.

FOOD AND AGRICULTURE ORGANIZATION. 1958. *Coffee in Latin America*. New York.

GUZMÁN CAMPOS, G., FALS BORDA, O. & UMAÑA LUNA, E. 1964. *La Violencia en Colombia*. Bogotá: Ediciones Tercer Mundo.

HALTER, A. N. & DEAN, G. W. 1965. Use of Simulation in Evaluating Management Policies under Uncertainty; Application to a Large Scale Ranch. *Journal of Farm Economics* 47(3): 557-573.

227

KATONA, G. 1953. Rational Behaviour and Economic Behaviour. *Psychological Review* **60**: 307-318.

MEIER, G. M. 1963. The Problem of Limited Economic Development. In A. N. Agarwala & S. P. Singh, 1963.

NEUMANN, J. VON & MORGENSTERN, O. 1964. *Theory of Games and Economic Behavior*. New York: Wiley.

OXENFELDT, A. R. (ed.). 1963. *Models of Markets*. New York: Columbia University Press.

OŻGA, S. A. 1965. *Expectations in Economic Theory*. London: Weidenfeld & Nicolson.

SAMUELSON, K. 1957. *Religion and Economic Action*. London: Heinemann.

SCHULTZ, T. W. 1964. *Transforming Traditional Agriculture*. New Haven: Yale University Press.

SIMON, H. A. 1959. Theories of Decision-Making in Economics. *American Economic Review* **49**: 253-283.

SMELSER, N. J. 1963. *The Sociology of Economic Life*. Englewood Cliffs, New Jersey: Prentice-Hall.

TAX, SOL. 1953. *Penny Capitalism, A Guatemalan Indian Economy*. Smithsonian Institution. Publication 16. Washington: U.S. Govt. Printing Office.

WOLF, E. 1955. Types of Latin American Peasantry: a Preliminary Discussion. *American Anthropologist* **57**: 452-471.

Scarlett Epstein

Productive Efficiency and Customary Systems of Rewards in Rural South India

INTRODUCTION

Economics is concerned with the phenomena of production and distribution. Market and non-market economies alike have to meet the same problems: goods have to be produced and distributed among the population. It is on the former that economists have concentrated their attention. At the same time they have tended to neglect the interactions and conflicts between the market and other social institutions. However, in the study of societies which are changing over from non-market to market economies such factors cannot be so easily ignored. Since the majority of the world's population lives in societies where this transition is now occurring, the development of underdeveloped areas has become a central problem in world affairs, and a central concern of economists and others. Ways and means have to be devised to increase output so as to allow for a surplus to be sold, by which the economy is incorporated in the market system. Economic development involves here not only the use of new and more productive methods, it also depends on the presence of appropriate incentives which will induce the population to adopt the new techniques. In these circumstances, therefore, the recognition of the interplay of all social institutions becomes particularly important. This probably explains why economists have developed so few models to show the working of traditional non-market economies. They have concentrated their attention rather on the emerging and growing capitalist sector (Lewis, 1954, pp. 139-191, and 1958; pp. 1-32). Yet in order to establish the conditions for the emergence and growth of a capitalist sector in underdeveloped countries an understanding of the principles underlying the customary non-market economies is essential. Apart from its purely theoretical interest, this is necessary to explain why some development schemes are successful and others fail; why the indigenous population of underdeveloped areas is prepared to react positively to some new economic opportunities and not to others.

Here I seek to explore some of these issues by focusing on hereditary labour relationships as they operate in India. My analysis is concerned to examine the implications of this system for productive efficiency, for the principles that underlie it and the way in which these differ from forms of capitalist economic organization. I shall show the importance of average productivity in underdeveloped Indian villages as opposed to the emphasis placed on marginal productivity in industrial economies.

THE JAJMANI SYSTEM

Economists sometimes assume that all farming economies are composed of self-sufficient owner-occupier households (e.g. Lewis, 1954, p. 148). However, there are many rural societies in which members perform specialized functions: Indian farming communities with their complex division of labour provide a good example. The character of economic relationships in Indian villages is largely determined by the high degree of specialization that exists and by the particular sets of beliefs and observances that underlie and perpetuate this division of labour. It is in fact the caste system that throws into relief the complex division of labour in Indian society. A major feature of the caste system is that labour relationships between the land-owning castes and their dependent servicing castes are usually hereditary and rewards are paid annually in the form of fixed quantities of farming produce.

In the past, villages were largely self-sufficient; goods and services were mutually exchanged by the different specialist castes within small rural communities. Services and duties which the various castes performed for one another and the rewards associated with these were regulated by a socio-economic system known as the *jajmani* system. According to Sanscritic Indian usage, '*jajmani*' refers to a client who receives religious services and gives gifts in return for them. But, following Wiser, the term *jajmani* has come to be accepted for the system as a whole. He defined *jajmani* as follows: 'These service relationships reveal that the priest, bard, accountant, goldsmith, florist, vegetable grower, etc. etc. are served by all the other castes. They are the *jajmans* of these other castes. In turn each of these castes has a form of service to perform for the others. Each in turn is master. Each in turn is servant. Each has his own clientele comprising members of different castes which is his *"jajmani"* or *"birt"*. This system of interrelatedness in service within the Hindu community is called the Hindu *"jajmani* system" ' (Wiser, 1958, p. xxi). Beidelman has criticized Wiser for describing a Hindu caste village as a system of idyllic mutuality, whereas in reality castes are linked in unequal relationships based upon power (1959, p. 6). This asymmetrical dimension of the *jajmani* system had its roots in land tenure, numerical predominance, political influence, and ritual differentiation in the caste hierarchy. From this point of view, Gould has described *jajmani* as 'a matter of landowning, wealth and power controlling castes providing a structurally fixed share of their agricultural produce along with numerous "considerations", in exchange for craft and menial services rendered by the mainly landless impoverished, politically weak lower castes' (1958, p. 431). Similarly, Beidelman speaks of *jajmani* as 'a feudalistic system of prescribed hereditary obligations of payment and of occupational and ceremonial duties between two or more specific families of different castes in the same locality' (1959, p. 6). In short, where Wiser talks of mutual rights and obligations, Beidelman and Gould emphasize the high degree of economic and political differentiation characteristic of India's customary system of labour relations. On the face of it, these views of the *jajmani* system are plainly inconsistent. I shall try to show later, however, that both are in a sense correct; the inconsistency arises from the fact that each stresses only one aspect of the total system.

All writers on the *jajmani* system stress the point that rewards and duties were strictly defined. The interdependence between the different caste occupations was based on hereditary ties. Rewards were in terms of agricultural produce, and quantities were fixed. As a result, methods of work were handed down from generation to generation and a certain rhythm of

Q   231

productive activities became a fixed aspect of the Indian villager's life.

TYPES OF TRADITIONAL LABOUR RELATIONS

In order to understand the traditional economic relationships which have been described as falling within the *jajmani* system, their component parts and variations in different places and under different conditions must be made clear. The extreme form of *jajmani*, that is the prescribed hereditary relationship involving all castes in any one rural settlement, appears to have been largely limited to certain areas in North India. Yet the division of labour supported by the caste system, and expressed in the hereditary ties between different caste households, occurred to some extent in most Indian villages. Thus in Mysore in South India I found two types of hereditary link in the villages: one between Peasant[1] masters and their Untouchable labourers, the other between Peasants and certain functionary castes, such as Washerman, Barber, and Blacksmith, whose services were continually required. Village craftsmen, such as the Goldsmith and Potter, whose services were not in regular demand, had no hereditary relationship with Peasant caste households; they were not rewarded annually, but rather on the occasions when their services were required. In these Mysore villages landholding was vested in Peasants, who possessed what Srinivas has called 'decisive dominance' (1959, pp. 1-16), that is they dominated numerically, economically, politically, and also largely ritually. (There were no Brahmins in this village.) Though most of the servicing caste households had some land of their own, their holdings were too small to suffice for their subsistence. Therefore the castes with little land contributed their labour and/or skills to the life of the community and in return received a fixed share of the total agricultural output produced. These economic relations were, however, only one aspect of the multiple relations which linked the different caste households in the Indian village. For instance, the hereditary relationship between a Peasant master and his Untouchable labourer operated not only in the economic but also in the political and ritual spheres. If an Untouchable was involved in a dispute with another, whether Untouchable or not, his Peasant master had to come to his support. Similarly, the Untouchable allied himself with his Peasant master in disputes. He was expected to be prepared to fight for the latter, even against Untouchables aligned with other Peasants in conflict with his own master. Perhaps even more important, the Untouchable had to perform a number of ritual services for his Peasant master, such as carrying a torch ahead of a funeral procession from his master's household. These different types of relations – political, economic, and ritual – reinforced each other and in turn helped to ensure the stability of Indian peasant economies. Furthermore, the Hindu concepts of Karma (destiny) and Dharma (innate endowment), as well as beliefs in ritual pollution, stressed the maintenance of the *status quo*. Caste indeed pervaded the total complex of Indian society. There are, therefore, many aspects to caste relations. For the purpose of the present argument, however, we need concern ourselves only with the way in which the different aspects of the hereditary ties affected the purely economic part of the relationship. The more general social and political advantages, which, as we have seen, are part of the system of customary labour relationships, acted as additional incentive to landowners to meet their economic liabilities in good and bad harvest years alike. The non-economic aspects of labour relations are probably even more important from the workers' point of view. Not only are Untouchable labourers assured of a minimum subsistence level in bad harvests, but the hereditary relationship provides them with a benevolent master who is expected to look after them as a father provides for his children. In fact, the customary relationship between Peasant masters and Untouchable labourers is couched in kinship terms; a Peasant calls his Untouchable labourer his 'Old Son' (*Hale maga*). Moreover, by leading the good life of an Untouchable, a labourer can hope to be reborn into a higher caste in his next existence.

The caste system incorporated two types of economic relationship. There were strictly hereditary ties between landowners and their servicing castes; these were highly prescribed. There were also the less prescribed but more personally contractual relationships between landowners and certain artisan castes, such as Basketmaker and Potter, whose services were not in regular demand. The establishment of links with outside markets brought new economic opportunities to Indian villages. The possibility of selling crops and labour offered incentives to enterprising men to improve their productive efficiency. We can investigate, therefore, whether these different types of socio-economic relationship produced different reactions to the new opportunities. I shall illustrate my discussion mainly with material from two villages: Wangala, with its strictly prescribed hereditary system of rewards; and Dalena, where the diversification of economic activities had already largely undermined the traditional relationships (Epstein, 1962).

CUSTOMARY SYSTEMS OF REWARDS AND IMPROVED PRODUCTION TECHNIQUES

Following irrigation, Wangala lands required more and deeper ploughing. Farmers, therefore, had to replace their customary wooden ploughs with iron ones. Not only did these need more maintenance than wooden ploughs, but repairs also demanded greater skill. Wangala's Blacksmith, who had hereditary relations with Peasant farmers in the village, found that he had to learn how to repair the new iron ploughs. He also found that he was kept busier by his Peasant clients than he had been prior to irrigation. Yet his annual reward in kind remained the same. When he approached Peasant elders about an increase in the customary reward, they flatly refused it. They argued that it had been fixed by elders in the distant past and they saw no reason to increase the quantity of agricultural produce given annually to the Blacksmith, since it was still adequate to feed him.

The Blacksmith then carefully considered his position and came to the conclusion that it would be in his best interest to discontinue his hereditary relations with Peasant households altogether and work instead for cash. However, when he proposed this to Wangala's Peasant elders, who composed the village *panchayat*, they opposed his suggestion most strongly. They pointed out to him that relations which had lasted through generations could not be broken off at one stroke. It was, of course, in their own interest that the traditional arrangement should be maintained. They threatened that if the Blacksmith refused to perform his customary duties they would make his life in the village pretty much impossible. Since he had a small landholding in Wangala he was reluctant to move to another village. Nevertheless, being a very enterprising man, he was determined to be rid of his customary obligations, which he regarded as obstacles in his way to success. He wanted to be able to branch out into other activities, not directly connected with his craft, such as making doors and window-frames. He continued to argue with the Peasant elders until they finally offered a compromise. They suggested that if he could find some other Blacksmith prepared to carry on the traditional relations on customary terms, he himself would then be free to work as he liked. Wangala's Blacksmith managed to find a classificatory brother from another village who, as the youngest of a large family, was pleased to be able to take over the position which Wangala's Blacksmith had come to find so burdensome. Thereafter the new Blacksmith repaired wooden ploughs and other traditional tools belonging to the Peasants for which he received his annual reward of a fixed quantity of agricultural produce; the indigenous Blacksmith repaired their more recently acquired iron ploughs, for which he was paid in cash. Whereas Peasant farmers had at first not been prepared to grant even a small increase in the quantity of annual reward in kind the blacksmith received, they were now quite ready to pay extra cash for the services, which they had previously expected from him as part of their customary arrangements. Though this behaviour may appear strange, I shall show that the rationale and the principles on which it was based are quite clear.

Admittedly irrigation had increased the productivity of land. However, Peasants tended to regard the greater yield as part of the normal windfall profits which had been associated with the system of prescribed hereditary rewards. They rationalized their argument in terms of subsistence requirements and told the Blacksmith that the customary reward was still sufficient to feed him and his family. But the expansion of a cash sector induced the Blacksmith to hold out for higher rewards; this meant that he was no longer prepared to work for a minimum of subsistence. After the Blacksmith had managed to disentangle himself from his customary obligations and had provided a substitute for himself, Peasants were quite prepared to pay different amounts of cash for the various jobs he performed for them and which his substitute was not able to do. As soon as the hereditary ties between Wangala's indigenous Blacksmith and his Peasant clients had been broken as a result of the contact with the wider cash economy, Wangala Peasants acted as typical entrepreneurs in advanced economies. They were prepared to pay extra for the blacksmith's work because it could be associated with a considerable increase in total output.

In the case of Wangala's Blacksmith we are dealing with an extremely enterprising man: he designed a new and improved iron plough and started making it himself; he branched out into house-building and other activities for which the growing prosperity in the area produced a demand. However, before he could take advantage of the new economic opportunities he had to disentangle himself from his hereditary relationship with his Peasant clients. Peasant elders, village *panchayat* members, had used their political influence and power to force the indigenous Blacksmith to provide a substitute for himself to carry out his traditional duties. Thus the customary system of rights and duties continued to exist and exert pressures to ensure conformity. Customary ties are obligatory not only for workers but also and equally, for employers. 'Workers were entitled to their rights from every villager, according to the rules of the village communities; and if the villagers declined to employ their services to which they were entitled, they must still pay the *bullcottee hucks* (reward in kind)' (Wiser, 1958, p. xxvi). What is also worth noting, incidentally, is how this system of relationships is modified to operate in India's large and rapidly growing cities. I became aware of this when I stayed with one of my English friends in Bombay. It appears that individual Washermen managed to establish a system of 'customary' relationships with tenants in particular blocks of flats. The Washerman washes all the clothes for the resident families and in turn receives a fixed monthly reward from each of them. When my hosts' Washerman decided to return to his natal village for a few months a year, he arranged for one of his kin to carry on his duties during his absence. Though my hosts were satisfied with their 'own' Washerman, they found the services of his substitute highly unsatisfactory; they therefore wanted to find a different Washerman. However, none of the many underemployed Washermen in Bombay was prepared to take on the job. They all regarded it as the prerogative of the 'customary' Washerman, who in turn had the right and duty to provide a substitute in his stead, if he went absent. In fact my hosts were boycotted by Bombay's Washermen, because they had attempted to change their 'customary' Washerman. The system of customary relationships in this way gives labour relations great stability and tends to eliminate competition, even in a highly competitive urban environment.

Similarly, Wangala's new Blacksmith continued to work according to long-established rules and was completely unaffected by the new economic opportunities in his environment. The existence of hereditary labour relations and fixed annual rewards, therefore, acted as a force to maintain the *status quo* and accordingly as an obstacle to economic growth and expansion. Wiser reports that 'there is very little stimulus for better work. The Washerman has no desire to buy a flat iron to iron his *jajmani's* clothes. If he were to get one, he would simply increase his own labour and get very little, if any more, pay for it' (1958, p. 142).

Craftsmen who have no such prescribed and highly formalized relations with their clients can much more easily branch out into new activities than those who, like Wangala's Blacksmith, are subject to traditional labour relations. For example, in Dalena there were a number of immigrant craftsmen caste households, such as the Basketmaker, whose enterprise was not in any way hampered by traditional agreements. When the growing urban demand for more colourful and nicely shaped mats and baskets became effective, Dalena's Basketmaker changed his products and methods of production. (There was no Basketmaker in Wangala with which to compare him but a comparable craftsman there, a Jeweller, preferred to cultivate his own small plot of land instead of seeking the advantage of the new urban market.) Moreover, the Basketmaker's close links with the nearby urban centre made him realize there was a big

237

demand for pork – which may be eaten by lower-caste Hindus. Accordingly, he started rearing pigs in Dalena itself and sold them with considerable profit at the nearest urban market. His enterprise proved so successful that he even sent word to his brother to join him. The latter came and they continued to expand their business. A comparison of the case of Wangala's indigenous Blacksmith with that of Dalena's Basketmaker clearly indicates the drawback of a prescribed system of rewards and obligations when it comes to economic expansion. This point can be further illustrated by the reaction of Wangala Peasants to the introduction of improved production techniques.

Wangala had had some tank-irrigated lands even before canal irrigation reached the village. Thus some of Wangala's peasants were already accustomed to growing paddy (rice) long before canal irrigation made the growing of wet crops a practical proposition. Traditionally, a *gumpu* group of ten or twelve women was employed as a team to transplant the paddy seedlings from the nursery to the paddy fields. Each *gumpu* had a leader, whose responsibility it was to see that her co-workers turned up on the day arranged between her and the Peasant: the leader also received a certain fixed amount of crops per acre of paddy her group transplanted. She gave equal shares of this agricultural produce to each member of her *gumpu* while she kept a slightly larger proportion for herself. Each Peasant always employed the *gumpu* of the wife of the Untouchable with whom he had hereditary relations. Accordingly, there was a traditional relationship between a Peasant farmer and his *gumpu*, involving fixed customary rewards. About 20 years after canal irrigation reached Wangala, the Agricultural Department tried to introduce the Japanese method of paddy cultivation to Wangala farmers. The officials stressed the considerable increase in yield which would result from the new method. Though farmers were quite prepared to believe this, only a few were ready to experiment with the new method, which involved a more laborious way of spacing plants properly. First of all, farmers were not prepared to pay the *gumpu* more for transplanting the new way, because there was pressure from the more conservative farmers against raising the fixed reward for the services of a group of women. Secondly, the few more enterprising men who were prepared to offer a higher reward to their *gumpu* found that the women had developed a certain rhythm of work and were reluctant to change it; besides no one was prepared to pay them for re-training. Similarly, when officials from the Agricultural Department tried to introduce a cheap and most efficient weeding hook, the use of which would have considerably reduced the cultivation labour required, Wangala farmers were not prepared to employ the new tool. At first sight their reaction appears difficult to understand, but it becomes more readily explicable when viewed in the context of hereditary relationships. These make them responsible for providing a minimum of subsistence for their Untouchable labourers. If they substituted tools for labour and therefore saved some agricultural produce in terms of rewards, they might then have to give in charity what they had initially saved. They would therefore have no net gain. Besides, they would be criticized for being mean and selfish.

In these instances we see the Peasants of Wangala rejecting new techniques which would have increased output. But their response cannot be atrributed simply to conservatism – which in any case often indicates a recognition of diffuse benefits not seen on the surface. For in other spheres, which were not covered by the hereditary system of rewards, Wangala Peasant farmers displayed a considerable degree of enterprise. They were, for example, extremely progressive in their attitude towards sugarcane cultivation, an entirely new venture to them. Since sugarcane had not been one of the traditionally cultivated crops, there were no customary production techniques or traditional rewards associated with it. Thus farmers felt free to experiment with the new techniques and methods and adopted those that proved most productive and efficient. They paid their labourers in cash on a daily basis. The number of labourers any one farmer employed was largely determined by the interaction between the wage-rate and marginal productivity, as is the case in any capitalist system. Since the problem of the subsistence for the village population was taken care of by the system of hereditary labour relations, a Wangala farmer could operate in spheres outside the customary system like any 'rational' employer in an industrial society: he attempted to maximize his returns by equating marginal returns with marginal costs. A Peasant's hereditary obligation to provide a minimum of subsistence for his dependent households provides an obstacle to improving productive efficiency and maximizing returns. Wherever this obligation is not in existence or has been abandoned, we can expect a more positive reaction to new economic opportunities. This becomes clear when we examine Dalena's economic activities.

Dalena lands had remained dry even after irrigation had reached the area. Dalena farmers therefore sought to participate in the growing prosperity of the region by diversifying their economic activities and by purchasing wet lands in neighbouring villages. This resulted in the breakdown of hereditary ties between Peasant farmers and their Untouchable labourers. In turn, this meant that farmers were left free to employ labourers with whom they had no customary arrangements. Nor were they bound by customary rewards in the form of a fixed quantity of agricultural produce. Unlike his Wangala counterpart, a Dalena Peasant farmer was thus able to select his labourers, who worked for him according to his instructions and under his supervision. His relationship with his labourers was mainly contractual; he paid them in cash on a daily basis. The better worker received a higher daily wage. Moreover, since his hereditary obligation to provide a minimum of subsistence for his dependent Untouchable households had already disappeared, he was keen to employ the new weeding hook, which Wangala farmers were reluctant to accept. This resulted in a considerable saving of labour and therefore in a sizeable gain. Paddy was a new crop to Dalena farmers. But, unlike Wangala landowners, Dalena Peasants were not tied to any customary techniques and arrangements for paddy cultivation, and they showed themselves eager to experiment with the Japanese method of paddy cultivation, which promised them greater returns. In fact, the adoption of the new method of paddy cultivation enabled Dalena farmers to get a considerably higher output per acre of paddy than Wangala farmers with their customary method. According to a stratified random sample, which I compiled in the same way in both villages in 1955 and 1956, the average output per acre of paddy cultivation by Dalena farmers was as much as Rs. 362 (1962, p. 218), while it amounted to only

Rs. 281 in Wangala (1962, p. 47). Thus the average yield per acre of paddy was about 30 per cent higher for Dalena than for Wangala farmers. As a matter of fact, Dalena's village headman won the prize in 1953 for the best yield per acre of paddy in the whole district. Although Dalena farmers have less wet land and have to walk longer distances to their fields than Wangala Peasant farmers, yet the disappearance of the prescribed hereditary system of labour relations enabled them to adopt more efficient and productive methods of paddy cultivation and therefore ensured them a considerably higher yield.

AVERAGE PRODUCT AND CUSTOMARY REWARDS

Having discussed the operation of customary systems of reward and shown that they provide serious obstacles to increasing productivity and economic growth in general I want now to attempt an analysis of the principles underlying these labour relations in stagnant village economies. Here I seek to suggest answers to such questions as: What determined the number of masters any one craftsman or agricultural labourer sought? What determined the number of customary labour relationships any one farmer was prepared to continue? And, again, what determined the amount of the fixed annual reward?

Since hereditary labour relationships still operate in Wangala, I shall utilize the numerical data I collected there as the basis for this discussion. Prior to irrigation, *ragi* (*Eleusine corocana*, a millet) used to be the major crop in Wangala; it also provided the staple diet for the villagers. The population was composed of 128 Peasant, 28 Untouchable, 2 Washerman, and 1 Blacksmith households. The total area of dry land cultivated by Wangala villagers was about 540 acres. Output of *ragi* varied from year to year according to climatic conditions. Bad years were those when rainfall was insufficient or fell at the wrong time; famine years were those when most crops failed and a considerable proportion of the population had to go hungry and many even died. Informants told me that bad years used to occur with a frequency of about one in every five or six years; this is borne out by Mysore rainfall statistics. Accordingly, we find that the output per acre of *ragi* varied from a minimum of just over two *pallas* (one *palla* of *ragi* equals 208 lb) in bad seasons to a maximum of about eight or nine *pallas* in good ones. The average daily subsistence requirement of *ragi* per household is just under two *seers* (one *seer* is one-hundredth of one *palla*, or 2 lb); this makes the annual *ragi* requirements for each household about seven *pallas* and for the whole village composed of 159 households 1,113 *pallas*. In bad years Wangala's total *ragi* output of approximately 1,300 pallas was thus slightly more than sufficient to keep all the households fed, provided it was distributed equally among all of them. The average output per household in bad seasons was, therefore, an important factor in determining the size of any one settlement. I shall subsequently return to the importance of the average in stagnant economies. At this stage in the argument it is sufficient to note that in bad years the total product of the village had to be distributed equally among all households in order to keep the population alive. Yet the discrepancy in the landholding by Peasants and their dependent Untouchable labouring households was, and still is, considerable. The average landholding per Untouchable household was about 1½ acres, while that of Peasants was about 4 acres. This meant that in bad years Wangala Untouchable households managed to produce only approximately 3½ *pallas of ragi*, while each needed at least 7 *pallas* to survive. By contrast, the average Peasant household produced over 9 *pallas* of *ragi*. Average labour requirements per acre of *ragi* amount to about 35 labour days in bad years. The average Peasant household thus needed a minimum of about 120 labour days to cultivate its *ragi* fields. As cultivation of *ragi* is concentrated into a short period in the year – *ragi* is a two to four months crop – each Peasant farmer needed at least one or two helpers. It is extremely difficult for the Indian farmer to know the marginal product of his labour, i.e. the addition to total output produced by the last unit of labour employed: sometimes two men produce as much as three do, at other times there are differences in return. For the Peasant farmer it is much easier and more reliable to calculate the average product per labourer: this can readily be done by sharing the output equally among all cultivators. In bad years Wangala villagers, Peasants and their dependent households alike, all received an equal share of the total quantity of *ragi* produced. This meant that each Peasant had to give 50 *seers* of *ragi* to each of his two dependent Untouchable households. Fifty *seers* of *ragi* is in fact the quantity of fixed annual reward given by Wangala Peasant masters to their Untouchable servants. Each Untouchable household had to have hereditary relationships with about eight or nine Peasant masters in order to make up the deficiency in bad years between his family's food requirements and his own output of *ragi*.

Clearly, in bad years Peasants had no more *ragi* supplies than their dependent Untouchables. However, masters were prepared to accept this egalitarian distribution always in the hope of better seasons. In years of bumper crops the average Peasant farmer could produce a surplus of about 25 *pallas* of *ragi* over and above his subsistence needs including the fixed rewards to his Untouchable labourers. This surplus enabled him to throw large feasts, arrange for elaborate weddings, invest in better bullocks or houses, etc. (cash saving was very rare). Good harvests, therefore, provided Peasants with the means with which to conduct their struggle for prestige. Economic differentiation was clearly taking place in good years, whereas in bad seasons the emphasis was on egalitarianism. In order to maximize his total product the Peasant farmer needed helpers; he needed them even more in good years than in bad. To make certain that his helpers were on the spot when required, he in turn was prepared to maintain hereditary relationships with them and give them fixed annual rewards. Other considerations besides the purely economic, such as ritual and political, reinforced the Peasant's preparedness to maintain his customary relationships.

Good years meant better yields also for Untouchables. However, since their landholdings were so much smaller than those of Peasants and their masters had prior claim on their work performance, their own output never reached the village maximum. Labour requirements per acre of *ragi* were higher in good than in bad years: bumper crops needed more weeding and more harvesting. Therefore, in good years Untouchables had even less time for their own fields than in bad seasons. The major part of their food requirements was always provided by

243

their Peasant masters in the form of fixed quantities of annual rewards. Untouchables were prepared to accept the system of fixed rewards because it provided them with security even in bad years. Though no dependent Untouchable ever managed to have a surplus even approaching that of Peasant households in good seasons, the servicing castes did also benefit indirectly from good harvests: they watched the Peasants' lavish weddings and collected food at feasts. They could also get loans from their masters to help purchase cattle. Moreover, the hereditary relationships offered to the dependent Untouchables a number of advantages of more diverse economic and social nature: each Untouchable could count on his Peasant masters to help him in arranging and conducting weddings and in settling disputes and to give him some degree of social security in general.

In our Wangala example we have seen how the small landholdings of the Untouchables buttressed the system of fixed customary rewards. On the basis of this, we may postulate that the quantity of fixed annual rewards will vary according to the total village produce in bad years, the size of the labourers' landholdings, and the number of labour relations any one of them can maintain. This statement may be verified in different ways: first, by examining the fixed annual rewards of landless dependent households; second, by finding out whether there is any correlation between the quantity of fixed rewards and the size of the dependent household's acreage; and, third, by establishing whether or not there are differences in the quantity of fixed rewards in different villages in the same area.

We can satisfy the first point by examining the hereditary relationships in which Wangala's two Washerman households were involved. Prior to irrigation they were completely landless. Each had hereditary relationships with 64 Peasant masters. In turn each Peasant gave his Washerman 15 *seers* of *ragi* per year. This meant that the Washerman households' annual income in terms of *ragi* amounted to 9½ *pallas*, which in bad years was probably more than the *ragi* intake in Peasant households. However, since these Washerman households were completely dependent for their own requirements on their annual rewards, which did not vary at all according to bad or good seasons, Peasants as a group were prepared to let them have slightly more than the average *ragi* output of a bad year. By contrast, the Blacksmith, who owned one acre of dry land and had hereditary relationships with all 128 Peasant households, received only 5 *seers* of *ragi* annually from each of them. Since one Blacksmith could quite easily meet the work requirements of 128 Peasant households and since he owned some land himself, his annual reward from each of his masters was only one-third of that of the Washerman. This clearly indicates that annual rewards were fixed regardless of the service involved.

Furthermore, neighbouring villages in the Wangala area, where the landholding pattern as well as the caste composition of the population is different, also had different quantities of *ragi* making up the annual rewards given by Peasant masters to their dependent households.

The importance of the average product in underdeveloped economies has already been emphasized by Lewis, when he referred to it as setting an objective standard for wages in the capitalist sector; 'men will not leave the family farm to seek employment if the wage is worth less than they would be able to consume if they remained at home' (1954, pp. 148-149). However, this is not entirely true, because other incentives besides wages may attract men to cities and often they do not understand how much subsistence costs in money terms. In any case, since Lewis's main concern at the time was to show how a newly emerging capitalist sector operates, rather than to analyse the subsistence sector, he did not pursue the point further.

In order to throw into relief the importance of the average product in Indian village economies I shall now describe the operation of a customary system of rewards by a composite picture of a traditional large settlement made up of one Peasant farmer, controlling 50 acres of dry land, and 14 dependent Untouchable households. The output of approximately 120 *pallas* of *ragi* in bad seasons was slightly more than sufficient to keep the small community alive – 7 *pallas* of *ragi* being the annual subsistence minimum per household. The Peasant master, who always hoped for better harvests, wanted to retain his labour force and, therefore, in bad years distributed his total product equally: his own as well as each of his 14 dependent households received 8 *pallas* each.

If, owing to the improvement in climatic conditions, a number of good harvests were experienced in succession, more labour was required to cope with cultivation and, in particular, with harvesting so as to maximize the total product. Thus one or more servicing households may have been attracted to join the 14 Untouchables' households. However, it probably took quite some time before the news of the more favourable harvests spread to less fortunate areas. Furthermore, time had to elapse before putative kinship ties – since hereditary labour relations are couched in kinship terms – could be manipulated so as to arrange for a grafting on to the system of hereditary labour relationships, as in the case of the Blacksmith cited earlier. Conversely, if after an increase in the number of dependent households once more some bad harvests occurred which reduced the output again to 120 *pallas* per year, pressures will have begun to operate on the last accepted member of the group to migrate and lighten the burden of the Peasant's obligation to provide subsistence for his labourers. The time-lag between the variations in harvests and the appropriate adjustment in the size of the labour force helps to explain cases of zero or even negative marginal productivity, as well as incidents of strains and stress in the political and social system of Indian villages.

The share of the Peasant landholder, who himself participated in cultivating, was in bad sessions no larger than the annual reward he had to give to each of his dependent Untouchable households. By contrast, good harvests gave him a surplus of as much as 300 *pallas* of *ragi* over and above the rewards he had to pay to his labourers. He could utilize this surplus to throw large feasts and establish status and prestige for himself. Labourers, on the other hand, were prepared to accept the system of fixed annual rewards, because it assured them of their subsistence requirements, even in bad seasons. Thus, it was the expectation of good harvests which induced the Peasant master to accept in bad years a share equal to the annual rewards his labourers received, whereas the continued threat of bad harvests induced Untouchable labourers to accept a reward which did not vary according to labour performed or according to harvest. The system was, therefore, maintained by the chance occurrences of good and bad harvests. Its essence was chance of profit for the

Peasant and assurance of security for the Untouchable. It broke down only in extremely bad harvests, when the total product was not sufficiently large to provide a minimum of subsistence for all the members of the society. Such years were famine periods, during which the customary system of rewards had to be completely suspended. But in normal times, when bad and good harvests occurred fairly regularly, the fixed rewards for customary services were based on the average product produced in bad seasons.

Indian villagers, rich and poor alike, used to be largely at the mercy of climatic conditions. In bad seasons 'share and share alike' was their motto, whereas good harvests facilitated large feasting and economic differentiation with its concomitant struggle for prestige. This may help to explain the contradictory views of the *jajmani* system expressed by Wiser, on the one hand, and by Gould and Beidelman, on the other. Wiser may have examined the *jajmani* system as it operated in bad seasons with its emphasis on equal distribution of output, while Gould and Beidelman may have concentrated their attention on good harvests when extreme economic differentiation occurred and when masters appeared to exploit their dependent helpers as capitalists are supposed to exploit their workers. But the difference may also be due to different philosophical approaches. However, while the success of a capitalist enterprise is largely due to the foresight and organizing ability of its managers, traditional Indian landowners and landless alike relied completely on favourable climatic conditions to provide them with good harvests. No one, of Wiser, Gould, or Beidelman, seems to appreciate that Indian villagers, rich and poor alike, were all subject to the hazards of their environment, over which they had very little control. Mere survival was therefore of the utmost importance to the population of these underdeveloped economies. Indian villagers did not have the technological know-how nor did they have any incentives to initiate growth in these economies, which were geared to stability.

In traditional Indian village economies with hereditary systems of reward, landowners were chiefly concerned with the quantity of the average product in bad years – or to put it in time-perspective: they were interested in the long-term average product, rather than in the marginal addition to total output which any one worker might contribute. This emphasis on the average is noticeable not only in economic relations; it pervades many other aspects of the culture. Beliefs in sorcery and witchcraft sanction 'average' behaviour. For instance, when a Wangala Peasant builds a new house with the surplus he produced in good years, he always hangs a broken pot on to the outside. This is done to protect the new house from evil and jealous spirits. The broken mudpot is supposed to give the impression that the house is not new but really old like all the other houses in the vicinity.

As soon as external forces break down the isolation of Indian villages and new economic opportunities are introduced, innovations and changes at the margin tend to become important. This is precisely what happened in Wangala after irrigation had facilitated cash cropping. As we have seen, Wangala Peasant farmers were not prepared to grant the Blacksmith even a small increase in his customary fixed reward of five *seers* per household. This had been based on the average product in bad years and was regarded as more than sufficient for subsistence. However, as soon as the Blacksmith managed to disentangle himself from his hereditary obligations, Peasants started to think of his work in terms of the contribution it made to the cultivation of their lands. The Blacksmith was obviously an innovator: he designed an improved plough and became a housing contractor. Peasants then began to appreciate their Blacksmith and his contribution to their output, i.e. wet crops, the cultivation of which necessitated iron ploughs in place of the customary wooden ones. Thus the transition from a non-market to a market economy involves a change from emphasis on average productivity to one on marginal productivity. However, before such change in emphasis can take place customary labour relations must be eliminated. Planners would be well advised to bear in mind that it may be easier to improve productive efficiency by introducing entirely new crops or products, rather than by attempting to change the traditional methods and techniques of production. For example, in Saurashtra 'attempts were made to introduce improved methods of cultivation like the Russian method of *bajri* cultivation and the Japanese method of paddy cultivation.

Only 34 acres were brought under the Russian method of b cultivation against the overall target of about 2,600 acres ai for the Japanese method, the respective figures were 52 acres and 865 acres' (Government of India, 1954, p. 247). If the agricultural officials responsible for this programme had appreciated the principles underlying the traditional organization of labour, they would never have attempted to introduce improved methods for cultivating customary crops, but would have tried to introduce entirely new crops, which could then have been cultivated outside the system of traditional labour relations.

This change-over from emphasis on the average product to stress on the marginal product is not only a symbol of important changes in the economic organization of previously isolated economies, but is also marked by radical changes in the social and political systems. In non-market economies nonconformity is usually penalized. By contrast, economic growth necessitates innovation and needs men who are prepared to take risks. These new entrepreneurs who try to take advantage of the new economic opportunities then want to translate their wealth into social status. They want to replace the system of ascribed social status with one in which status can be achieved. This has been happening in Dalena (Epstein, 1962, pp. 276-293) and is evidenced in a great number of societies which are in the process of being integrated into the wider economy and polity. The strains and stresses associated with these changes provide a fascinating field for study and analysis.

CONCLUSION

A prescribed hereditary system of rights and duties of the kind I have been describing is a mark of a stagnant rather than a developing economy. India's customary systems of rewards and obligations placed great emphasis on stability. In a country such as India, with low soil fertility and little and/or irregular rainfall, there are usually great fluctuations in harvests occurring side by side with small margins of agricultural profits. Accordingly, the security value offered by the stable system of prescribed rights and duties was of great importance. Landowners knew in advance the exact quantity of agricultural

249

produce they had to give as reward for services rendered them throughout the year. A good harvest brought them windfall profits. However, making allowances for differences of individual skill – and some were very adept in getting the best yield out of a poor soil – the greater yield was due primarily not to any positive efforts of their own, but to more favourable climatic conditions. On the other hand, a good harvest also meant more work for labourers, as well as for certain functionaries, for which they received no extra rewards, though they did get greater fringe benefits. Yet a poor harvest still provided the dependent castes with a minimum of subsistence. Since Indian villagers, landowners and landless alike, were all subject to the hazards of their climate and environment, they were all prepared to participate in a system which offered all of them at least the minimum necessities of life, except in times of extreme crop failure and general famine. There were, therefore, no incentives to initiate growth in these stagnant economies. The relative isolation of traditional Indian villages and the absence of outside markets helped to perpetuate the system of hereditary relationships, which defined most obligations and rewards.

The equal distribution of the total output in bad seasons may help to explain migration whenever population increased to such an extent that the average product in bad years became insufficient to provide a minimum standard of subsistence for villagers. There may be also some correlation with infanticide and the frequency of abortion though this is much more difficult to measure. Moreover, the appreciation of fixed annual rewards, i.e. fixed labour costs, associated with variations in output may clarify the fact of economic differentiation in traditional non-market peasant economies as well as the forms such differentiation has taken.

If my analysis of traditional Indian peasant economies is valid – and I hope I have shown that it is – it may also be relevant to other pre-industrial societies. For instance, we may find that many societies with a low level of technological knowledge and consequent inability to control their environment tend to distribute produce in a standard pattern equally in bad as in good seasons. What good seasons do is to facilitate economic differentiation. This tentative suggestion gains support from a study of African farming practices. Allan, an agriculturalist, reckons that before the introduction of cash crops to Africa, men cultivated enough land to bring them in a small surplus in normal years – he calls this a normal surplus. However, in good seasons, when there were favourable climatic conditions, they had bumper harvests with a large surplus; in bad years they went on short commons. Allan worked this out in trying to explain the considerable annual variations in the crops that African tribes now sell on the open market. Before the creation of this external European market, the bumper seasons presumably produced large-scale feasting, while bad harvests involved mutual assistance in terms of the same relations (Allan, 1965, pp. 38-49). Though African landholding patterns and labour relations differ from those in India, there seems to be a general similarity. The emphasis on average productivity in bad seasons may also help to throw light on witchcraft beliefs and sorcery in many primitive societies. These are but a few of the many interesting problems raised by the preceding analysis of Indian village economies.

NOTE

1. Caste names are written with capital initials: thus a Peasant is a member of the Peasant caste, whereas a peasant is a farmer.

REFERENCES

ALLAN, W. 1965. *The African Husbandman*. London: Oliver & Boyd.
BEIDELMAN, T. O. 1959. *A Comparative Analysis of the Jajmani System*. New York: J. J. Augustin.
EPSTEIN, T. S. 1962. *Economic Development and Social Change in South India*. Manchester: Manchester University Press.
GOULD, H. A. 1958. The Hindu Jajmani System. *Southwestern Journal of Anthropology* 14: 428-437.
GOVERNMENT OF INDIA. 1954. *Evaluation Report*. Delhi: Planning Commission.
LEWIS, W. A. 1954. Economic Development with Unlimited Supplies of Labour. *The Manchester School of Economic and Social Studies* 22: 139-191.

LEWIS, W. A. 1958. Unlimited Labour: Further Notes. *The Manchester School of Economic and Social Studies* **26**: 1-32.

SRINIVAS, M. N. 1959. The Dominant Caste in Rampura. *American Anthropologist* **61**: 1-16.

WISER, W. H. 1958. *The Hindu Jajmani System*. Lucknow: Lucknow Publishing House.

Lorraine Barić

Traditional Groups and New Economic Opportunities in Rural Yugoslavia[1]

In this study, I attempt to isolate social variables associated with low productivity and low investment in Yugoslav agriculture. The analysis thus deals with a practical economic problem, and one that is singled out as crucial by Yugoslav writers on the subject (see, for instance, Bakarić, 1960, and Kardelj, 1959, 1962); it is not, however, an analysis of the complexities of the Yugoslav economy, since I would say that an extended study of the purely economic variables in a completely monetized, increasingly industrialized economy is not the task of an anthropologist or a sociologist.

Economic anthropology, although it has a long history, has of recent years been expanding in many different directions. For example, the applicability of the terminology and theories of current economics to technologically primitive and to peasant societies has interested some anthropologists; the analysis of the actual processes of production, distribution, exchange, consumption, and investment in small-scale economies has been the concern of others; while studies in the field of applied economic anthropology (concentrating on social problems of growth points) are becoming more numerous. Sometimes a single study contains elements of these and other approaches to the field of inquiry.

The aims of a particular piece of research must determine the degree to which an economic anthropologist needs to borrow assumptions, concepts, models, and data from economics. Here extreme caution is advisable, since there is no general guarantee that communication between disciplines must always be of mutual benefit; it all depends on what is communicated.

Therefore, in studying the social context of productivity and investment in traditional agriculture in a country such as

253

Yugoslavia, one must be clear about the form in which questions can be posed. If one asks 'Why is investment in Yugoslav agriculture falling below desirable levels?', the answer could involve a discussion of data and concepts derived from economics, law, sociology/anthropology, psychology, political science, and Marxism-Leninism, as well as reference to historical events of the nineteenth and twentieth century in Eastern Europe. On the other hand, questions in the form 'What major social variables are associated with lack of investment?' or 'What is the social context of situations in which decisions about investment or technical innovations are taken?' are amenable to sociological or anthropological analysis.

It is important to note that answers to these modified questions, although they may provide an adequate descriptive model of some aspects of social action, are only part of a model that would explain 'why' investment does or does not occur. Another model or part of a model could be a wholly economic one. The isolating of social variables in a situation is, moreover, only one step in making a model of the actual process of decision-making or of the forms decisions could take. The study of decisions demands the posing of quite different questions.

In studying the social variables associated with investment, some simplifying assumptions have to be made: it is necessary to assume that it is possible to discuss the effect of social factors on economic action, without simultaneously discussing the fact that social variables themselves are changing under the impact of economic growth, although in Yugoslavia the latter fact is clearly evident. In addition, in order to describe a situation in these terms, it is necessary to assume that an anthropologist can meaningfully distinguish 'social' and 'economic' in an empirical situation. Operationally, activities or aspects of activities have to be allocated to one or other category, although in 'real life' the aspects may be almost inextricably interwoven.

In this context, I designate as 'economic' the aspects of behaviour that are specifically related to the material advantage of mixed 'socio-economic' acts. In other contexts, other definitions would be appropriate.

New Economic Opportunities in Rural Yugoslavia

Agriculture in old Yugoslavia

The policy of Yugoslavia in the period following World War II has included the encouragement of rapid growth in agricultural production as well as in industrial production, but the policy has been much more successful in the latter sector than in the former. A major Yugoslav theoretician and active shaper of policy, Kardelj, has written 'It is no exaggeration to say that a fundamental increase in agricultural production, based on radical technical refashioning of agriculture and increased labour productivity has become a basic precondition of the further development of our industry in general, and for the steady improvement of the living conditions of our working population' (Kardelj, 1962, p. 44).

Agriculture in Yugoslavia is overwhelmingly one of small private farms. This present state has a short enough history for peasants to recall and describe the preceding state of feudalism existing three or so generations previously. In a northwestern Croatian area that I studied peasants may be found who know the family history of the former feudal lords of their grand-parents' and greatgrandparents' time, and speak of them as if they had died within the past few years instead of more than a hundred years ago.

The legal relations of feudalism were abolished in the countries that make up present-day Yugoslavia during the nineteenth and early twentieth centuries. The socio-economic system that existed before abolition is always referred to as 'feudalism' although it lacked features sometimes taken to be characteristic of feudalism in Western Europe. For example, land was held by many feudal lords under allodial tenure and was not in general a fief entailing vassalage or service. In Croatia, the peasants on the lord's land were bound by urbarial laws, which were regulations promulgated by Habsburg rulers in the eighteenth and nineteenth centuries, setting out rights and duties of serfs. By the laws, peasants had to deliver to their lord certain specified proportions of their annual production and stock,

Lorraine Barić

to provide labour according to the lord's assessment, and sometimes to make money payments.

Abolition of feudal land tenure was accomplished to the slogan 'The land belongs to the man who tills it'. After abolition, a huge population of peasants found themselves able for the first time to rent, buy, sell, and mortgage their land.

An intricate series of legal provisions for land reform began in the nineteenth century and has continued up till the present day. Briefly, the land reform has aimed at the expropriation of large private landowners and foreigners and the redistribution of land to the smallest holders, landless peasants, and, latterly, socialized enterprises. The upper limit of land that any farm was permitted to own has been progressively lowered. At present the upper limit for an individual holding is 10 hectares (1 hectare = 2·47 acres). As Bakarić (1960, p. 11) has pointed out, Yugoslav agriculture has never passed through a type of post-feudal production in which landlords disposed of a reasonable amount of capital and employed agricultural workers, but remained, in his term, 'precapitalistic'.

The characteristic productive group in most parts of Yugoslavia in the nineteenth century and earlier was the *zadruga*.[2] The *zadruga* has generally been accepted into the inventory of social forms as a type of 'extended family' (cf. Bottomore, 1962, p. 165). This is not quite precise. The *zadruga* had elements of the patrilineal joint family, and was a corporate group in the Fried (1957) sense. It was not merely an extended family taking the form of a residential unit. In addition, it had a collective element, since in the more recent period it was possible for a person who was not related by kinship or marriage to any existing member of the *zadruga* to join as a full member. It was thus a cooperative with a kin core (see A. Mayer, 1910).

The word *zadruga* itself merely means 'collective', 'cooperative', or 'community'. Nowadays it is applied to modern cooperative and collective undertakings. As far as the traditional kin-based *zadruga* is concerned, the term has been applied largely after the event. In the pre-nineteenth-century period, those who lived in *zadrugas* usually referred to them as 'families', 'households', or 'big families'.

Segmentation or division similar to that which takes place

in kin groups such as lineages did not occur in *zadrugas*: legal permission had to be sought in order to dissolve or divide them. Towards the end of the nineteenth century the authorities attempted to discourage dissolution of *zadrugas*, since, as cooperatives, they were considered to be an efficient protection against fragmentation of land and landlessness, as well as a way of economizing on capital equipment.

Nevertheless, dissolution and division of *zadrugas* occurred widely after the feudal laws were abolished and peasants had obtained greater freedom of action. As a result of this tendency, the primary form of unit in agricultural production became the *inokosna kuća* or individual household. Even where it is extended to three generations or extended by the accretion of collaterals, it cannot be considered to be a *zadruga*.

Present-day agriculture

Agriculture (broadly interpreted) provides the income for a major proportion of all households in Yugoslavia. Approximately twelve million people out of the total population of eighteen and a half million in 1961 obtained their income wholly or partly from agriculture. The table below shows the situation.

Population by Source of Income of Household—
Yugoslavia, 1961

Income from	Male ('000)	Female ('000)	Total ('000)
Agriculture	3,600	3,847	7,447
Agriculture and non-agricultural occupations	2,363	2,419	4,782
Non-agricultural occupations	3,021	3,190	6,211
Collective and not known	45	54	99
Total	9,029	9,510	18,539

Source: *SGJ* – 62, p. 62; 5 per cent sample.

The area under production in agriculture in 1961 was 12,358,000 hectares. Of this total, an area of 1,794,000 hectares, or 14·5 per cent, was under the control of social undertakings. As much as 10,564,000 hectares, or 85·5 per cent, was under cultivation by family farms. Despite collectivization, most agricultural production is in the hands of private producers.

Collectivization and the creation of cooperatives[3] have been the most important ways in which the government has attempted to change the structure of Yugoslav agriculture. The policy of transformation has also included the industrialization of the countryside.

Yugoslavia emerged from World War II as a Federated People's Republic (now Socialist Republic), with a one-party government headed by Communist leaders who had distinguished themselves as partisan fighters against enemy occupation. By the end of 1946, industrial mining and quarrying enterprises, employing over 80 per cent of workers in these industries, had been nationalized, as were all wholesale trading firms and all banks and transport companies (cf. Waterston, 1962, p. 7). All private industrial concerns over a very small size were taken over by the government, and also about 97 per cent of retail establishments. The private owner of agricultural land was permitted by law to hold up to 25 hectares, but land over this amount was confiscated and either converted into state farms or distributed among peasants and to war veterans. This was the first post-war land reform.

The first five-year plan – for 1947-1951 – was as much political in aim as economic. In this phase, the strongest attempts were made to collectivize peasant holdings. The 1947-1951 plan was modelled on the Russian five-year plan, and aimed at raising industrial production to about five times the 1939 level, and also at raising agricultural production, but to a lesser extent. The plan set out detailed, quantitative, physical targets for commodities. In agriculture, the production targets were remarkably specific; for example, the actual number of pear, apple, or plum trees to be planted each year was laid down.

After 1949, when a sharp division of interest arose between Yugoslavia and the Cominform countries, new routes towards socialism were sought. The watershed year between the old, centralized system and the new, decentralized, more pragmatic system was 1953. The trend after 1953 has been a movement away from centralized, quantitative setting of economic targets towards using the forces of supply and demand to set levels of production. The government tends to rely more and more on indirect monetary and fiscal instruments to achieve the aims of the federal plans. There have been phases in which the tendency towards growing independence of enterprises and decentralization of control has been checked, in the interests of rationalizing certain industries in which there has been an over-enthusiastic proliferation of similar, competing firms. There has, however, been no change of overall policy.

The trend towards independence has been important in agriculture. Apart from collectivization, early plans for agriculture included compulsory deliveries at extremely low prices, detailed sowing plans – so that farmers no longer had any control over the crops in which they would specialize – and discriminatory income tax. In line with post-1953 developments, the changes from the initial position included: letting up on the pressure on peasant farmers to join cooperatives and collectives; replacement of income tax by a tax based on the cadastral valuation of land, thus providing farmers with incentives to increase output to raise their incomes; and a free possibility for peasants to plant the most profitable crops instead of those indicated by the plan, and to sell either on the free market or at guaranteed prices at their own will. These policies have had their effect on production. Agricultural production was, in 1961 and 1962, roughly half as high again as during the period 1947-1956, when production fluctuated considerably, but rose very little.

There are three types of cooperative and collective in present-day Yugoslav agriculture: the *poljoprivredna dobra*, 'Agricultural Estates' or collectives, which are run as socialized farms with workers and employees; the *seljačke radne zadruge*, or 'Peasants' Working Cooperatives', which have peasant members as well as workers and employees, and were meant at the beginning of the new agrarian policy to provide the backbone of collectivization; and the *opšte zemljoradničke zadruge*, or 'General Agricultural Cooperatives', which provide capital equipment for members, such as tractors and combines, marketing facilities, and other forms of aid. They also have recently gone in for agricultural production.

There are now fewer of all forms of collective and cooperative. From 1959 to 1961 the Agricultural Estates (collective socialized farms) declined from 559 to 469; the Peasants' Working Cooperatives declined from 232 to 127; and the General Agricultural Cooperatives declined from 4,817 to 3,228 (*SGJ* – 62, pp. 361-364). This was a considerable decrease in a short time.

The critical category is that of the Peasants' Working Cooperative, which was to have been the means of organizing the peasants in political as well as economic terms, but in which achievement has been low. After 1953, laws were passed that permitted any peasant who had joined a Peasants' Working Cooperative in the first phase of collectivization to withdraw from it. A widespread exodus immediately ensued.

The Agricultural Estates and the General Agricultural Cooperatives, although fewer in number, are efficient as compared with private agriculture. The areas cultivated have been increased, particularly the holdings of the General Agricultural Cooperatives, which are being pressed to extend their functions of aid and marketing into the sphere of actual production. Cooperation between individual peasants and the General Agricultural Cooperatives has increased.

Peasants' Working Cooperatives on the other hand are further losing their importance in the socialization of the countryside: permanent full-time workers were introduced in 1959 – over 22,000 of them – and this situation is a negation of the original conception. The number of actual members dropped from 38,660 in 1959 to approximately 19,000 in 1961 (*SGJ* – 62, p. 362).

The increase of productivity in the socialized sector of agriculture is at the same time an encouraging demonstration of the value of new mechanized methods of production and a source of frustration to Yugoslav administrators, when they compare it with the low achievement in the large private sector.

Private peasant farmers still follow the methods of what may be called 'traditional' agriculture. In most parts of Yugoslavia, the technology involved is comparatively simple, primarily labour-intensive plough and hoe agriculture. The largest proportion of useful land is arable, a smaller proportion grazing land, an even smaller proportion orchards, and a still smaller proportion vineyards. What is produced varies according to region. Wheat, maize, barley, oats, rice, millet, buckwheat, hemp, flax, cotton, sugarbeet, tobacco, hops, sunflower seeds, soya, and many kinds of vegetables and fruit, as well as other crops, are cultivated. Stock raised includes cattle, sheep, and pigs. Raising of poultry and beekeeping are widespread. Few farms specialize in one product; many are mixed and provide for a large part of the subsistence needs of those working on them, together with an additional cash-production component, to be sold on the market, privately or through General Agricultural Cooperatives. Sometimes the cash crop can be easily converted in whole or part to consumption, sometimes not. There is no general picture.

A major problem – and one officially much discussed – lies in the small supplies coming on to the market. This is associated with low productivity, although it is also due to a rise in consumption by peasants. Expenditure on the cheaper carbohydrates, such as maize flour and beans, fell during the period 1954-1955 to 1960-1961, while expenditure on meat, milk, eggs, and fruit rose. Consumption of meat, milk, and eggs now provides a larger proportion of the nutritional intake of peasants (*SGJ –* 62, p. 257). Peasants would rather eat their own 'luxury' produce than sell it. In Yugoslav analyses, the underlying difficulty is seen as lack of investment, and as need for modernization and mechanization (cf. Kardelj, 1962, pp. 61-63).

ALTERNATIVE POSSIBILITIES FOR ECONOMIC ACTION

To show that a course of action, given certain circumstances, is financially less profitable or more profitable is not necessarily a sufficient explanation of the emergence of a certain form of behaviour in a field of action which is essentially social as well as economic. But some idea of the possible material advantage of certain actions helps to clarify the context of the situation in which social variables are significant.

The units involved are farm households rather than individuals: they are units of production, units of consumption, and units of investment. I emphasize groups, since decisions are a function of a number of variables, of which one is the structure of the household unit, considered as a reference group (cf. Merton, 1957, *passim*). In some circumstances it could be useful to simplify the situation by maintaining that decisions were individual ones, taken perhaps by the head of the family; the head's relation to other members of the productive group and the influence of their opinions of him could then be incorporated as factors influencing the individual's decision. Nevertheless, this simplification cuts out some important aspects of analysis.

As I shall try to show, the structure of the group and the stage of its domestic cycle are relevant to the question of investment in traditional agriculture. The unit of analysis must be the group. But, first, the economic variables involved should be outlined.

Yugoslav peasant farmers are constantly being exhorted to be more efficient, to do everything possible to increase production and productivity, to invest in such equipment as they can, to use the resources of the General Agricultural Cooperatives, including taking their advice and using their equipment, and to make as much of their produce as possible available for general consumption. A major difficulty in the application of modern methods lies in the widespread fragmentation of land. Consolidation of landholding, by sale of outlying parcels and purchase of contiguous plots where possible would also be a contribution towards raising productivity.

It is clear that the farms, deliberately kept below 10 hectares in size, are not in a position to undertake any large-scale mechanization of agriculture. This leaves four feasible possibilities for peasants who remain on the land. Productive groups can increase investment in traditional agriculture; they can join cooperatives and collectives; they can diversify income by having some members enter non-agricultural occupations; and they can continue customary forms of traditional agriculture, aiming at a holding operation: maintenance of the *status quo* rather than growth. In the face of information and propaganda directed at the peasant sector, concerning the agricultural problem, a decision to take the last course emerges as a positive decision, not an absence of action.

In effect, the last two possibilities are those most frequently followed: diversification and maintenance. Where investment in

traditional agriculture occurs, it does not meet planned requirements.

Investment in traditional agriculture, aiming at increased
productivity, means the purchase of more ploughs, of plough
animals and other stock, of traditional machinery and equipment
(e.g. wagons, harrows, rakes, rollers), of farm buildings, and of
more land, to be cultivated in the traditional manner. The
number of ploughs in Yugoslavia has been increasing only slowly
in the past ten years: from 1,179,000 in 1951, they rose to
1,333,000 in 1961. Investment in traditional agriculture in
1960 was a little over 14 per cent of total peasant expenditure;
this represented an average amount of 38,200 dinars per household. In the same year, 15,000 dinars per household was spent on
alcohol and tobacco and 40,500 dinars per household was spent
on clothes and shoes. The table below shows the general situation
for two years, 1959 and 1960.

Expenditure by Peasant Households—Yugoslavia

| Type of Expenditure | Amount of Expenditure by Household | | | |
| | 1959 | | 1960 | |
	'000 *dinars*	%	'000 *dinars*	%
For agricultural production (seed, seedlings, artificial fertilizer, minor repairs, paid labour)	31·4	13	31·2	12
Investment in land, stock, machines, equipment, agricultural buildings	36·8	15	38·2	14
Expenditure on household (food, drink, tobacco, shoes, clothing, electricity)	113·2	45	123·2	45
Other including taxes	68·9	27	78·9	29
Total	250·3	100	271·5	100

Source: *SGJ* – 62, p. 365.

Peasants can sell their produce by contracting with the
government in advance (through Cooperatives) or they can
sell privately. The index of prices of all agricultural products, as
received by producers, rose fairly steadily from 1953 to 1960,
by about one-third (*SGJ* – 62, p. 239). A major economic
problem is the slow increase in farm produce available for urban

Lorraine Barić

consumption. But it is difficult to know whether, although the demand exists, the actual cost of investment involved in increasing cash-crop production is too high.

Some indirect evidence on this point is provided by Schultz (1964, pp. 85, 90-94), who has attempted to show that investment in traditional agriculture (as distinct from modern, 'industrialized', or mechanized agriculture) is hardly worth while for peasant cultivators. He uses Tax's data on Panajachel (1953, p. 116) to demonstrate that the net return on Panajachel peasant farmers' investment was about 4 per cent or, as he prefers to put it, in a more vivid way, a peasant has to spend 25 dollars – a sum, moreover, subject to much risk and uncertainty – to obtain an annual income stream of one dollar. Looked at in this context, the investment could well appear unattractive.

There are very few empirical, quantitative comparative data on return to investment in land and capital goods in traditional agriculture. Schultz presents a good deal of material in building up a theory, which is both convincing and enlightening, of the interrelatedness of problems in the study of the profitability of investment in traditional agriculture, and does much with some quantitative and rather more qualitative and descriptive material. It may perhaps be assumed that his model fits Yugoslavia also. But the data necessary to test the hypotheses and theories involved in the model are lacking, here, as in most other peasant societies. Since it is difficult in this case to examine investment on the basis of profitability alone, an examination of this important economic variable is in effect of little help in explanation.

One might argue that, since machinery and equipment are available for those peasants who wish to cooperate with General Agricultural Cooperatives, while still retaining control of their farms, there is no need for peasants to invest in these items. Tractors, seed drills, mowers, binders, threshing machines, trucks, and combine-harvesters are available for cooperators in ever increasing numbers. The number of tractors in Yugoslavia increased from 6,266 in 1951 to 33,680 in 1961, almost all in the hands of Cooperatives and Collectives. Here, investment has been kept at as high a level as possible.

In 1960, 1,463,000 peasants had been enrolled as members of

General Cooperatives, and in that year approximately 850,000 cooperated in agriculture and stockraising (*SGJ* – 62, p. 132). Cooperators must pay for use of equipment and for services. The proportion of cooperators, although high, is perhaps less than one might expect, considering the extensive encouragement that peasants are given to join, since there are 12 million people in agriculture, living on approximately 2,629,000 private farms. Those who are not members, and those who are nominal members but do not cooperate, manage without the apparatus of modern agriculture. They continue in the traditional system, carrying on a 'holding operation', contributing their part to the picture which shows that peasant households spend about two or three times as much on investment in land and capital equipment as on tobacco or additional alcohol; or spend about as much on this investment as on new clothes.

New economic opportunities are there: even if investment in traditional agriculture could be shown to be too costly, peasant productive groups could cooperate with General Agricultural Cooperatives, at lesser cost, while remaining private and autonomous. But, in fact, most peasant productive groups do not take advantage of these opportunities.

An examination of the material consequences, particularly profitability, of investment has thus revealed an ambiguous situation and no clear answers. In the next section I turn to an exploration of peasants' reactions to these possibilities of economic action, in terms of social variables.

SOCIAL VARIABLES

The social variables of this analysis have emerged from anthropological fieldwork, but wherever possible they have been checked by statistical data or by reference to legal rules. Since this paper is concerned with applied economic anthropology, I have concentrated on the most easily identifiable variables and attempted to fit them closely to empirical reality, while bearing in mind that the variables may have meaning at two levels: that of the overall structure and that of the individual productive group. A more clearly specified relationship among variables would be valuable; nevertheless, connections can be explored only to a small extent, since each connection is a study in itself, as in, for example, the relationship between kinship and social mobility, or the relationship between flexibility of manoeuvre and patterns of inheritance. Each variable can change, become greater or lesser, but this can only be expressed in a qualitative way. Identification of variables and the elaboration of some of the effects of qualitative changes are the aims of the present analysis.

Kinship

Yugoslavia is a 'kinship' society. By this I mean that rights and obligations among kin are accepted as more binding than they are among kin of corresponding genealogical distance in most sectors of, for example, English society. This is a broad generalization and difficult to document, but it is clearly evident to Western and Yugoslav fieldworkers (cf. Halpern, 1958, 1965; Erlich, 1964; Balen, 1962). It can be supported by reference to Yugoslav family law, which provides evidence as to the formalized relationships of the system. As Yugoslavia is a planned society, written law enters more intimately into the nature of personal relations than in many other countries. The Basic Law on Relations between Parents and Children, for instance (Sect. 32, §2) (see Bakić, 1962), specifies the material support which it is the duty of everyone to supply to all lineal ascendants and descendants in need as well as to brothers and sisters. Kin can apply for support from relatives when they can prove they are incapable of working through old age, illness, or accident, and when any income they may have is insufficient for their support (Sect. 36). The needy person applies for aid to his closest kinsman, as defined by law, and then to those more and more distant. The law is clear about the binding nature of these claims and the fact that the source of the claims is degree of kinship alone. The claims are irrevocable and permanent and cannot be waived or mortgaged.

Forms of behaviour appropriate to kin roles are, for a European society, comparatively precisely defined. The solidarity and identity of the family still form an important value, although the concept of the former patrilineal descent group has changed in a number of intricate ways.

The solidarity of the family is centred on property. In towns, this frequently takes the form of a dwelling (since Yugoslavia has an urban housing problem). Kin may have residence rights in a family apartment. In the country, the land and the house form a focus of family support and identity which peasants are reluctant to give up. This means that the primary interest need not be in running the farm as`an efficient business, but rather in preserving it as an entity. Here, maintenance and not expansion is important; thus, expenditure on the house itself and not on farm buildings and other types of investment is encouraged. Even in non-farm families, houses provide one of the few legitimate avenues for private investment in a society such as Yugoslavia. There are no channels for private productive investment in industry on anything but a minute scale.)

Maintenance without expansion is associated with the fact that geographical mobility in Yugoslavia is high, and is increasing (see Halpern, 1965, for an excellent description of what this means in personal terms to urbanized peasants). In 1959-1961, over one million people migrated from one part of Yugoslavia to another (*SGJ* – 62, p. 56). A large part of the migration is to towns and cities. Families frequently have a town branch and a country branch. The town branch needs the house and farm of the country branch as a holiday residence, as a place in which to store, and from which to obtain, extra food, as a place to send children to, and occasionally as a place of security. In these circumstances, some peasants do not consider a farm to be a firm or business.

Cycle of development

Another social variable associated with the expansion implied by investment and attempts to raise productivity and production brings in the cycle of development of the group and the ages of its members. It is for this reason that I earlier emphasized the fact that the decision-taking unit was a group and that the structure of the group had a part to play in decisions. The phase in which a domestic group finds itself, at the point of time at which an opportunity for investment arises, is a variable that must be taken into account. The concept of developmental cycles in domestic groups (see Goody, 1958) is a straightforward one: it refers primarily to expansion and contraction in size of households and corresponding alterations in composition and other aspects of structure during phases in cyclical change over time. By convention, the phase of expansion is usually taken to begin with marriage; it continues through the period of pro-creation and rearing of children, until they are ready for marriage; a phase of dispersion may begin when children marry and leave the group, a final phase of dissolution or replacement marks the end of the cycle. Fewer or more numerous phases may be dis-tinguished according to the needs of analysis. In Yugoslavia, the phase of dispersion may not occur in a clear-cut way, since a three-generation family household is a type of domestic unit frequently found. In this case there may be a transfer of authority within the domestic group from the older generation to some members of the younger generation, but no decrease in numbers. Dissolution occurs when the original couple dies and the farm is sold or divided. But the original couple may be replaced on the farm by one or more of their children, with the children's own families of procreation.

Where younger members of a group have already opted for work in a non-agricultural occupation – a very frequent situation – the old people remaining on the farm are again merely attempt-ing to keep going. They see little point in investment from which they may derive small benefit and in which their children are not interested.

The phase of the domestic cycle is thus relevant to the context of situation in which investment decisions are taken. One might imagine that, from the point of view of the overall structure, no clear conclusions about investment could be drawn, since one could expect that throughout the whole society there would be a distribution of groups in different phases. But this is not a repetitive society: changes have occurred which leave the dis-persed phase a frequent one in rural areas.

Ownership and inheritance of land

Patterns of ownership of land in Yugoslavia arise as a result of buying and selling, of allocation by a government agency in the course of redistribution in land reform, and of inheritance. Yugoslavia has a monetized economy. Although there are reciprocal exchanges of gifts at *rites de passage* such as christenings, weddings, and funerals, exchange of aid between households in productive tasks, and exchange of goods and services between households that maintain friendly relations, nevertheless almost all goods and services can be bought and sold. The concept of segregated spheres of exchange is not helpful in understanding the distribution of goods in the economy or the economic activity of villagers. Labour is, most frequently, purchased. Overall, the cash proportion of incomes and expenditures of peasants is considerable.

Land, however, stands somewhat outside the general picture in that peasants still obtain most of their land by inheritance, although there is no stigma attached to buying and selling. Thus the legal form of inheritance is a social variable of some significance. The patterns that emerge from the operation of customary rules provide part of the land-holding situation, as a given factor in production.

In law, no person can inherit more land than the maximum allowed. Both women and men can inherit. An inheritance consists of a 'necessary part' (half the property for the first line of inheritance) and a disposable part; the latter can be disposed of by will, but the distribution of the former is specified by law.

The property, either the minimum 'necessary part' or any larger part up to the whole, is divided into as many portions as there are children plus spouse. If one of the children dies before the testator, the proportion that would have gone to him goes to his spouse and children. If the testator's spouse dies before the testator, his or her portion is divided among their children. This is the first line of inheritance. The second line of inheritance consists of spouse plus parents, on the same principle. This means that if parents are dead, then their other children may inherit i.e. the testator's siblings. There are third and fourth lines of inheritance, which may bring in first cousins and second cousins (see Law of Inheritance, FNRJ, 1961). The partible principle is carried to an extreme, which means that, on death, landed property may be subdivided into minute fractions.

If this is considered together with the fact that women can inherit land and bring it under the control of the productive group at marriage (virilocal residence being customary in the countryside), then it can be seen that the land of the productive group may consist of scattered parcels. A large proportion of peasant men and women who marry come from the same area. In 1960, 168,120 marriages were contracted. In 90,914 of these marriages, husbands and wives came from the same village, and in a further 39,781 marriages, husbands and wives came from the same commune (*SGJ* – 62, pp. 478). If peasant spouses came from further afield, the situation would perhaps be improved, as there might be more incentive to sell the outlying land; but as it is, the tendency is to keep the inherited land rather than to go through the difficulties of selling and buying from neighbours with the aim of consolidating holdings.

Inheritance, combined with customary forms of kinship and marriage, has the effect of scattering landed property among men and women, which, combined with post-marital residence patterns, leads to fragmentation. Fragmentation due to partible inheritance is common in peasant economies. For obvious practical reasons, it inhibits investment in modern agricultural techniques, and even in traditional agriculture.

Since it is a most visible failing of Yugoslav agriculture, fragmentation is frequently singled out by Yugoslav commentators as a major brake on investment, and, in this, social variables are basic.

Mobility and status

A further social variable associated with the question of investment lies in occupational status. There is much greater occupational mobility now that Yugoslavia, although still largely agricultural, is becoming rapidly more industrialized. In accordance with Yugoslav policy, industries have been established in country towns and villages as well as in the cities. The peasant farmer has the possibility of moving to the city to take up industrial employment, in which case some of the familiar characteristics of migrant labour prevail. But the other possibility is a popular one: that of combining factory work with farming, either through daily commuting or through working in one of the factories in the countryside.

Given the importance of the farm and farmland, which I stressed earlier, it is not surprising that so many peasants choose to combine the two occupations. In this way they may have the benefit of the farm as a focus for family relations and for security, while obtaining all the ideological and material benefits of being a worker. On the national scale of prestige, worker is on a higher level than peasant; in the village, the status of worker is ambiguous, at least among younger peasants, since the traditional peasant form of life seems to many of them to be one with no long-term future.

In these circumstances, farms are no longer vital from the point of view of material subsistence, merely an advantage. They turn into country gardens. What is produced on them tends to be consumed and does not enter the market, since worker-farmer households do not need the cash from crops.

The implications of this situation are that the necessity of modernizing their agricultural methods and of investing for greater productivity does not seem to households to be very pressing.

From the point of view of government policy, this conflict of roles is severely to be discouraged (cf. the very enlightening discussion by Bičanić, 1956). It is thought to lead to a lack of interest in farming (as it does) but, just as serious, inefficiency in the worker role. The transformation of former bourgeois ideas which, it is believed, must take place when a peasant becomes a worker is not forthcoming; the peasant-worker hurries home to his house and garden-farm, either to work or to be with his family who continue to work as peasants.

A case-study illustration of the situation is provided by data I collected in 1961-1962 during fieldwork in a Zagorje commune with a recently built factory. The first intake of factory workers consisted of 116 men and women, mostly under 30. Of these, 76 had worked before at industrial or commercial occupations and had been accepted as factory workers largely because of this experience. For the most part their previous employment had been in Zagreb, and those who lived in the commune had commuted to town daily or stayed there for various periods. Most now welcomed the opportunity of combining more work on their family land with work in the factory. Some hoped that, as the factory expanded, farmer brothers and sisters would be able to work there also. As many as 96 workers came from local peasant households which obtained their income wholly or partly from cultivating their fields, and almost all of these said they would continue to help with the work in the fields when necessary. Nevertheless, they did not expect their future to lie in peasant farming and spoke of their farm work in terms of helping out the old people.

From the point of view of agriculture, the importance of this occupational opportunity lies also in the unexpected way in which industrialization has acted not as the enemy of the peasant, but as his ally, even though a temporary one. It provides a situation in which many peasant productive groups can keep their farms going, while discouraging any tendency to invest a great deal in them except as places of residence.

The 'maze' effect

The productive group in Yugoslav agriculture operates in a framework of constantly changing economic opportunities, arising through political or legal changes. The situation may be described by analogy with a maze, where there are a number of apparently equally attractive paths to be followed, and one does not know until one goes down each one which path is or will be blocked. Yugoslavia is a country run through an elaborate system of economic and social laws. Laws and regulations can be changed very rapidly indeed, with little warning, so that a situation which could give a peasant an economic advantage, if he were to take steps to utilize it, may alter very quickly and put him at a severe disadvantage. This is not merely a question of choice in a situation of uncertainty, but rather of a constant changing of the rules of the game. This state is one of the by-products of detailed planning, and is one of the social variables involved in investment.

In view of the 'maze' effect, the safest situation as interpreted by many peasants is to consume and not to invest. It is not even safe to save or hoard, since savings may be eroded, as in 1965, by a combination of a sudden decision to abandon supply and demand as determinants of prices in some sectors of consumer goods, and to fix high prices, together with a decision to devalue. The 'maze' effect is more important according to the extent to which an economy is controlled by frequently changed law and regulation, while keeping a large private sector. In Yugoslavia it inhibits investment and encourages consumption expenditure. But it does not go so far as to encourage peasants to sell their land and consume the proceeds, since, whatever else may happen, it seems very unlikely that the government would expropriate peasant land, or would again, as in the four years after 1948, induce collectivization through Peasants' Working Cooperatives. It means, rather, that it is not worth making risky expenditures to increase future income that demand the forgoing of present consumption.

The social variables I have so far discussed are associated with lack of investment in traditional agriculture. There is, however, the alternative of industrialized and mechanized farming. In a country short of capital in agriculture, Cooperatives and Collectives provide a way of economizing in capital equipment. But peasants have avoided joining the crucial Peasants' Working Cooperatives. They cooperate to an increasing extent with the General Agricultural Cooperatives, as I have said. This involves, for example, buying from Cooperative shops (seed,. fertilizer, consumption goods), selling their produce to Cooperatives, and hiring from them machinery and equipment. (The Agricultural Estates are socialized enterprises with paid labourers, not involving peasant farmers.)

When peasants who had entered the Peasants' Working Co-operatives were legally permitted to leave without difficulty in 1953, large numbers opted out. Nevertheless, properly run, these Cooperatives were expected to be extremely efficient, to increase productivity, to produce a great deal of marketable surplus, and at the same time to provide members with high incomes and high levels of living in comparison with traditional peasant cultivators. Indeed, peasants in Cooperatives were frequently materially better off.[4] But still they reject the Working Co-operatives.

Two further social variables, which are integrated with and reinforce those discussed earlier, are associated with this fact: they are flexibility in social manoeuvre and the decline of the traditional *zadruga*.

Lorraine Barić

FLEXIBILITY IN SOCIAL MANOEUVRE

Flexibility in social manoeuvre is reflected in and influenced by various characteristics of a society: complex societies may be considered to have more and small-scale societies less; the degree to which basic roles and roles ascribed by custom or law dominate behaviour is also relevant, as is the ease or difficulty of joining or leaving groups. Flexibility, in general, varies with social mobility.

Ownership of land provides the Yugoslav peasant with a possibility of manoeuvre which is immediately lost if he enters a Peasants' Working Cooperative. Being a member may provide more security and possibly a higher income, but its main social implication is that it limits freedom of action and social mobility.

The Cooperative Council, which may have as many as 80 members, makes decisions. Action is joint action. Once a member has entered, the conditions on which he can withdraw his land or the monetary value of his share depend on the regulations of each Cooperative. In practice, it is extremely difficult, and even if a member leaves a Cooperative, his property is still considered as a security for any commitment the Cooperative undertook while he was a member. Furthermore, even if he sells his land and becomes a worker, he is still responsible to the extent of the monetary value of his former share (see Law on Agricultural Cooperatives, FNRJ, 1958, §§3, 4).

Independence is lost, and individual aims can be achieved only through influencing decisions taken in the Cooperative Council. The loss, real or assumed, of independence of action was frequently given by peasants as an important deterrent to entering or creating Cooperatives. It is bound up with the idea of the 'free' peasant. In terms of traditional social values, the landless man was at the mercy of all and his status was the lowest in the hierarchy of peasant status groups. To keep land was to keep freedom and security, or at least have the impression of doing so.

THE DECLINE OF TRADITIONAL ZADRUGAS

The rejection of the traditional *zadruga* (see pp. 256-257) was a phenomenon that changed the pattern of traditional agriculture from one of comparatively large, cooperative, productive groups with a kin base, to one of small farms. It was largely through the dissolution of *zadrugas* that so many peasants were able to own the rights to land and achieve personal control of the manner of production. Under the *zadruga* system, the head (the *domaćin* or *starešina*) dominated economic and social activity with his patriarchal authority. Other adults had their rights as members, but were subordinate to the head in all spheres of activity.

In some ways the traditional *zadrugas* resembled the present-day Peasants' Working Cooperatives as productive groups. *Zadrugas* were cooperatives too. But in many ways they were different: the means of recruitment was different and the internal structure of roles was different. The kin-based *zadruga* was a community, in the sense that it formed a local unit within which the greatest share of daily activities was regularly carried out, and relations among its members were multi-dimensional and not primarily economic. Modern cooperatives are not supported by the customary rights and obligations of kinship.

Since *zadrugas* and Cooperatives have important differences and since the *zadrugas* had largely disappeared a generation before the Cooperatives were created, one cannot expect them to form a developmental sequence. Nevertheless, many Yugoslav politicians and agricultural economists, before the last World War, were impressed by the similarity between *zadrugas* and Cooperatives and hoped that a revival of the '*zadruga* spirit' would permit the establishment of modern Cooperatives, which would solve some of the problems of production. It is more significant to compare the reasons for which peasants rejected *zadrugas* and the reasons for which peasants largely reject Peasants' Working Cooperatives. There are similarities. The increasing differentiation in levels of consumption within *zadrugas*, which came with the growing heterogeneity of Yugoslav society and the greater possibilities for individual mobility, was one important reason for the breaking up of *zadrugas*. Customary forms of behaviour had subordinated the elementary family components of the *zadruga* to the general good; but, in time, some elementary families attempted to gain a higher level of living than others, while the growing diversity of extra-agricultural occupations made supplementation of farm income

275

possible. The discrepancies of consumption and of inputs of labour among component elementary families, and sometimes individuals, encouraged division. Division made it possible for younger members, together with their elementary families, to settle on smaller farms, which they themselves managed.

Modern Cooperatives have some of the disadvantages (in a social sense) imputed to *zadrugas*, without a framework of customary forms of behaviour, such as the kin rights and obligations of the *zadruga*, to support them. Some of the forces that led peasants to opt out of traditional *zadruga* cooperatives thus still operate, to the detriment of modern Peasants' Working Cooperatives, and a study of the old *zadrugas* throws some light on the present.

CONCLUSION

In this study I have attempted to isolate certain variables important in examining the social context of the situation in which decisions about investment or technical innovation are taken by Yugoslav peasants. I have not studied the process of decision-making, nor have I attempted to provide an economic model of the situation, apart from showing that some obvious economic explanations are ambiguous. I arrived at the variables from an examination of case studies, and it is through case studies also that some idea of the relative importance of different variables and their interconnections, in individual instances, can be obtained. Where kinship obligations are strongly recognized, and the category of effective kin a large one; where the older generation of peasants are left on the farm while members of the younger generation have gone elsewhere; where land is fragmented and will be further fragmented through inheritance; where the proximity of industry and a high evaluation of being a worker have given rise to the worker-peasant; where there is a period of rapid administrative change; and, under the conditions that flexibility of manoeuvre is preferred to constraint, and that membership of certain types of groups, which restrict mobility in a society with growing geographical and social mobility, is rejected – then, a great deal of private investment for increased production in traditional Yugoslav agriculture is unlikely to occur.

New Economic Opportunities in Rural Yugoslavia

Seeing the forces operating, which preserve a system of maintenance, modified to meet changing conditions, and do not encourage growth, one may doubt whether planned increases of material incentives to peasants would have much short-term effect in leading them to invest or produce a great deal more, either privately or through Cooperatives. Incentives may have to be high. At the same time it seems obvious that the importance of the private peasant agricultural sector will decrease, not so much through increasing membership of Cooperatives as through the very industrial employment often chosen by peasant productive groups as a means of preserving their existence.

NOTES

1. The fieldwork on which this paper is partly based was carried out during the period 1960 to 1963 (in all, approximately a year). I am grateful to the Ford Foundation for a grant to cover field expenses.
2. In some parts of Yugoslavia the *zadruga* did not exist. One might say, for Yugoslavia as a whole, that it was characteristic but not universal.
3. There is no general agreement about the usage in English of 'cooperative' and 'collective'. Lopandić (1959) uses 'collective' to comprise general social ownership (as in the State farm) and cooperative ownership (p. 263). But in the course of his paper he uses 'cooperative' and 'collective' more or less interchangeably, and also refers, for instance, to 'collective peasants' cooperatives' (p. 269). I have used 'Collectives' to refer to units mainly composed of 'workers' and 'employees' (officially so defined); and 'Cooperatives' where the significant criterion is or should be the major importance of members or cooperators.

It is worth noting that the deputy director of the Institute of Social Sciences, Belgrade, has pointed out that the Yugoslav economy is not a collective economy but a socialist economy (I. Maksimović, 1962).
4. Average income of farm households from agriculture in 1960 was 162,300 dinars; the total net personal income of Peasants' Working Cooperatives as divided among persons employed gives an average per person of 198,000 dinars for the same year (*SGJ* – 62, pp. 127, 130, 133).

REFERENCES

BAKARIĆ, V. 1960. *O poljoprivredi i problemima sela.* Beograd: Kultura.

BAKIĆ, V. 1962. *Porodično pravo.* Beograd: Savremena Administracija.

BALEN, M. 1962. Family Relations and their Changes in the Village of Jalžabet. *Sociologija* 4: 254-283.

BIČANIĆ, R. 1956. Occupational Heterogeneity of Peasant Families in the Period of Accelerated Industrialization. *Third World Congress of Sociology* **4**: 80-96.

BOTTOMORE, T. B. 1962. *Sociology*. London: Unwin University Books.

ERLICH, V. 1964. *Porodica u transformaciji*. Zagreb: Naprijed.

FNRJ 1958. *Uredba o zemljoradničkim zadrugama* (Law on Agricultural Cooperatives). Beograd: Službeni List.

—— 1961. *Zakon o nasledjivanju* (Law of Inheritance). Beograd: Službeni List.

FRIED, M. 1957. The Classification of Corporate Unilineal Descent Groups. *Journal of the Royal Anthropological Institute* **87**: 1-29.

GOODY, J. (ed.). 1958. *The Developmental Cycle in Domestic Groups*. Cambridge Papers in Social Anthropology 1. Cambridge: Cambridge University Press.

HALPERN, J. 1958. *A Serbian Village*. New York: Columbia University Press.

—— 1965. Peasant Culture and Urbanization in Yugoslavia. *Human Organization* **24**: 162-174.

KARDELJ, E. 1959. *Problemi socijalističke politike na selu*. Beograd: Kultura. (Trans. Sonja Bičanić, 1962, as *Problems of Socialist Policy in the Countryside*, London: Lincolns-Prager.)

LOPANDIĆ, D. 1959. Development and Mutual Relationships of the Collective and Private Sectors of Yugoslav Agriculture. *Annals of Collective Economy* **30**: 267-300.

MAKSIMOVIĆ, I. 1962. Collective Economy and Socialist Economy. *Annals of Collective Economy* **33**: 283-288.

MAYER, A. 1910. *Die bäuerliche Hauskommunion (Zadruga) in der Königreichen Kroatien und Slavonien*. Heidelberg.

MERTON, R. K. 1957. *Social Theory and Social Structure*. (Revised and enlarged edition). Glencoe, Ill.: Free Press.

SCHULTZ, T. W. 1964. *Transforming Traditional Agriculture*. New Haven and London: Yale University Press.

(*SGJ—62*) *Statistički Godišnjak FNRJ*. 1962. Beograd: Savezni zavod za statistiku.

TAX, S. 1953. *Penny Capitalism*. Washington: Smithsonian Institution. Publication 16. Washington: U.S. Govt. Printing Office.

WATERSTON, A. 1962. *Planning in Yugoslavia*. Baltimore: Johns Hopkins Press.

NOTES ON CONTRIBUTORS

BARIĆ, LORRAINE. Born 1928, Australia; studied at the University of Sydney, B.A.; London School of Economics and Political Science, University of London, Acad. Postgrad. Dip. Anthropology; Ph.D.

Research Economist, Research Service, Sydney, 1949-52; Assistant Lecturer, London School of Economics, 1957; Lecturer, 1961; Chief Assistant Planning Officer, Liverpool City Planning Department, 1963; Temporary Lecturer, Manchester University, 1964; Lecturer, Royal College of Advanced Technology (University of Salford), 1964; Senior Lecturer, University of Salford, 1966.

Author of 'Kinship in Anglo-Saxon Society' (*British Journal of Sociology*, Sep., Dec., 1958); 'Some Conceptual Problems in the Study of Family and Kin Ties in the British Isles' (*British Journal of Sociology*, Dec., 1961); 'Some Aspects of Credit, Saving and Investment in a "Non-Monetary" Economy' in R. Firth and B. S. Yamey (eds.), *Capital, Saving and Credit in Peasant Societies*, 1964.

BARTH, THOMAS FREDRIK W. Born 1928, Norway; studied at University of Chicago, M.A.; London School of Economics and Cambridge University, Ph.D.

Research Associate, University of Oslo, 1953-60; Visiting Professor, Columbia University, 1961; Associate Professor, University of Bergen, 1962-63; Visiting Professor (UNESCO), University of Khartoum, 1963-64, Professor, University of Bergen, 1965.

Author of *Principles of Social Organization in Southern Kurdistan*, 1953; *Political Leadership among Swat Pathans*, 1959; *Nomads of South Persia*, 1961.

COHEN, PERCY S. Born 1928, South Africa; studied at Witwatersrand, B.Comm.; London School of Economics, B.Sc.(Econ.), Ph.D.

Lecturer in Sociology, University of Leicester, 1960-64; Lecturer in Sociology, London School of Economics, 1964; Reader, 1967.

DOUGLAS, MARY. Born 1921, Italy; educated at Oxford University, B.A., B.Sc., D.Phil.

Lecturer in Social Anthropology, Oxford, 1950-51; Lecturer in Social Anthropology, University College, London, 1951-63; Reader, 1963.

T 279

Author of *The Lele of the Kasai*, 1963; *Purity and Danger*, 1966.

EPSTEIN, TRUDE SCARLETT. Born 1922, Austria; studied at University of Manchester, B.A.(Econ.), Ph.D.

Research Assistant, Manchester University, 1954-58; Research Fellow, Australian National University, 1959-61; Senior Lecturer, Royal College of Advanced Technology, Salford, 1962-65; Visiting Fellow, Australian National University, 1966. Author of *Economic Development and Social Change in South India*, 1962.

FIRTH, RAYMOND WILLIAM. F.B.A., Hon.D.Ph.(Oslo). Born 1901, New Zealand. Studied at Auckland University (College), B.A., M.A.; London School of Economics, Ph.D.

Lecturer in Anthropology, University of Sydney, 1930-31; Acting Professor of Anthropology, University of Sydney, 1931-32; Lecturer in Anthropology, London School of Economics, 1933-36; Reader in Anthropology, University of London, 1936-44; Professor of Anthropology, University of London, 1944.

Author of *Primitive Economics of the New Zealand Maori*, 1929 (Second edition as *Economics of the New Zealand Maori*, 1959); *We, The Tikopia*, 1936 (Second edition, 1957); *Primitive Polynesian Economy*, 1939 (Second edition, 1965); *Work of the Gods in Tikopia*, 1940 (Second edition, 1967); *Malay Fishermen: Their Peasant Economy*, 1946 (Second edition, 1966); *Elements of Social Organization*, 1951 (Third edition, 1961); *Social Change in Tikopia*, 1959; *History and Traditions of Tikopia*, 1961; *Essays on Social Organization and Values*, 1964; *Tikopia Ritual and Belief*, 1967.

FRANKENBERG, RONALD. Born 1929, London. Studied at Gonville and Caius College, Cambridge, B.A.; and Manchester University, M.A.(Econ.), Ph.D.

Research Assistant, University College, Cardiff, 1954-56; Education Officer in Trade Union, 1957-60; Lecturer in Sociology Manchester University, 1960-65; Senior Lecturer, 1965; in 1966 seconded as Professor of Sociology, University of Zambia.

Author of *Village on the Border*, 1957; *Communities in Britain*, 1966; joint editor, *African Social Research*, from 1966.

JOY, JACK LEONARD. Born 1928, London; studied at the London School of Economics, B.Sc.(Econ.).

L.S.E. Economics Research Division, 1951-53; Makerere College (Lecturer in Agricultural Economics, 1953-60); Farm Economics Branch, Cambridge (Senior Research Officer 1961-

62); L.S.E. (Lecturer in Economics 1962-63, Senior Lecturer, 1964). Professorial Fellow (in Agricultural Development), Institute of Development Studies, University of Sussex, 1966. Author of articles on agricultural development and of reports on such topics as coffee-marketing, irrigation development, agricultural development strategy, etc. for governments and international agencies.

ORTIZ, SUTTI. Born 1929, Buenos Aires; studied at University of California at Berkeley, B.A., M.A. (Anthropology); London, Ph.D.

Assistant Lecturer in Social Anthropology, London School of Economics, 1964.

Index

Abortion, 250
Abraham, R. C., 137
Acholi, 36, 45n.
Administration/Administrators, 210, 260; business, 22; change, 276; procedures, 11
Admiralty Island, 124
Affinal ties, 164
Africa, 16, 18, 24, 26n., 37, 57, 71, 80, 95, 142, 149, 251
Agarwala, A. N., 191, 192
Agriculture, 6, 26n., 44n., 53, 75, 106, 123, 150, 155, 156, 165, 168, 201, 202, 207, 214, 218, 219, 223, 231, 232, 234, 235, 238, 240, 241, 249, 251, 254-256, 264, 270-272, 277; economists, 109; produce/production, 239, 255, 257, 259; traditional, 260, 262-265, 270, 273, 274, 276
Agronomy, 36
Allan, W., 251
Allcorn, D. H., 77
Allocation, 19, 59, 60, 108, 268; v. also Resource allocation
America, 50, 62, 98, 133
Andes, 199
Arab, 155, 163, 171
Arensberg, C., 64
Armstrong, W. E., 2, 48, 134
Arrow, K. J., 193, 226n.
Art, 50, 56
Asia, 24
Australia, 129, 142
Authority, 60, 80, 101, 106, 110, 113, 127, 129, 136, 138, 139, 199, 201, 210, 212, 213, 226n., 268, 275

Baggara Arabs, 160
Bakarić, V., 253, 256
Bakić, V., 266
Baldwin, J., 25n.
Balen, M., 266

Banking, 1, 93, 94, 123, 134, 139, 258
Baran, P., 48
Barić, L., 22, 23, 43, 134, 135
Barotse, 85n.
Barter, 104, 105, 121, 123, 140, 141
Barth, F., 23, 41, 45n., 58, 61-65, 162, 167, 171, 175-188
Basutoland, 26n.
Beals, L., 24n.
Beidelman, T. O., 231, 247
Beliefs, 35, 76, 230, 233, 248, 251; v. also Religion
Belshaw, C. S., 19, 20, 22, 25n., 85n.
Benedict, R., 56
Benham, F., 74
Berliner, J., 55-57, 81, 85
Bernal, V., 202
Bičanić, R., 271
Bilateral kinship system, 201
Bismarck Archipelago, 136
Blau, P., 25n.
Bohannan, P., 24n., 41, 50, 65, 66, 83, 84, 95, 96, 113, 137, 138, 156
Bombay, 236, 237
Bottomore, T. B., 256
Bougainville, 124
Boulding, K., 70
Brahmins, 232
Bribery, 16
Bride-price/Bride-wealth, 38, 59, 128, 131, 132, 143, 151, 156, 159, 160, 185
Bücher, K., 2, 49, 83, 84
Buganda, 185
Buin, 135
Bunzel, R., 79
Burling, R., 50, 51, 57-60, 78, 81-84, 96, 97, 104
Bushong, 141

Caja Agraria (Governmental credit), 207

283

Index

Linear programming, 38, 182, 185, 187, 224
Loans, 97, 134, 207, 209, 212, 222, 244
Lopandić, D., 277n.
Lowie, R. H., 79
Lupton, T., 77
Luxury, 71, 73, 79, 94, 124, 140, 210, 261

MacRae, D. G., 49
Madagascar, 137
Maine, H. S., 111, 116
Maksimović, I., 277n.
Malay, 12, 13, 15, 94
Malinowski, B., 2, 3, 8, 10, 11, 13, 24n., 25n., 32, 49, 51, 55, 70, 91, 92
Management, 8, 22, 34, 52, 151, 153, 157, 158, 162, 165-166, 168, 169, 197, 206, 213-219, 226n.
Manus, 125
Maori, 25n.
Marcovitz, H., 38
March, J. G., 34
Marginality, 6-8, 12, 18, 25n., 39, 42, 44n., 60, 71, 103-105, 107, 191, 198, 203, 205, 206, 217, 221, 230, 239, 246, 248, 249
Marindanim, 136
Market, 1, 6, 7, 21, 24n., 30, 35, 39-41, 48, 50, 52, 60, 65-70, 72, 77, 78, 83, 91, 94-97, 101-103, 106, 108, 113-115, 119-125, 130-132, 135, 141, 144, 151, 154-163, 165, 167, 169, 172, 173, 178, 182, 188, 198, 202, 204, 206, 207, 209, 211, 217, 220, 224, 234, 238, 250, 251, 259-261, 273; concept, 5; economy, 65, 194, 229, 248; marketeers, 53; non-market economy, 7, 69, 115, 206, 229, 248-250
Markov Process analysis, 39
Marra, 161, 166, 171
Marriage, 50, 64, 112, 123, 130-132, 134, 136, 137, 151, 157, 162, 201, 202, 213, 256, 268-270
Marshall, A., 48
Marx, Karl, 1, 21, 25n., 47-49, 53, 54, 69, 70, 79, 81, 83, 84, 102, 254

Massa, 140
Matrix, 56, 132, 152, 175, 176, 178, 179-185, 186-188; analysis, 182
Matrilineage, 92
Maximization, 5, 6, 8, 32, 35, 37-41, 43, 58-61, 64, 67, 92, 97, 104-107, 115, 165, 168, 181, 182, 186, 194, 203, 223, 239, 240, 243, 246
Mauss, M., 8-13, 15-17, 24n., 25n., 71
Mayer, A. C., 256
McFarquhar, A. M. M., 185
Mead, M., 124, 125
Mecca, 160
Meek, R., 101
Meier, G. M., 192
Melanesia, 18, 20, 78, 123
Meillassoux, C., 24n.
Menger, K., 119, 121, 138
Merton, R. K., 62, 63, 262
Methodism, 47, 56
Mexico, 24n.
Mintz, S. W., 24n.
Mobility, 270-272, 275; v. also Social mobility
Models, 31, 32-35, 37-39, 41-44, 57, 58, 82-84, 99, 101, 102, 116, 127, 128, 156, 158, 173, 175, 181, 184, 192, 196, 197, 218, 222-224, 226n., 229, 253, 254, 264; v. also Economic
Money, 1, 11, 12, 15, 18, 20, 32, 52, 64, 65, 68, 72, 73, 75, 79, 94, 96, 104, 106, 119-121, 126, 129, 131, 136, 139, 140, 142, 155, 156, 168, 193, 194, 210, 212, 220, 245, 256; monetary/mone-tized, 43, 59, 74, 95, 102, 107, 124, 130, 156, 253, 259, 274; non-monetary economy, 7, 18, 19, 21, 105, 107, 108, 135, 136; primitive, 119-124, 126, 130, 134, 135, 138, 140, 142, 143
Moral values/Morality, 5, 8, 10, 11, 13, 14, 16, 17, 50, 92, 94, 95, 98, 100, 101, 103, 106, 156, 165, 194, 203; constraint, 62, 105; rights, 210; sanctions, 210
Morgan, L. H., 82
Morgenstern, O., 193
Moskowski, M., 2

288

Index